MAX ANDERSSON   LARS SJUNNESSON
BOSNIAN FLAT DOG

fantagraphics books

FANTAGRAPHICS BOOKS
7563 Lake City Way NE
Seattle WA 98115

Translated (from the Swedish), designed and produced by Max Andersson
Edited by Kim Thompson
Promoted by Eric Reynolds
Published by Gary Groth and Kim Thompson

Originally published in slightly different form in Death and Candy # 2-4.

Cover photo by Daniel Munoz
Photo on back cover flap by Helena Ahonen

To receive a free catalog of comics, call 1-800-657-1100 or write us at
Fantagraphics Books, 7563 Lake City Way NE, Seattle, WA 98115.

Distributed in the U.S. by W.W. Norton and Company, Inc. (212-354-5500)
Distributed in Canada by Raincoast Books (800-663-5714)
Distributed in the United Kingdom by Turnaround Distribution (208-829-3009)

Visit the Fantagraphics website: www.fantagraphics.com
Visit the Max Andersson website: www.maxandersson.com

First printing: July 2006

ISBN-10: 1-56097-740-X
ISBN-13: 978-1-56097-740-7

Printed in Singapore

TABLE OF CONTENTS

Long ago in the year 1982, when I as a postgraduate student began to study economic and social geography in Lund, I moved to a room in a student corridor. There I met a group of young Swedish students and among them Lars Sjunnesson. I was 35 years old at this time already and coming from Slovenia (at that time a part of former Yugoslavia) I was a complete "greenhorn" in Sweden despite my knowledge from books. And to live in daily contact with such a group of young Swedish students was a quite unusual but positive experience for me. Many of them only began their student life and were on one hand full of enthusiasm to experience their freedom and life to the greatest possible extent, and on the other hand they were faced with study obligations and worries. But their enthusiasm, their critical and unconventional attitude to the society around them prevailed. Slowly this attitude influenced me too and I felt as if there was a humorous, nonconformist, creative child in them sometimes ironically reacting to what happened in society, being fed up with all logical explanations. The prime example of such a student was Lars.

Already at the beginning of his student life he recorded many events that happened around him in a series of comic drawings. They also described some funny events that happened in our student corridor and from time to time they appeared at the door of the refrigerator in our common corridor kitchen. In this way I regularly appeared in his comics as a figure with a special personality and absurd eating and other habits, surviving bomb explosions and meals made of litter etc., being undestroyable as in some kind of modernised absurd fairy tale. Looking back I find now that already at this time it was evident that the prime channel of communication for Lars was drawing comics and that already then he developed his own graphic style. In them he is critically observing the world reacting in an ironical and absurd manner criticism. Or maybe to show his own anger and to more easily overcome his own pain caused by what happened, as I sometimes do.

After a very long time I met Lars again and saw the new comics done by him and his colleague Max Andersson, which consider the cruelties that happened in Bosnia. My basic reaction to these cruelties was: that they are so terrible that because of this they are out of reach of my understanding, of my mind, of my world. And I was unsure whether my emotional reactions to them are appropriate. I am from Slovenia and one would expect that having some contacts (although few) with people from Bosnia and a certain knowledge about the circumstances in Bosnia, I should have anticipated what would happen. But I was surprised as much as other people around Europe and couldn't believe the truth.

The new drawings in this book very much reflect the horrors that happened and the situation after the war. Among other things I noticed the wide opened eyes that show the fear and horror, the emptiness and the vanity of life without perspective. Lars and Max are showing considerable psychological sensitivity, which is reflected in their drawings. There is a lot of irony directed towards the former regime. When it collapsed, the devil, which was hiding under the carpet, immediately showed up. On the other hand there is humor which shows that there is still hope, that everything is not lost, that the human soul can survive in spite of all that happened. I look forward to seeing more of their comics for adults.

Štefan Skledar
Ljubljana, September 2003

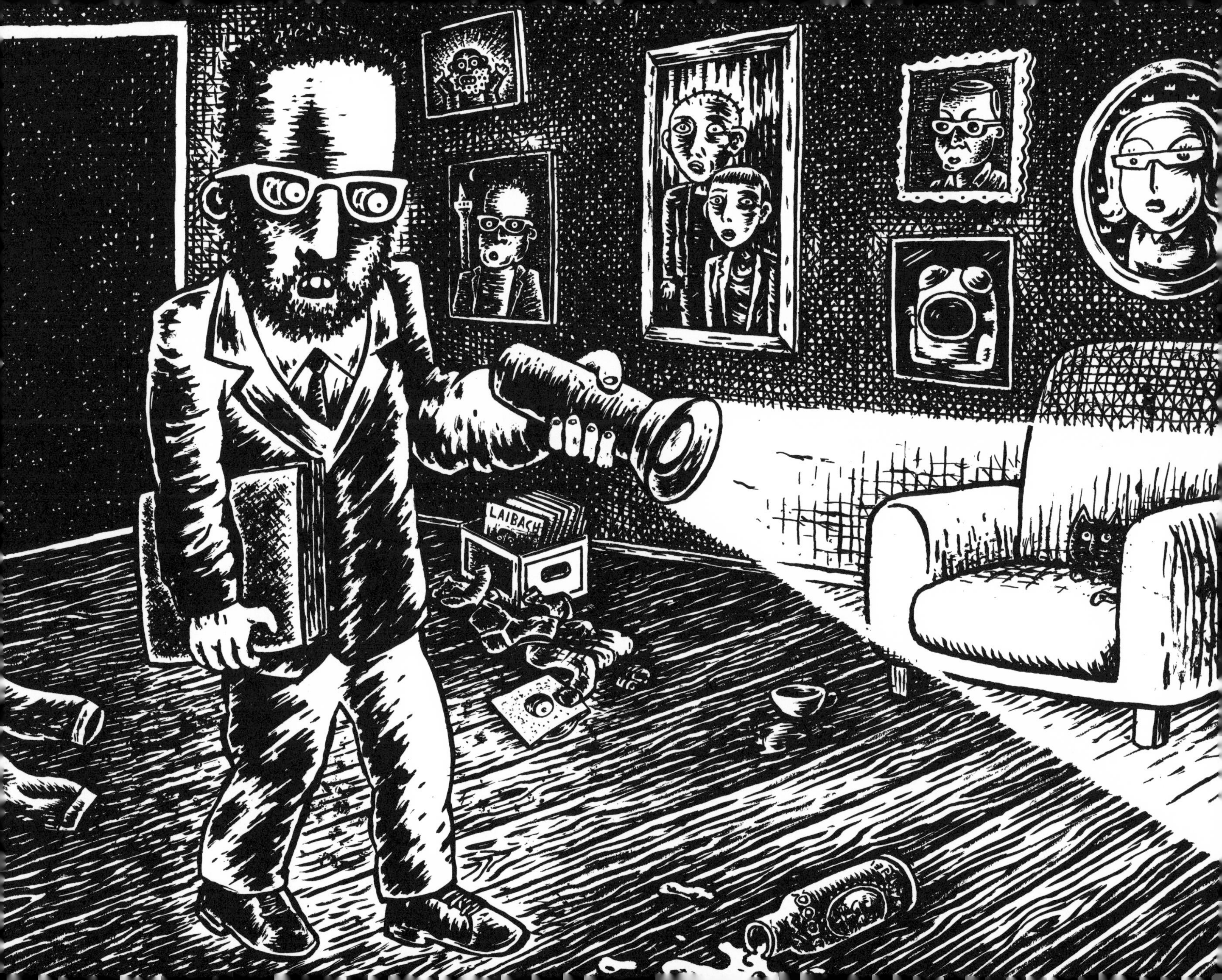
LAIBACH

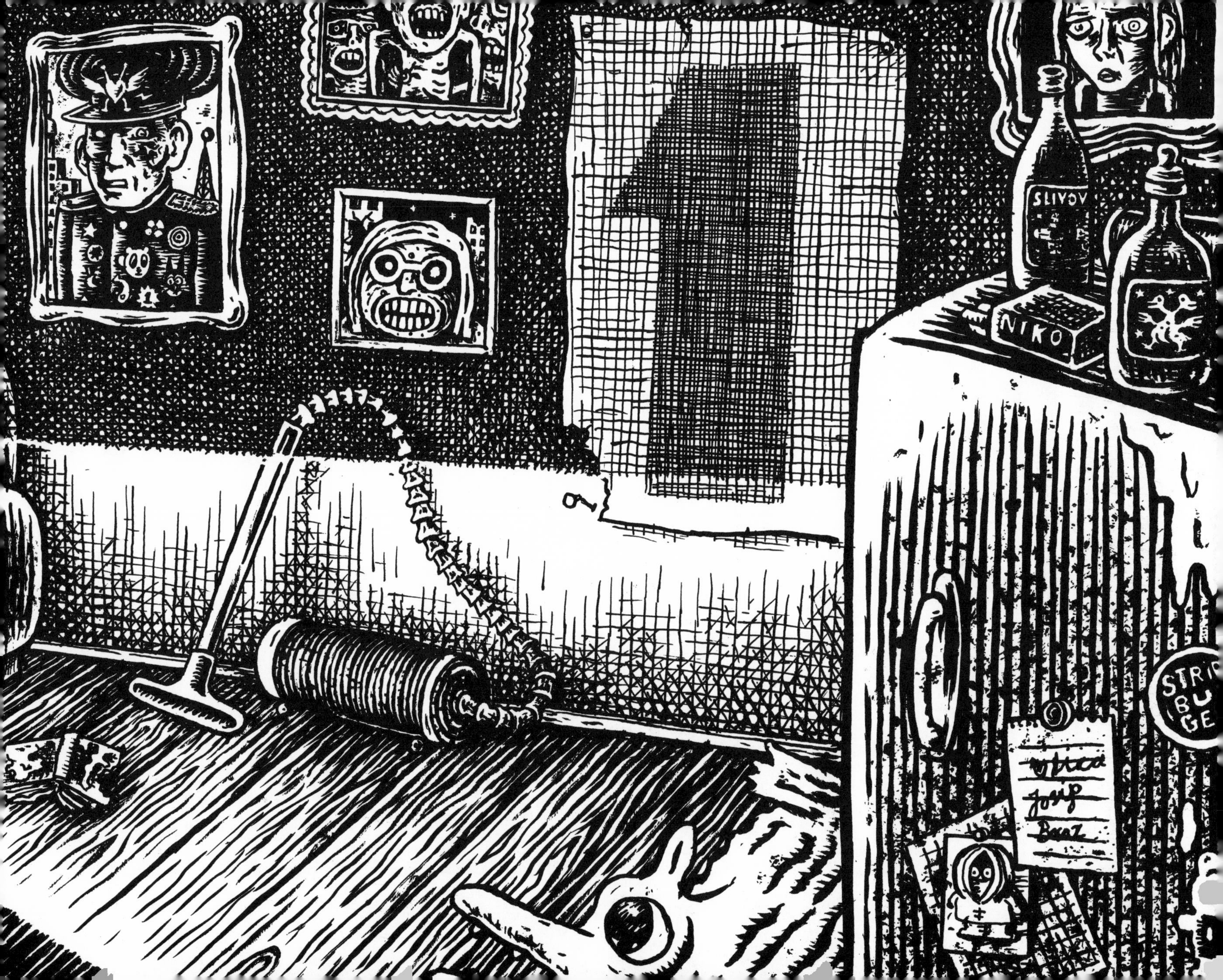
SLIVOV
NIKO

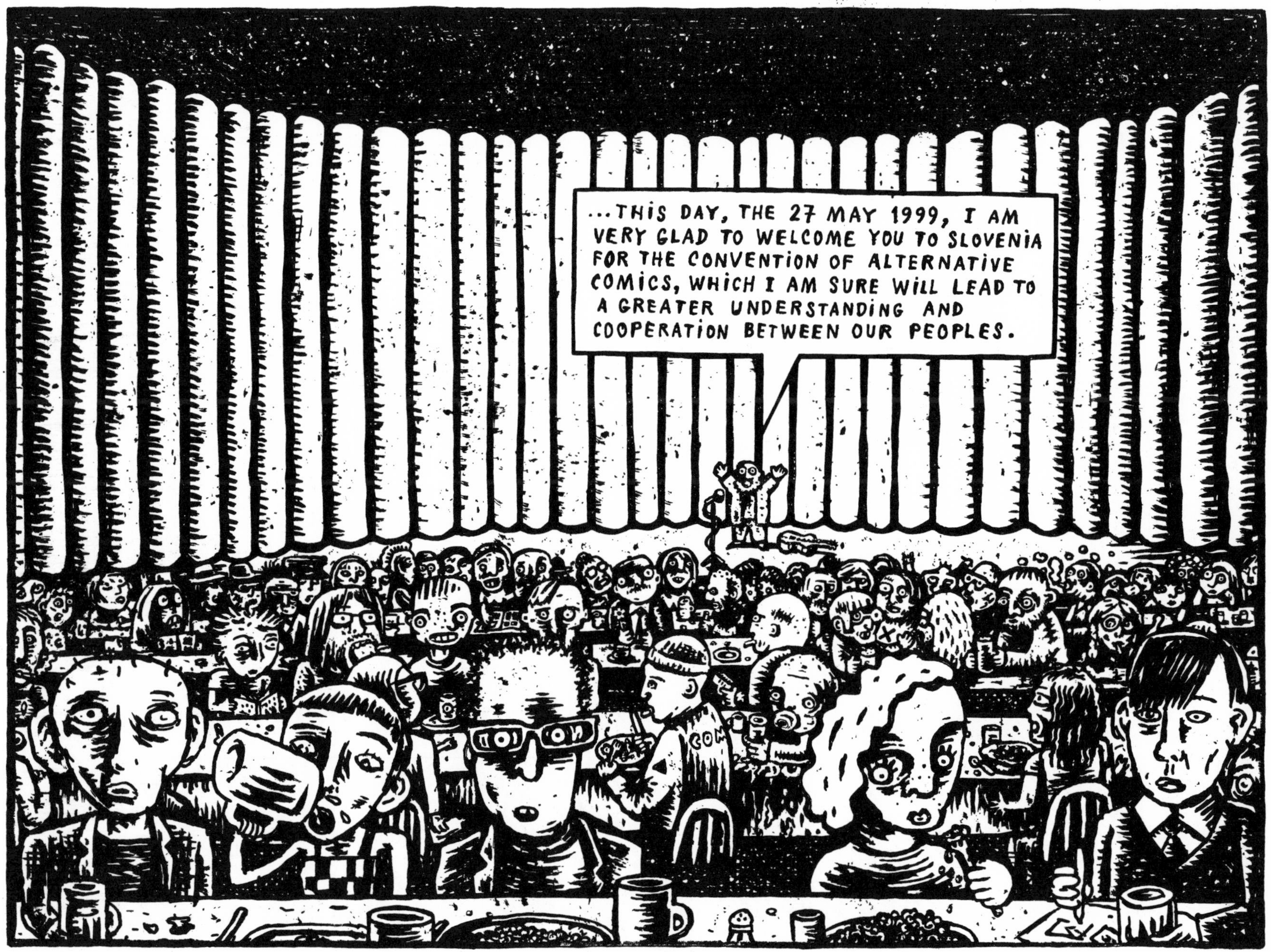
...THIS DAY, THE 27 MAY 1999, I AM VERY GLAD TO WELCOME YOU TO SLOVENIA FOR THE CONVENTION OF ALTERNATIVE COMICS, WHICH I AM SURE WILL LEAD TO A GREATER UNDERSTANDING AND COOPERATION BETWEEN OUR PEOPLES.

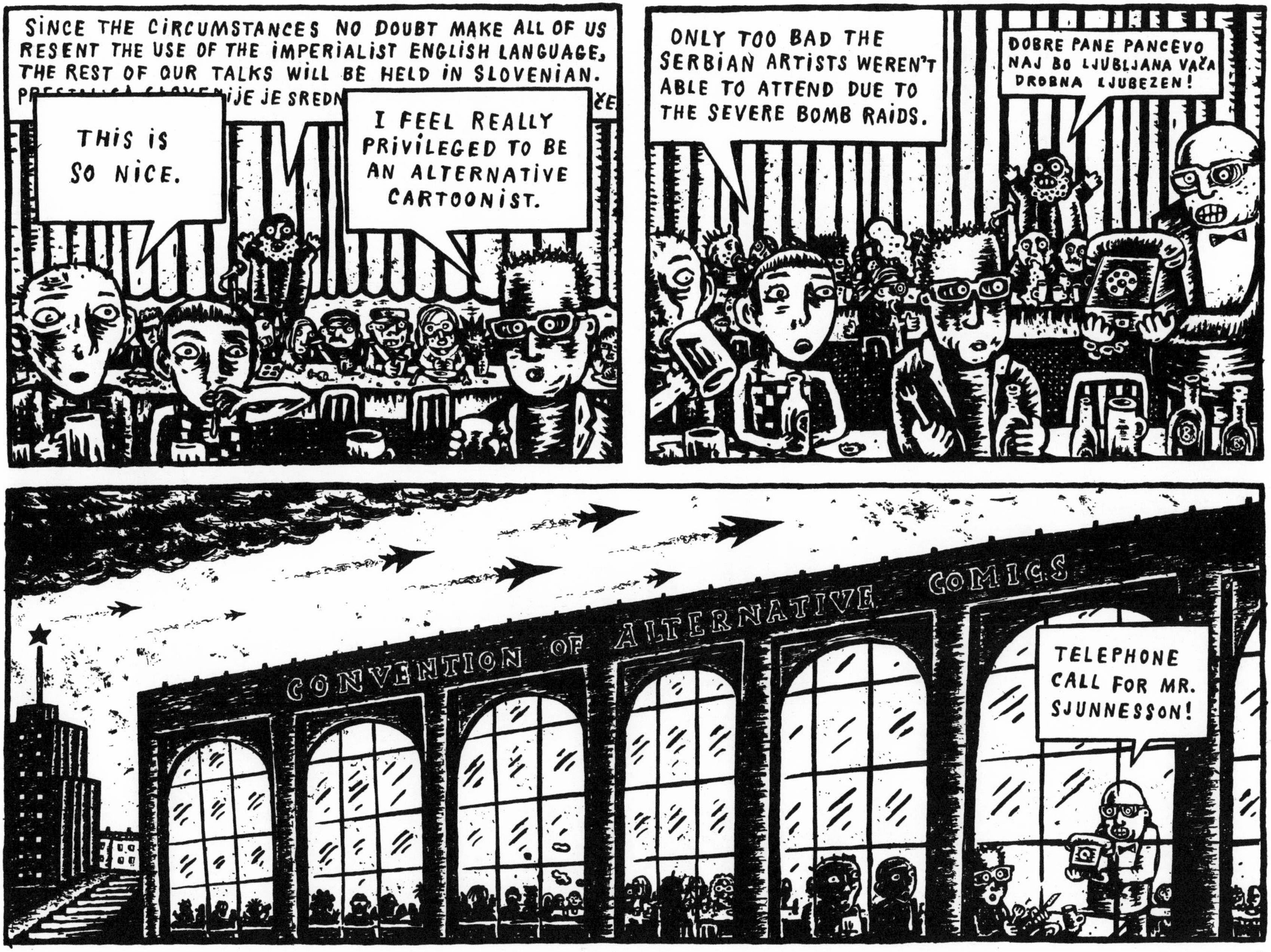

SINCE THE CIRCUMSTANCES NO DOUBT MAKE ALL OF US RESENT THE USE OF THE IMPERIALIST ENGLISH LANGUAGE, THE REST OF OUR TALKS WILL BE HELD IN SLOVENIAN.
THIS IS SO NICE.
I FEEL REALLY PRIVILEGED TO BE AN ALTERNATIVE CARTOONIST.
ONLY TOO BAD THE SERBIAN ARTISTS WEREN'T ABLE TO ATTEND DUE TO THE SEVERE BOMB RAIDS.
DOBRE PANE PANCEVO NAJ BO LJUBLJANA VAČA DROBNA LJUBEZEN!
CONVENTION OF ALTERNATIVE COMICS
TELEPHONE CALL FOR MR. SJUNNESSON!

HELLO, STEFAN SKLEDAR HERE... YOU USED ME AS A CARTOON CHARACTER WITHOUT ASKING FOR PERMISSION... *crackle*... NOW I WANT YOU TO PAY!

BUT...

YOU USED ME! EXPLOITED MY LIFE TO MAKE FABULOUS PROFITS! ...*crackle*...

TEMVEČ TUDI KULTURNO

BUT I DIDN'T MAKE ALL THAT MUCH...

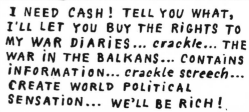

I NEED CASH! TELL YOU WHAT, I'LL LET YOU BUY THE RIGHTS TO MY WAR DIARIES... *crackle*... THE WAR IN THE BALKANS... CONTAINS INFORMATION... *crackle screech*... CREATE WORLD POLITICAL SENSATION... WE'LL BE RICH!

I'M A BIT TIED UP RIGHT NOW... THERE'S A COMICS CONVENTION...

WE HAVEN'T GOT MUCH TIME... I'M BEING FOLLOWED... THEY ARE EXTREMELY DANGEROUS! MEET ME AT 7 O'CLOCK ... THE WASTE-BASKET IN FRONT OF THE LJUBLJANA CASTLE... BRING 500 DEUTSCHE MARKS IN SMALL BILLS ...GOT IT? *Click!*

PODNEBIJE JE SREDNJEEVROPSKA CELINSKO Z VPLIVI

HELLO... HELLO! GODDAMMIT, HE HUNG UP!

KULTURE, OD KATHERI JE VSAKA, PUSTILA

WHO WAS THAT?

WHEN I WAS LIVING IN A STUDENT DORM IN SWEDEN IN THE 80'S THERE WAS THIS SLOVENIAN STUDENT OF ARCHITECTURE CALLED SKLEDAR. EVENTUALLY WE LOST TRACK OF EACH OTHER... THEN I USED HIM AS A CHARACTER IN MY COMICS...

NOW HE WANTS ME TO PAY!

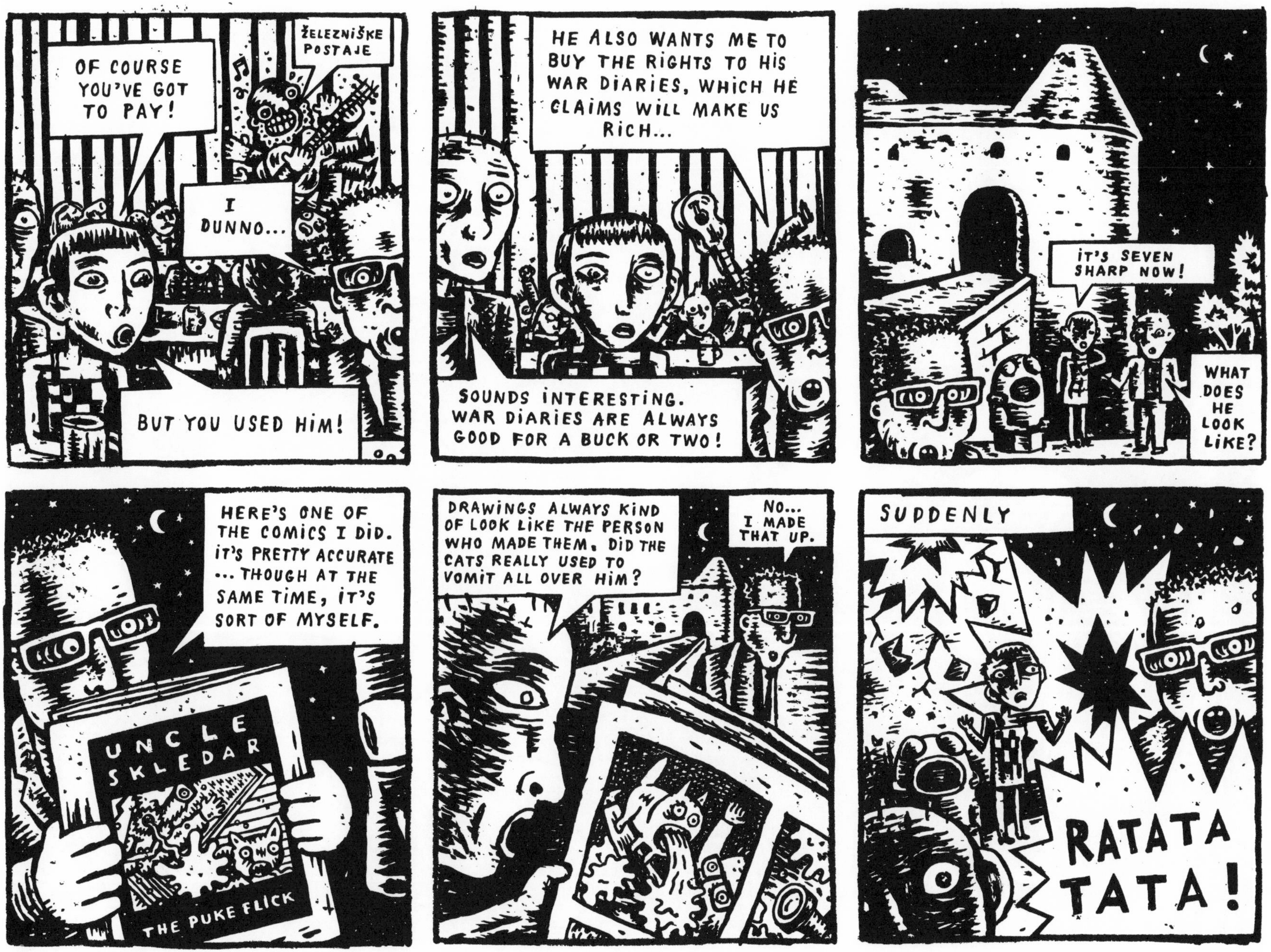
OF COURSE YOU'VE GOT TO PAY!
ŽELEZNIŠKE POSTAJE
I DUNNO...
BUT YOU USED HIM!
HE ALSO WANTS ME TO BUY THE RIGHTS TO HIS WAR DIARIES, WHICH HE CLAIMS WILL MAKE US RICH...
SOUNDS INTERESTING. WAR DIARIES ARE ALWAYS GOOD FOR A BUCK OR TWO!
IT'S SEVEN SHARP NOW!
WHAT DOES HE LOOK LIKE?
HERE'S ONE OF THE COMICS I DID. IT'S PRETTY ACCURATE ... THOUGH AT THE SAME TIME, IT'S SORT OF MYSELF.
UNCLE SKLEDAR
THE PUKE FLICK
DRAWINGS ALWAYS KIND OF LOOK LIKE THE PERSON WHO MADE THEM. DID THE CATS REALLY USED TO VOMIT ALL OVER HIM?
NO... I MADE THAT UP.
SUDDENLY
RATATA TATA!

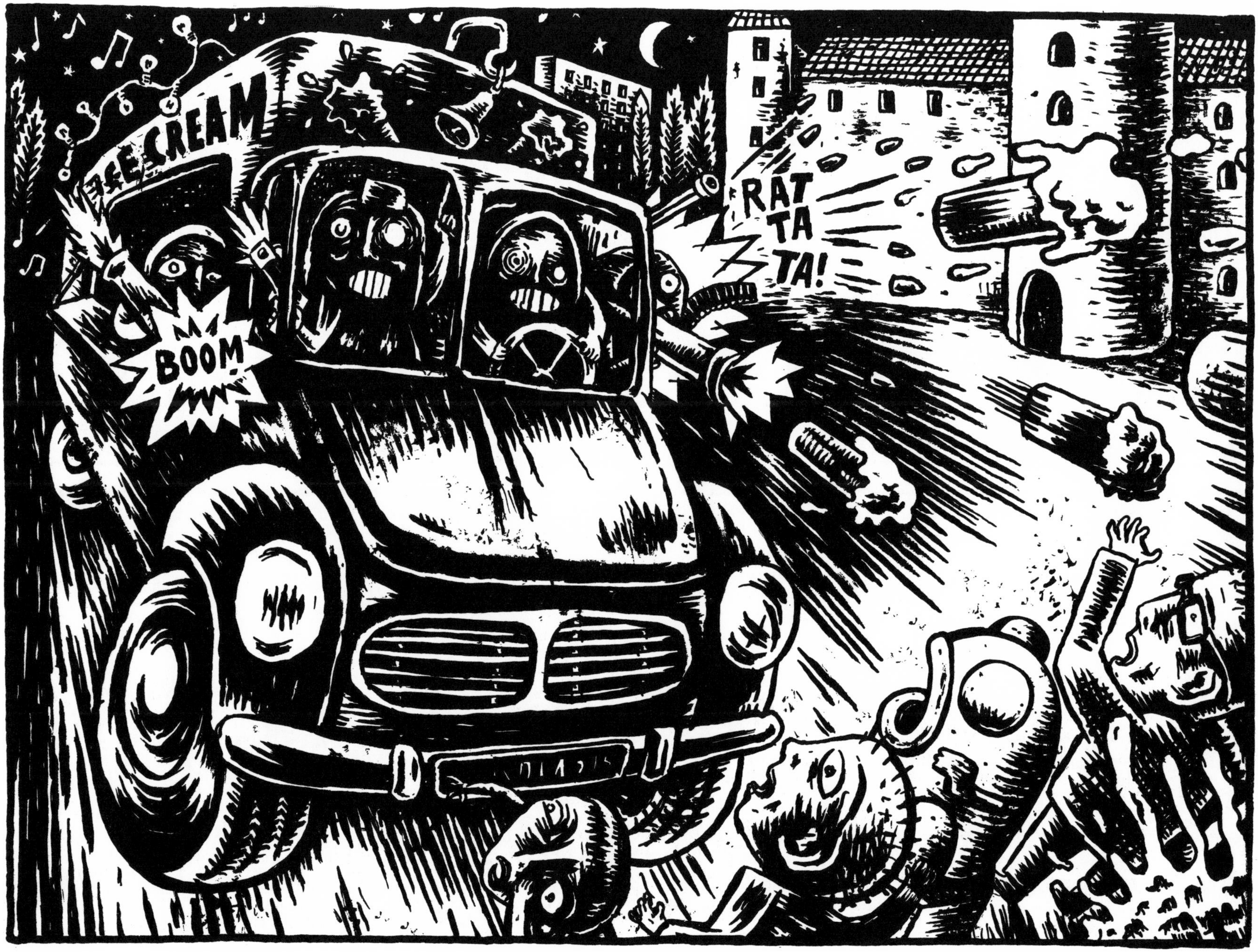
CE CREAM
BOOM
RAT TA TA!

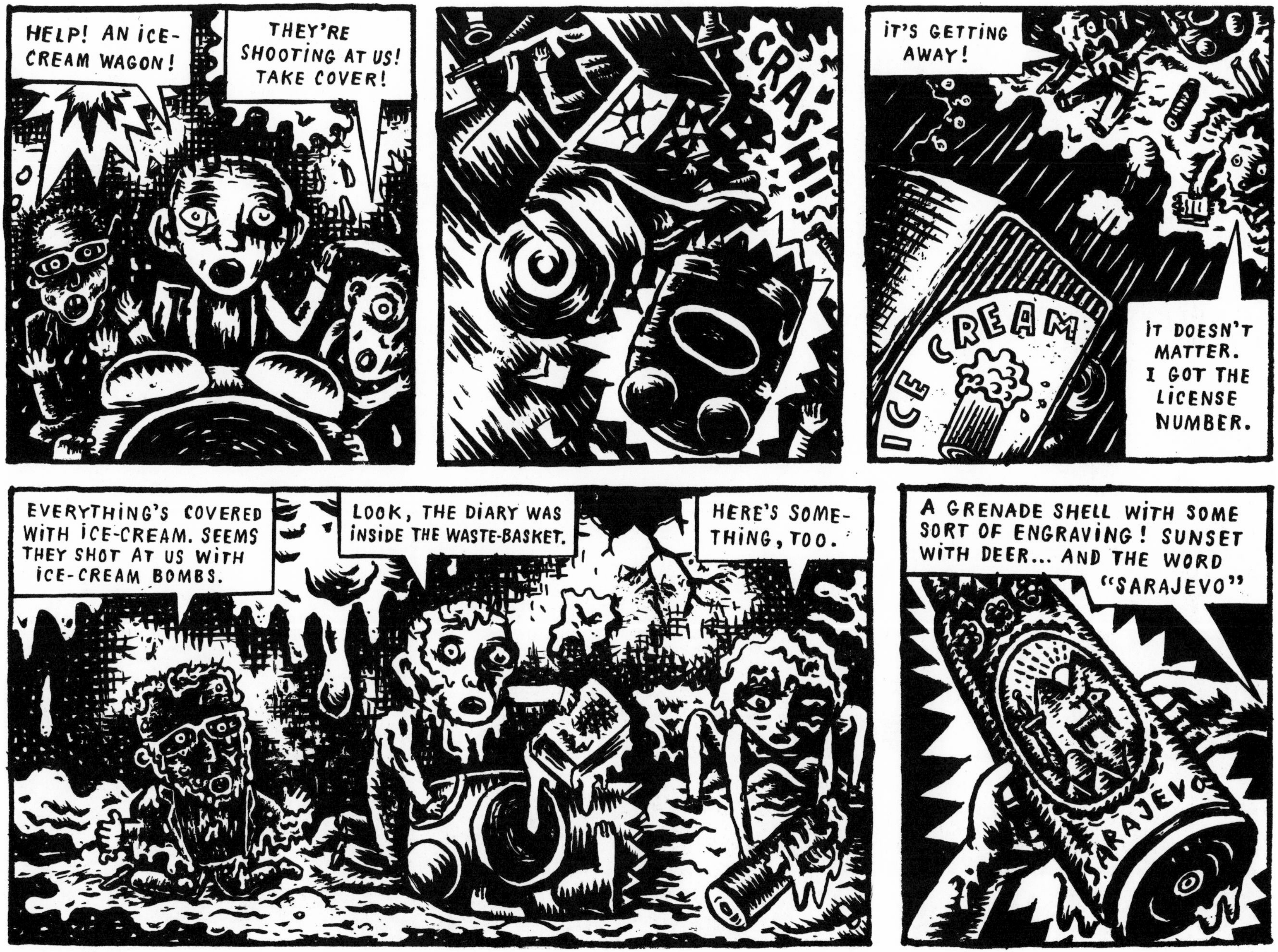
HELP! AN ICE-CREAM WAGON!
THEY'RE SHOOTING AT US! TAKE COVER!
CRASH!
IT'S GETTING AWAY!
ICE CREAM
IT DOESN'T MATTER. I GOT THE LICENSE NUMBER.
EVERYTHING'S COVERED WITH ICE-CREAM. SEEMS THEY SHOT AT US WITH ICE-CREAM BOMBS.
LOOK, THE DIARY WAS INSIDE THE WASTE-BASKET.
HERE'S SOMETHING, TOO.
A GRENADE SHELL WITH SOME SORT OF ENGRAVING! SUNSET WITH DEER... AND THE WORD "SARAJEVO"
SARAJEVO

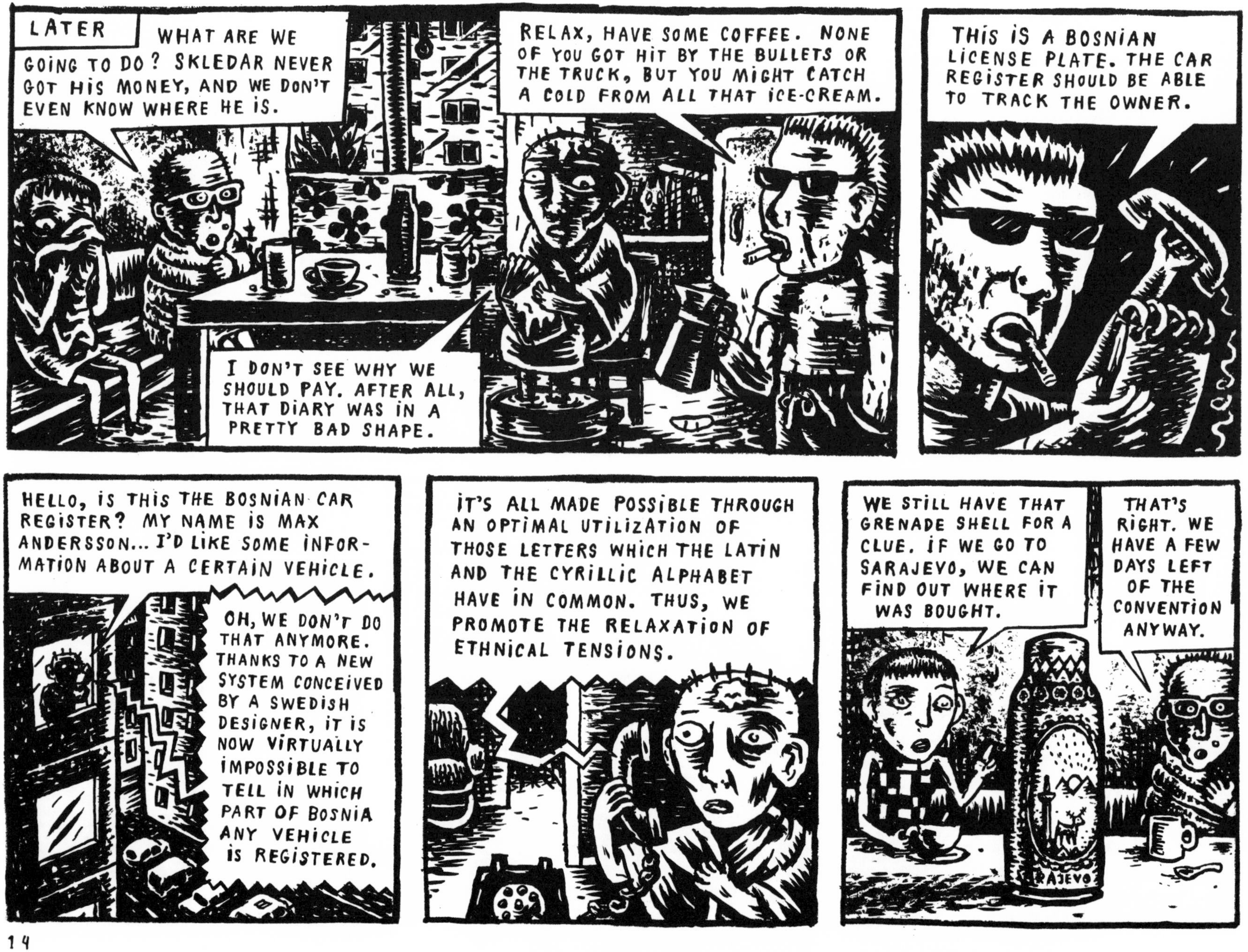
LATER
WHAT ARE WE GOING TO DO? SKLEDAR NEVER GOT HIS MONEY, AND WE DON'T EVEN KNOW WHERE HE IS.
I DON'T SEE WHY WE SHOULD PAY. AFTER ALL, THAT DIARY WAS IN A PRETTY BAD SHAPE.
RELAX, HAVE SOME COFFEE. NONE OF YOU GOT HIT BY THE BULLETS OR THE TRUCK, BUT YOU MIGHT CATCH A COLD FROM ALL THAT ICE-CREAM.
THIS IS A BOSNIAN LICENSE PLATE. THE CAR REGISTER SHOULD BE ABLE TO TRACK THE OWNER.
HELLO, IS THIS THE BOSNIAN CAR REGISTER? MY NAME IS MAX ANDERSSON... I'D LIKE SOME INFORMATION ABOUT A CERTAIN VEHICLE.
OH, WE DON'T DO THAT ANYMORE. THANKS TO A NEW SYSTEM CONCEIVED BY A SWEDISH DESIGNER, IT IS NOW VIRTUALLY IMPOSSIBLE TO TELL IN WHICH PART OF BOSNIA ANY VEHICLE IS REGISTERED.
IT'S ALL MADE POSSIBLE THROUGH AN OPTIMAL UTILIZATION OF THOSE LETTERS WHICH THE LATIN AND THE CYRILLIC ALPHABET HAVE IN COMMON. THUS, WE PROMOTE THE RELAXATION OF ETHNICAL TENSIONS.
WE STILL HAVE THAT GRENADE SHELL FOR A CLUE. IF WE GO TO SARAJEVO, WE CAN FIND OUT WHERE IT WAS BOUGHT.
THAT'S RIGHT. WE HAVE A FEW DAYS LEFT OF THE CONVENTION ANYWAY.
SARAJEVO

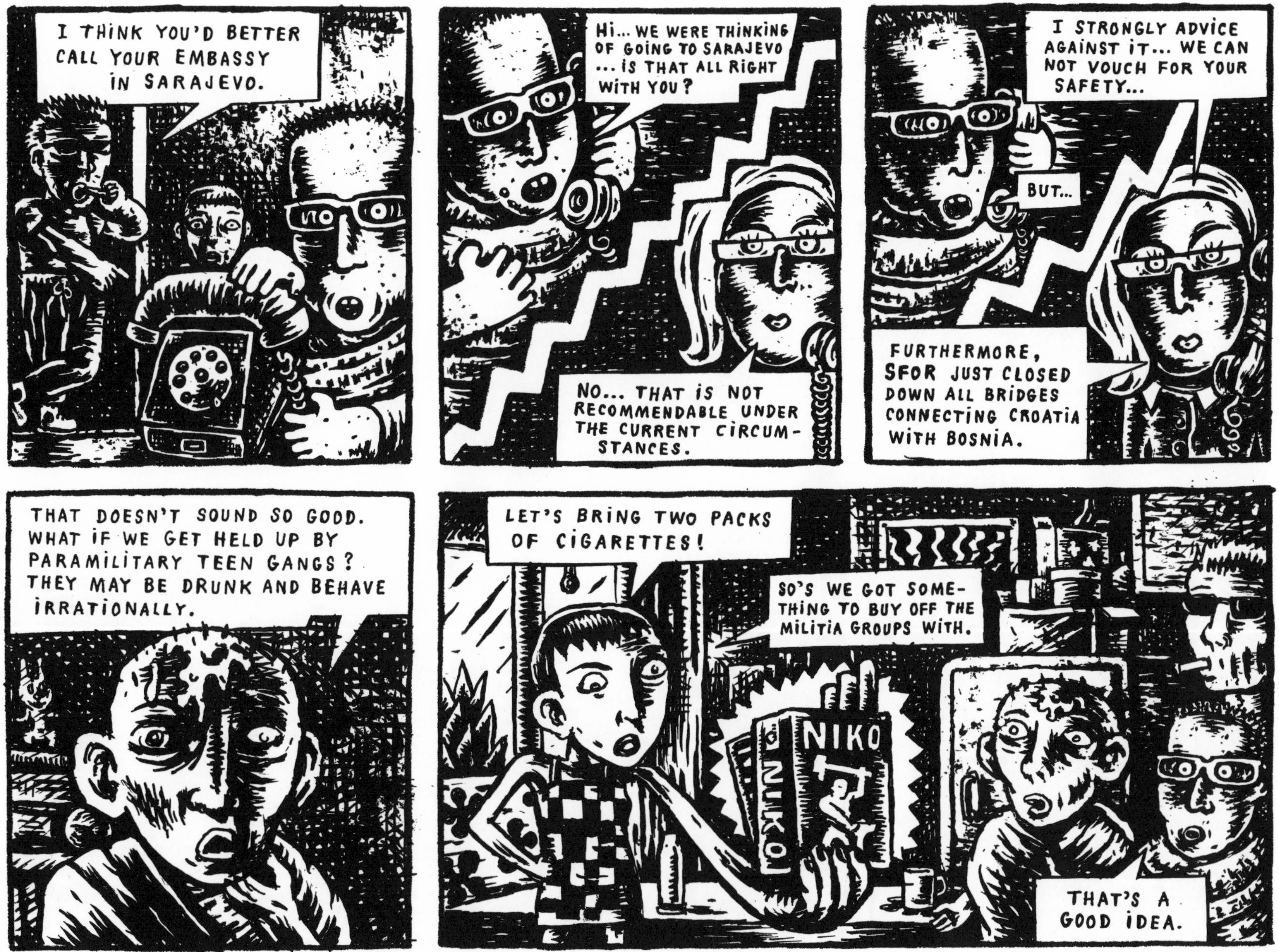
I THINK YOU'D BETTER CALL YOUR EMBASSY IN SARAJEVO.
HI... WE WERE THINKING OF GOING TO SARAJEVO ... IS THAT ALL RIGHT WITH YOU?
NO... THAT IS NOT RECOMMENDABLE UNDER THE CURRENT CIRCUM-STANCES.
I STRONGLY ADVICE AGAINST IT... WE CAN NOT VOUCH FOR YOUR SAFETY...
BUT...
FURTHERMORE, SFOR JUST CLOSED DOWN ALL BRIDGES CONNECTING CROATIA WITH BOSNIA.
THAT DOESN'T SOUND SO GOOD. WHAT IF WE GET HELD UP BY PARAMILITARY TEEN GANGS? THEY MAY BE DRUNK AND BEHAVE IRRATIONALLY.
LET'S BRING TWO PACKS OF CIGARETTES!
SO'S WE GOT SOME-THING TO BUY OFF THE MILITIA GROUPS WITH.
NIKO
NIKO
THAT'S A GOOD IDEA.

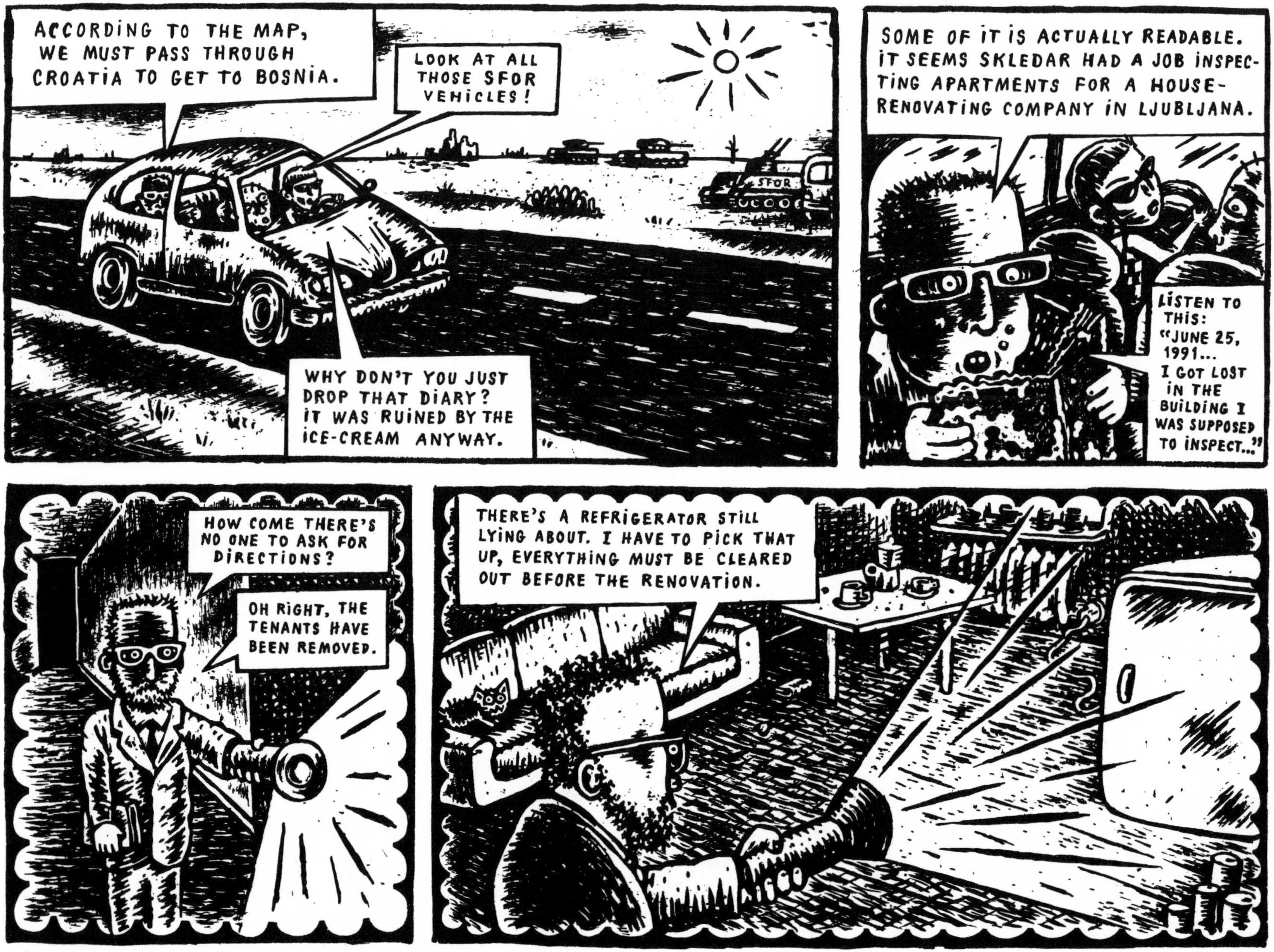
ACCORDING TO THE MAP, WE MUST PASS THROUGH CROATIA TO GET TO BOSNIA.
LOOK AT ALL THOSE SFOR VEHICLES!
SFOR
WHY DON'T YOU JUST DROP THAT DIARY? IT WAS RUINED BY THE ICE-CREAM ANYWAY.
SOME OF IT IS ACTUALLY READABLE. IT SEEMS SKLEDAR HAD A JOB INSPECTING APARTMENTS FOR A HOUSE-RENOVATING COMPANY IN LJUBLJANA.
LISTEN TO THIS: "JUNE 25, 1991... I GOT LOST IN THE BUILDING I WAS SUPPOSED TO INSPECT..."
HOW COME THERE'S NO ONE TO ASK FOR DIRECTIONS?
OH RIGHT, THE TENANTS HAVE BEEN REMOVED.
THERE'S A REFRIGERATOR STILL LYING ABOUT. I HAVE TO PICK THAT UP, EVERYTHING MUST BE CLEARED OUT BEFORE THE RENOVATION.

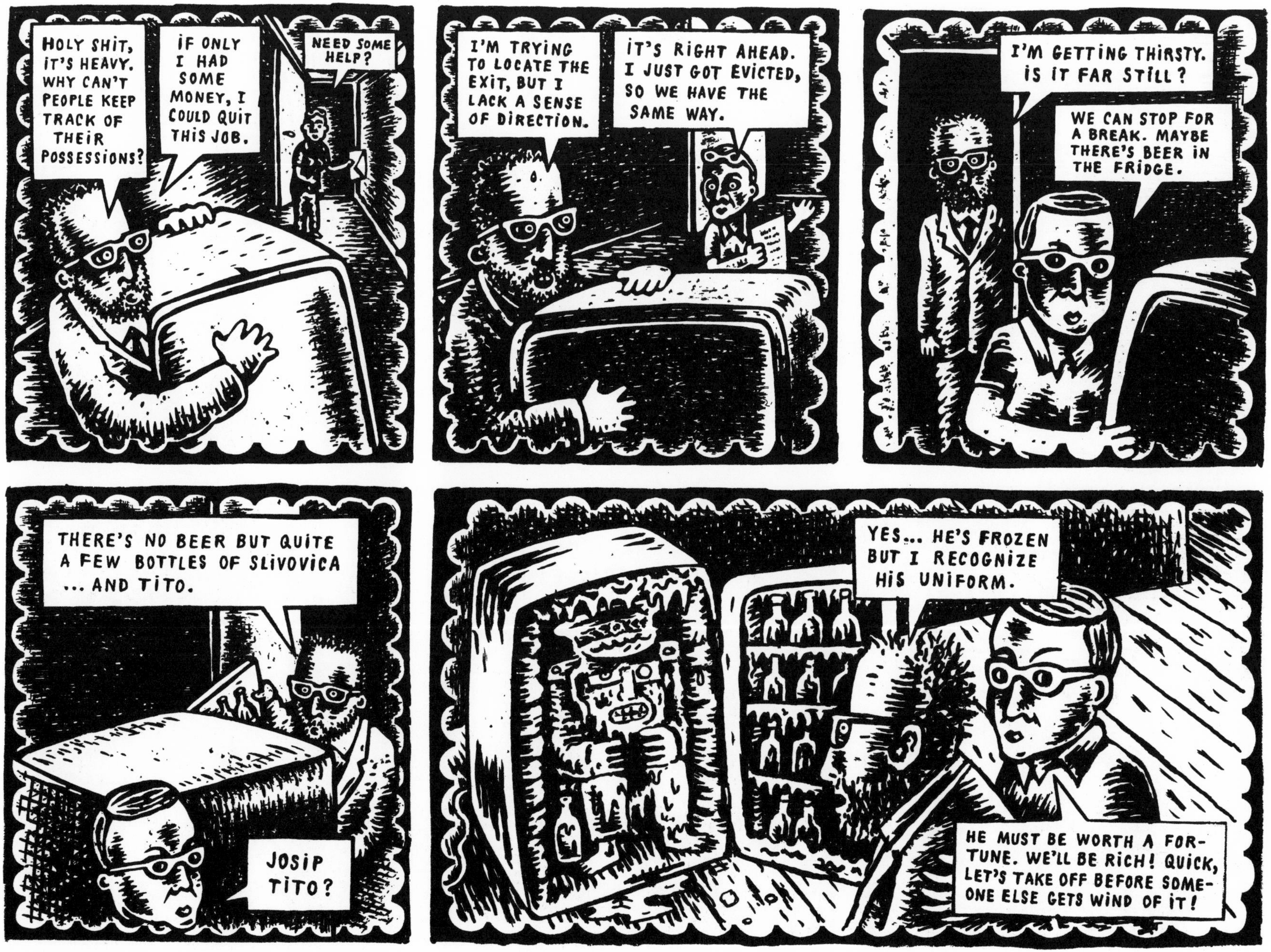
HOLY SHIT, IT'S HEAVY. WHY CAN'T PEOPLE KEEP TRACK OF THEIR POSSESSIONS?
IF ONLY I HAD SOME MONEY, I COULD QUIT THIS JOB.
NEED SOME HELP?
I'M TRYING TO LOCATE THE EXIT, BUT I LACK A SENSE OF DIRECTION.
IT'S RIGHT AHEAD. I JUST GOT EVICTED, SO WE HAVE THE SAME WAY.
I'M GETTING THIRSTY. IS IT FAR STILL?
WE CAN STOP FOR A BREAK. MAYBE THERE'S BEER IN THE FRIDGE.
THERE'S NO BEER BUT QUITE A FEW BOTTLES OF SLIVOVICA ... AND TITO.
JOSIP TITO?
YES... HE'S FROZEN BUT I RECOGNIZE HIS UNIFORM.
HE MUST BE WORTH A FORTUNE. WE'LL BE RICH! QUICK, LET'S TAKE OFF BEFORE SOMEONE ELSE GETS WIND OF IT!

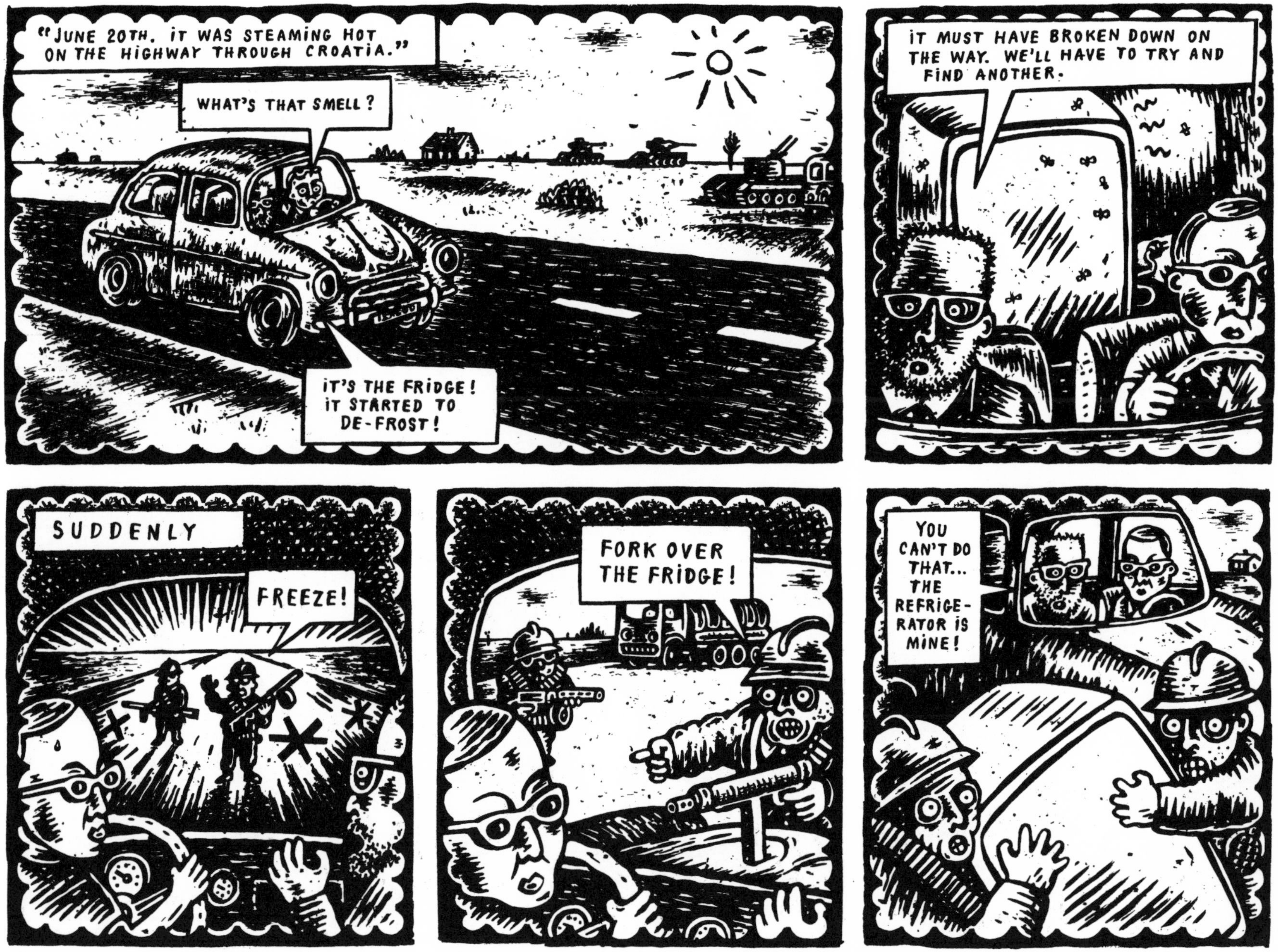
"JUNE 20TH. IT WAS STEAMING HOT ON THE HIGHWAY THROUGH CROATIA."
WHAT'S THAT SMELL?
IT'S THE FRIDGE! IT STARTED TO DE-FROST!
IT MUST HAVE BROKEN DOWN ON THE WAY. WE'LL HAVE TO TRY AND FIND ANOTHER.
SUDDENLY
FREEZE!
FORK OVER THE FRIDGE!
YOU CAN'T DO THAT... THE REFRIGE-RATOR IS MINE!

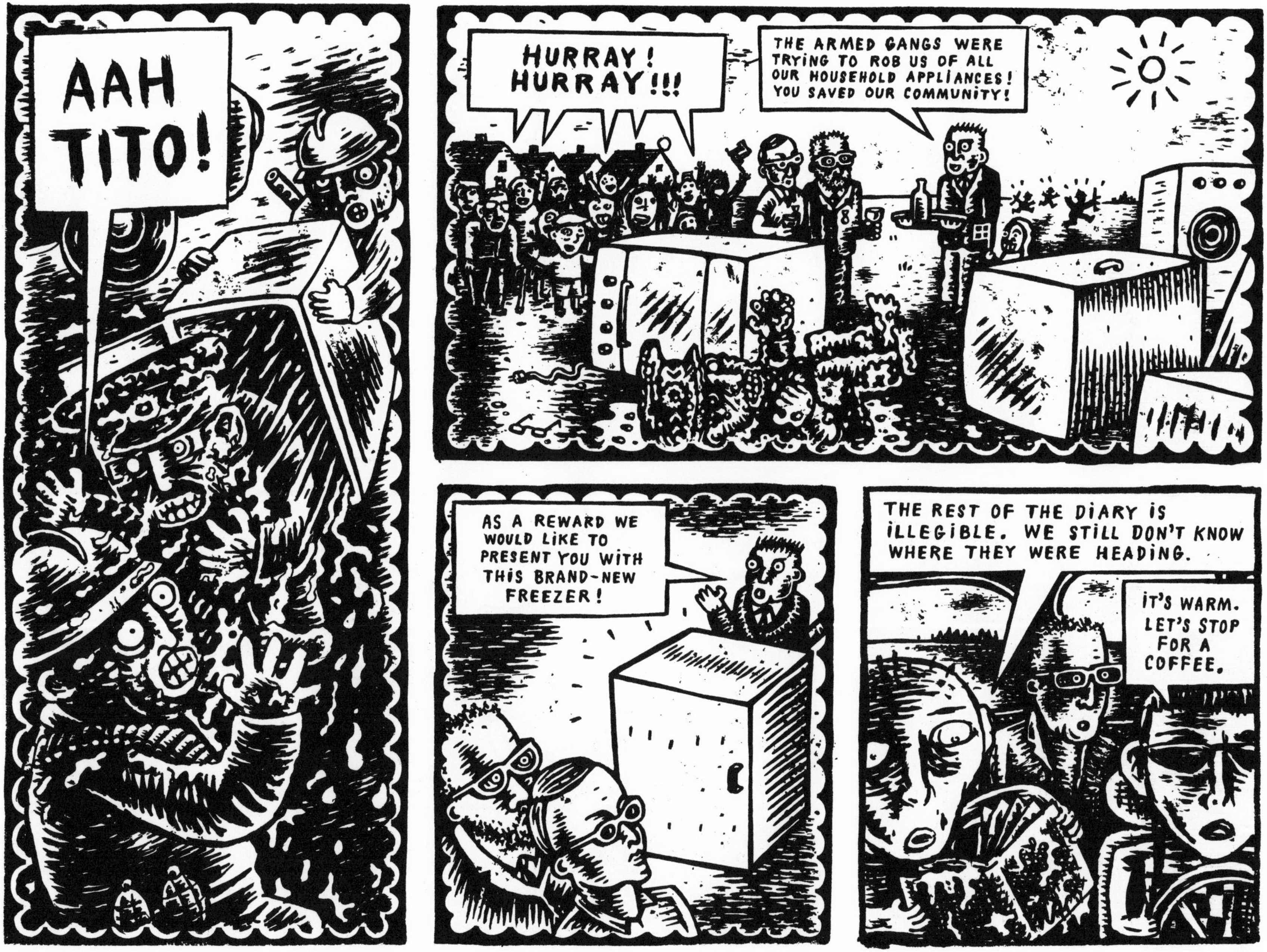
AAH TITO!
HURRAY! HURRAY!!!
THE ARMED GANGS WERE TRYING TO ROB US OF ALL OUR HOUSEHOLD APPLIANCES! YOU SAVED OUR COMMUNITY!
AS A REWARD WE WOULD LIKE TO PRESENT YOU WITH THIS BRAND-NEW FREEZER!
THE REST OF THE DIARY IS ILLEGIBLE. WE STILL DON'T KNOW WHERE THEY WERE HEADING.
IT'S WARM. LET'S STOP FOR A COFFEE.

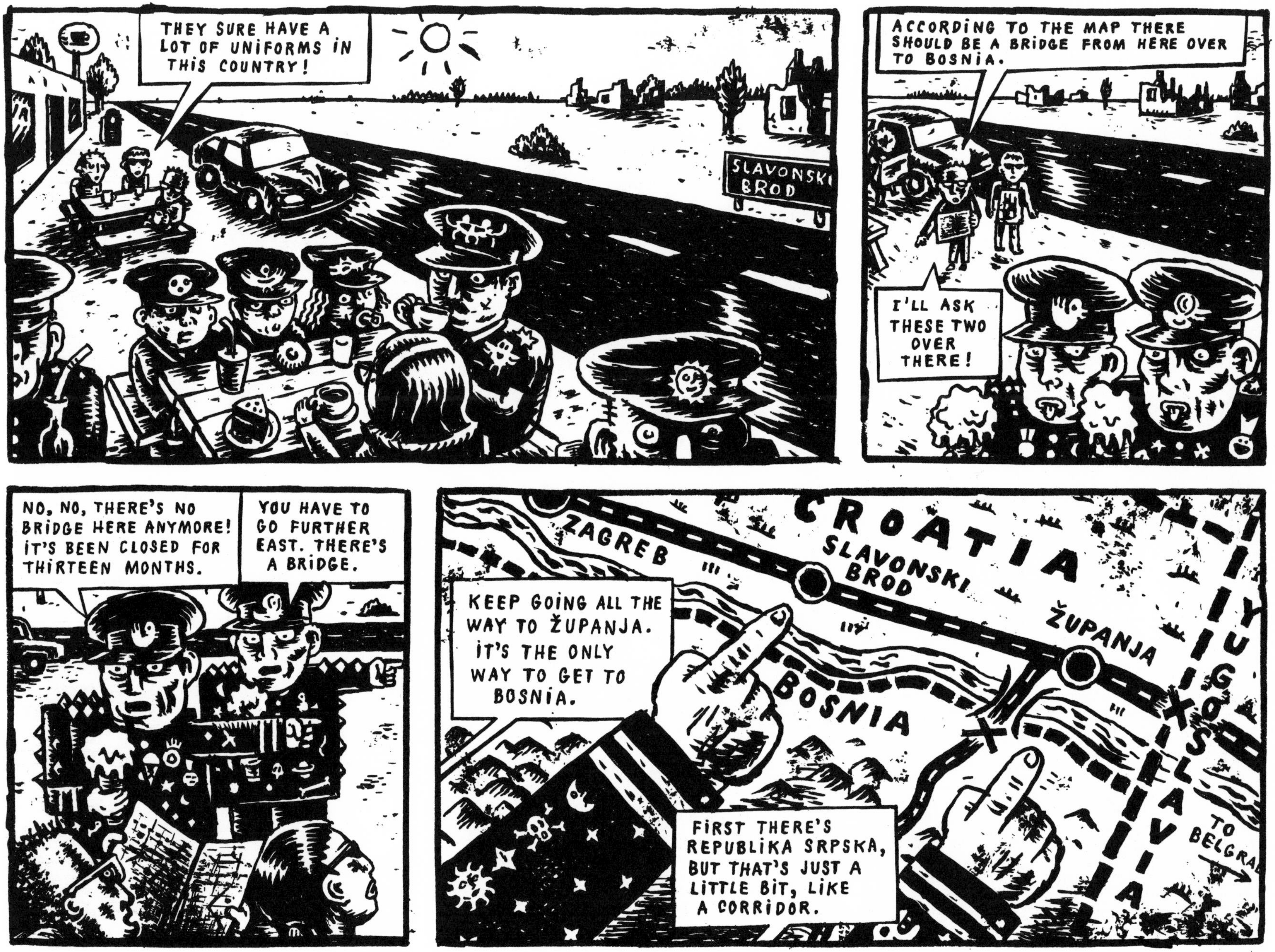
THEY SURE HAVE A LOT OF UNIFORMS IN THIS COUNTRY!
SLAVONSKI BROD
ACCORDING TO THE MAP THERE SHOULD BE A BRIDGE FROM HERE OVER TO BOSNIA.
I'LL ASK THESE TWO OVER THERE!
NO, NO, THERE'S NO BRIDGE HERE ANYMORE! IT'S BEEN CLOSED FOR THIRTEEN MONTHS.
YOU HAVE TO GO FURTHER EAST. THERE'S A BRIDGE.
CROATIA
ZAGREB
SLAVONSKI BROD
ŽUPANJA
BOSNIA
YUGOSLAVIA
TO BELGRA
KEEP GOING ALL THE WAY TO ŽUPANJA. IT'S THE ONLY WAY TO GET TO BOSNIA.
FIRST THERE'S REPUBLIKA SRPSKA, BUT THAT'S JUST A LITTLE BIT, LIKE A CORRIDOR.

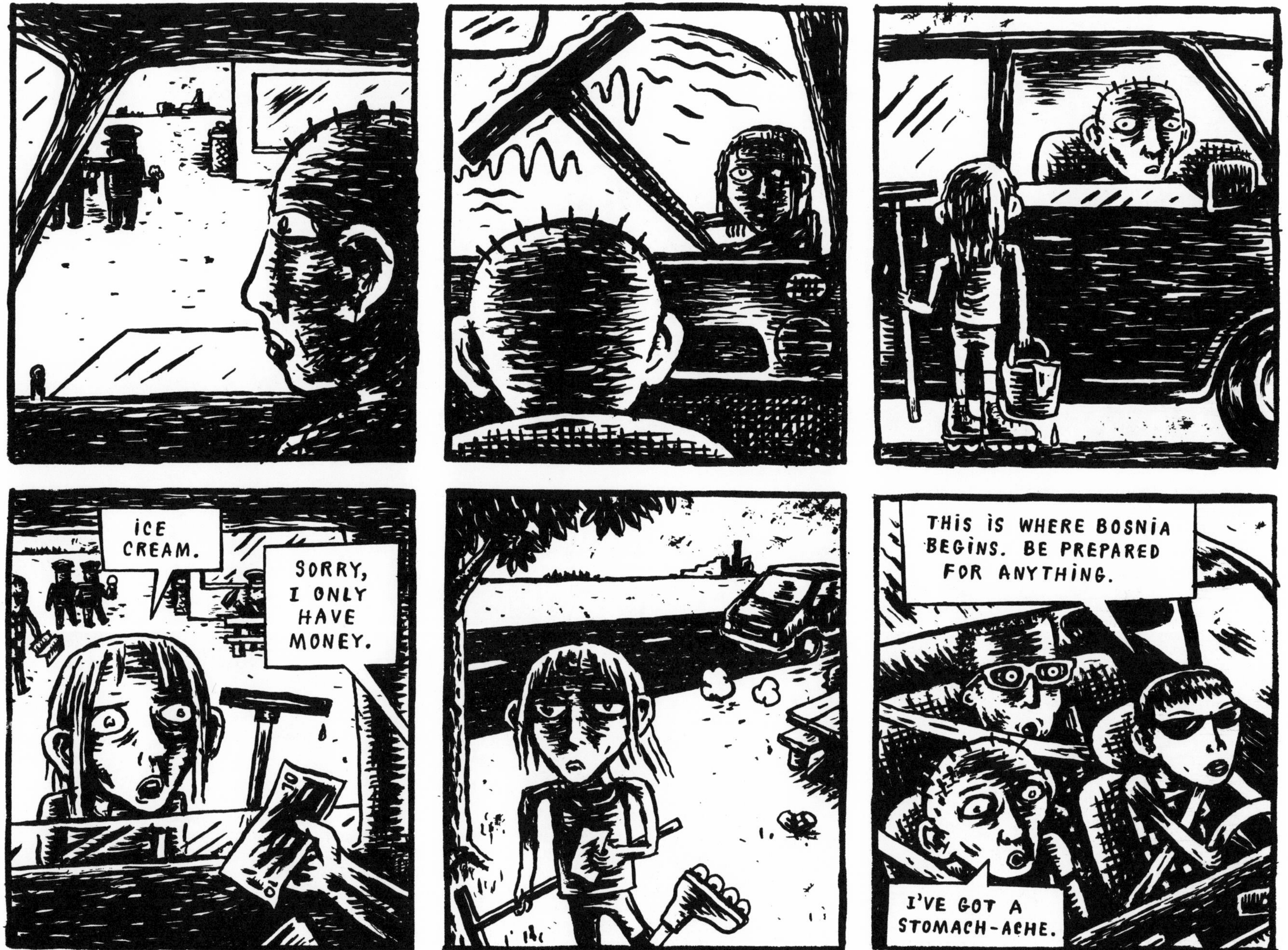
ICE CREAM.
SORRY, I ONLY HAVE MONEY.
THIS IS WHERE BOSNIA BEGINS. BE PREPARED FOR ANYTHING.
I'VE GOT A STOMACH-ACHE.

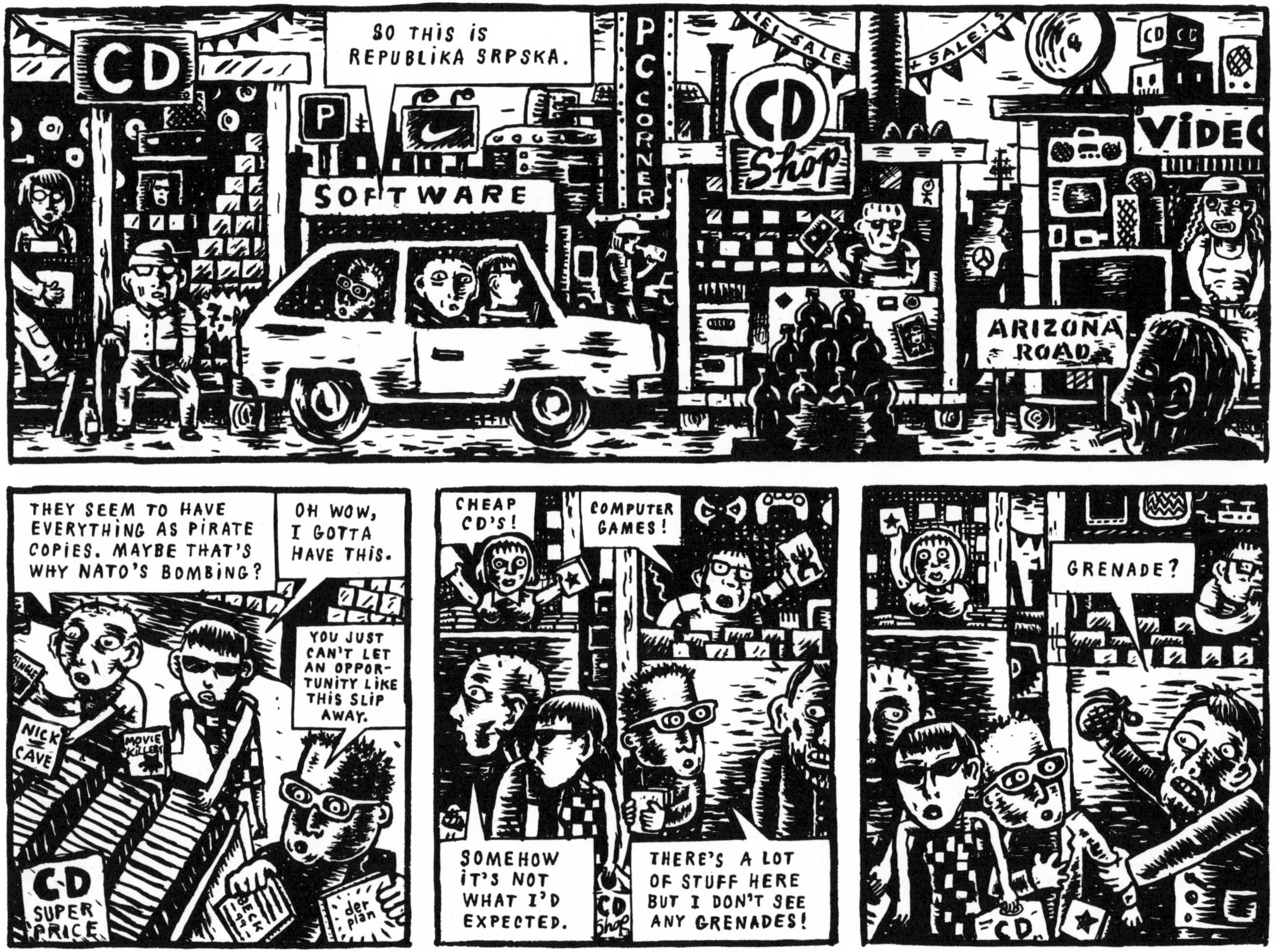
SO THIS IS REPUBLIKA SRPSKA.
CD
SOFTWARE
PC CORNER
CD Shop
SALE!
ARIZONA ROAD
THEY SEEM TO HAVE EVERYTHING AS PIRATE COPIES. MAYBE THAT'S WHY NATO'S BOMBING?
OH WOW, I GOTTA HAVE THIS.
YOU JUST CAN'T LET AN OPPORTUNITY LIKE THIS SLIP AWAY.
NICK CAVE
MOVIE KILLERS
CD SUPER PRICE
der plan
CHEAP CD'S!
COMPUTER GAMES!
SOMEHOW IT'S NOT WHAT I'D EXPECTED.
THERE'S A LOT OF STUFF HERE BUT I DON'T SEE ANY GRENADES!
GRENADE?

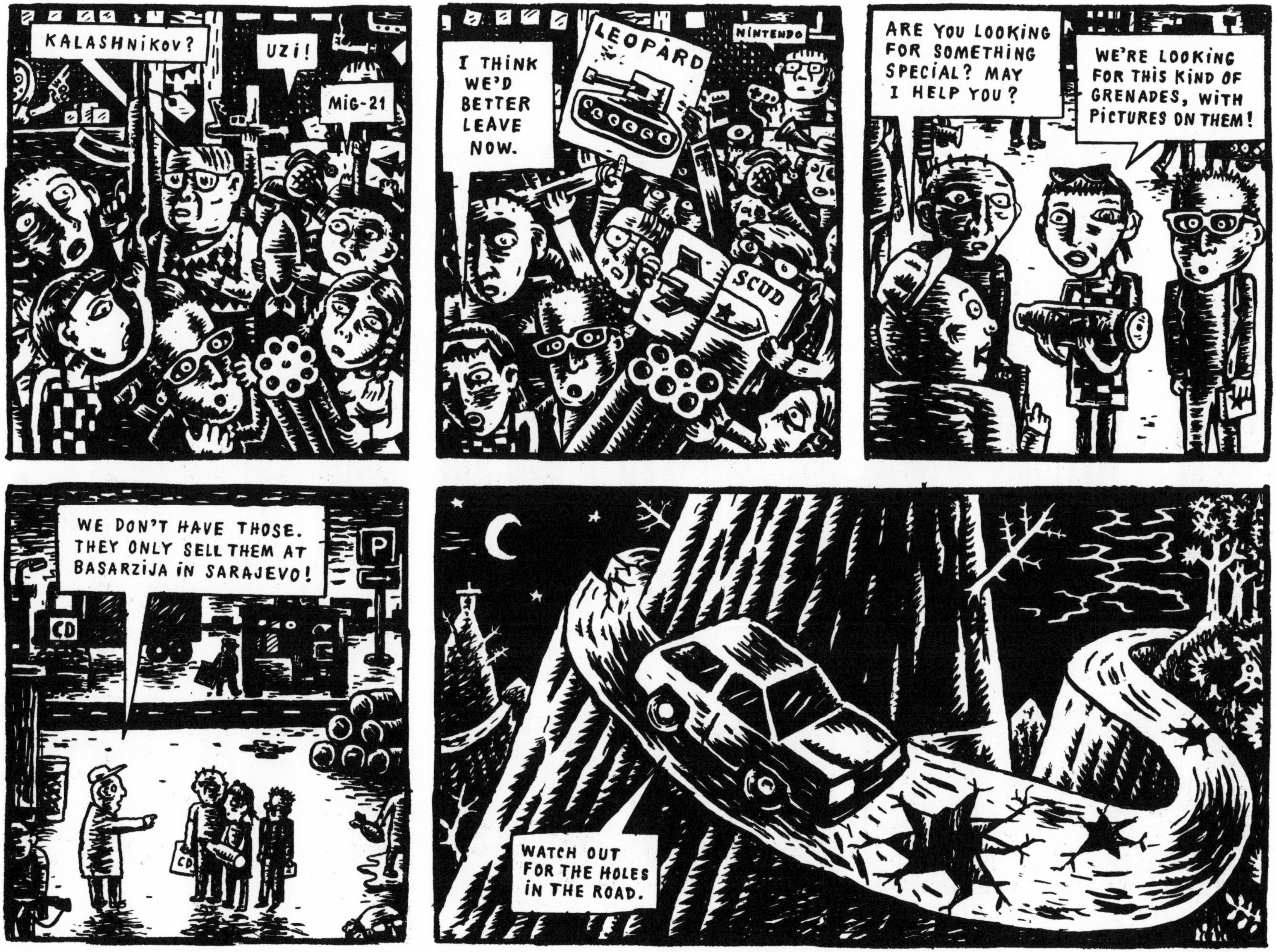

KALASHNIKOV?
UZI!
MIG-21
I THINK WE'D BETTER LEAVE NOW.
LEOPARD
NINTENDO
SCUD
ARE YOU LOOKING FOR SOMETHING SPECIAL? MAY I HELP YOU?
WE'RE LOOKING FOR THIS KIND OF GRENADES, WITH PICTURES ON THEM!
WE DON'T HAVE THOSE. THEY ONLY SELL THEM AT BASARZIJA IN SARAJEVO!
P
CD
CD
WATCH OUT FOR THE HOLES IN THE ROAD.

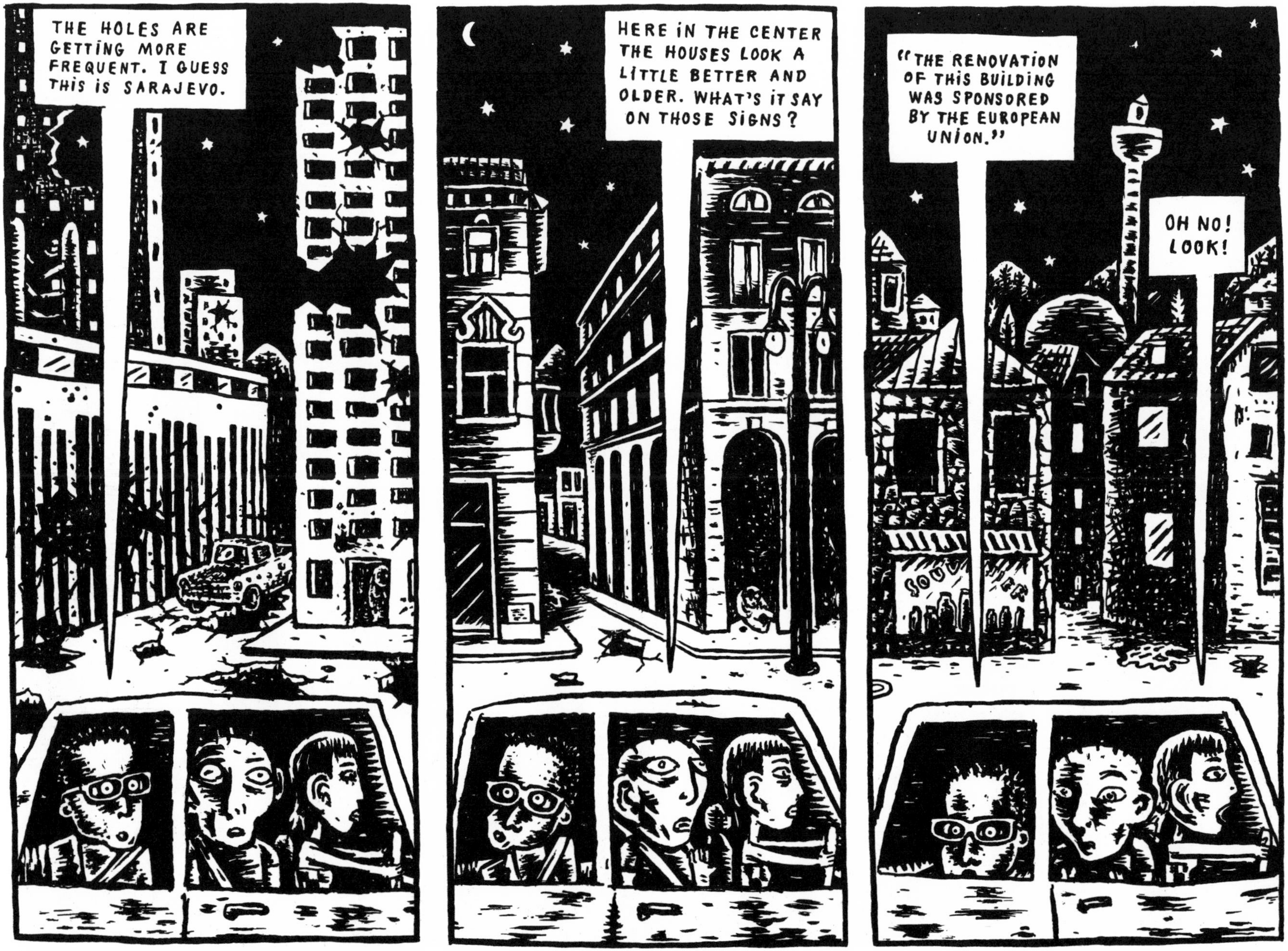
THE HOLES ARE GETTING MORE FREQUENT. I GUESS THIS IS SARAJEVO.
HERE IN THE CENTER THE HOUSES LOOK A LITTLE BETTER AND OLDER. WHAT'S IT SAY ON THOSE SIGNS?
"THE RENOVATION OF THIS BUILDING WAS SPONSORED BY THE EUROPEAN UNION."
OH NO! LOOK!

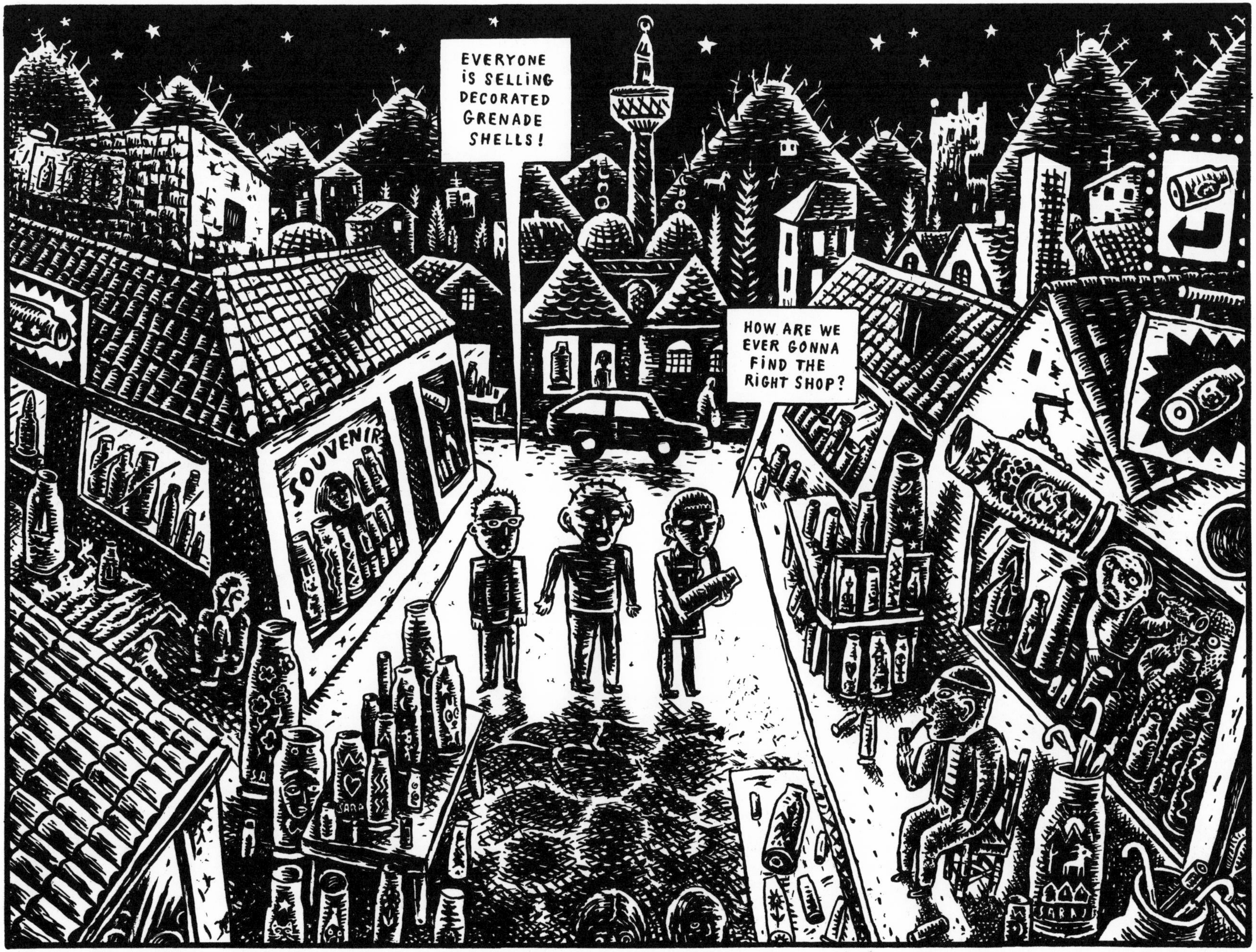
EVERYONE IS SELLING DECORATED GRENADE SHELLS!
HOW ARE WE EVER GONNA FIND THE RIGHT SHOP?
SOUVENIR

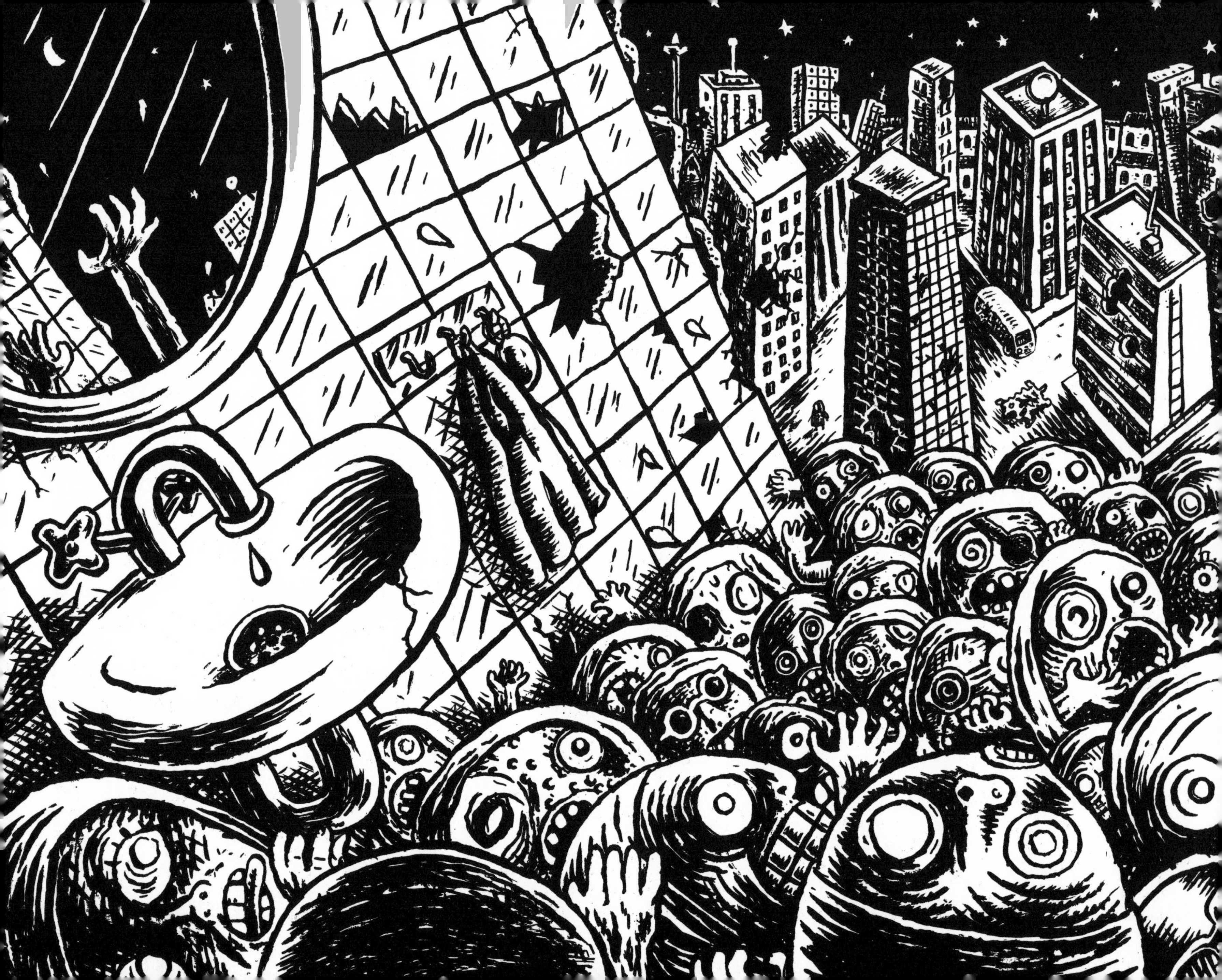

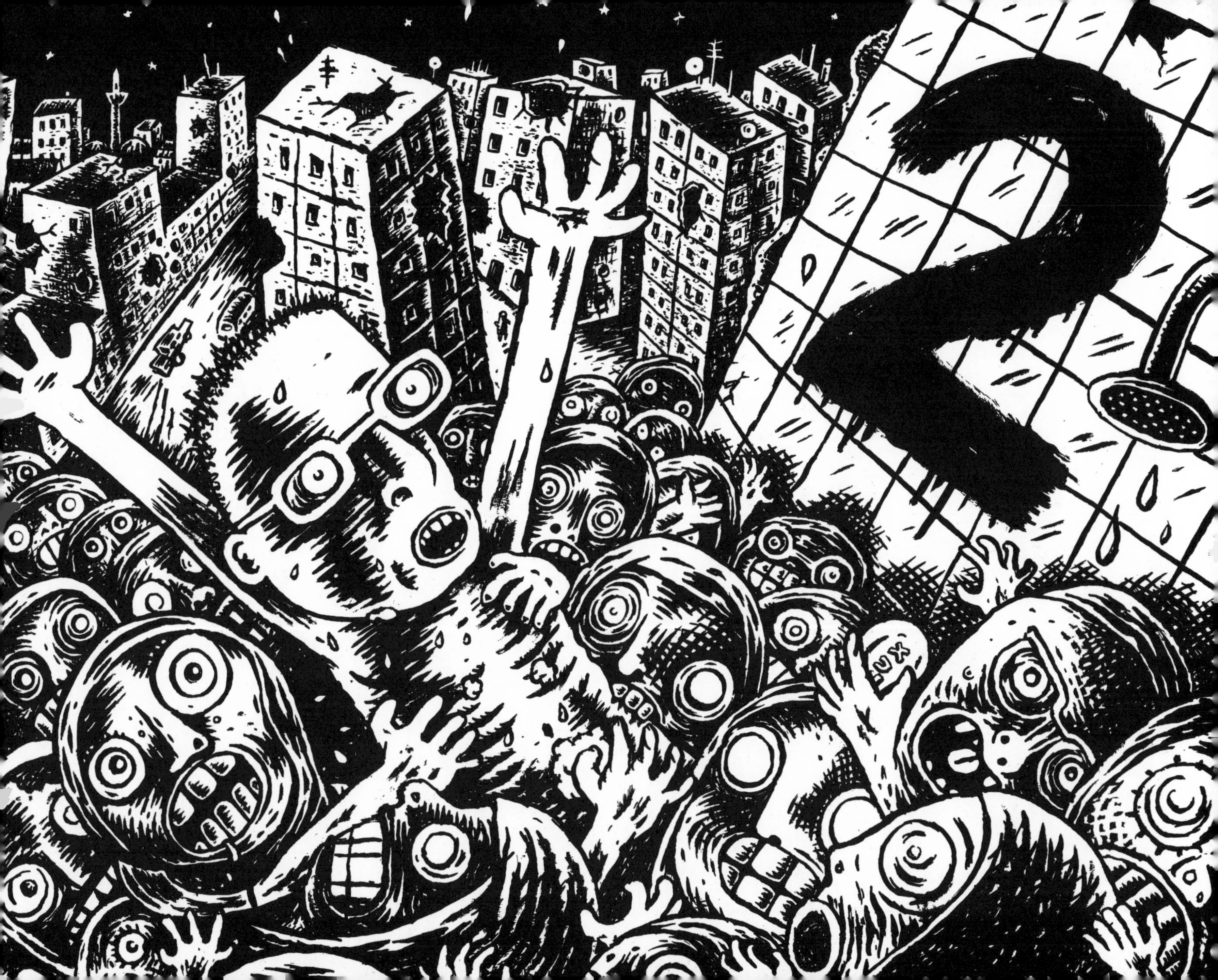
2

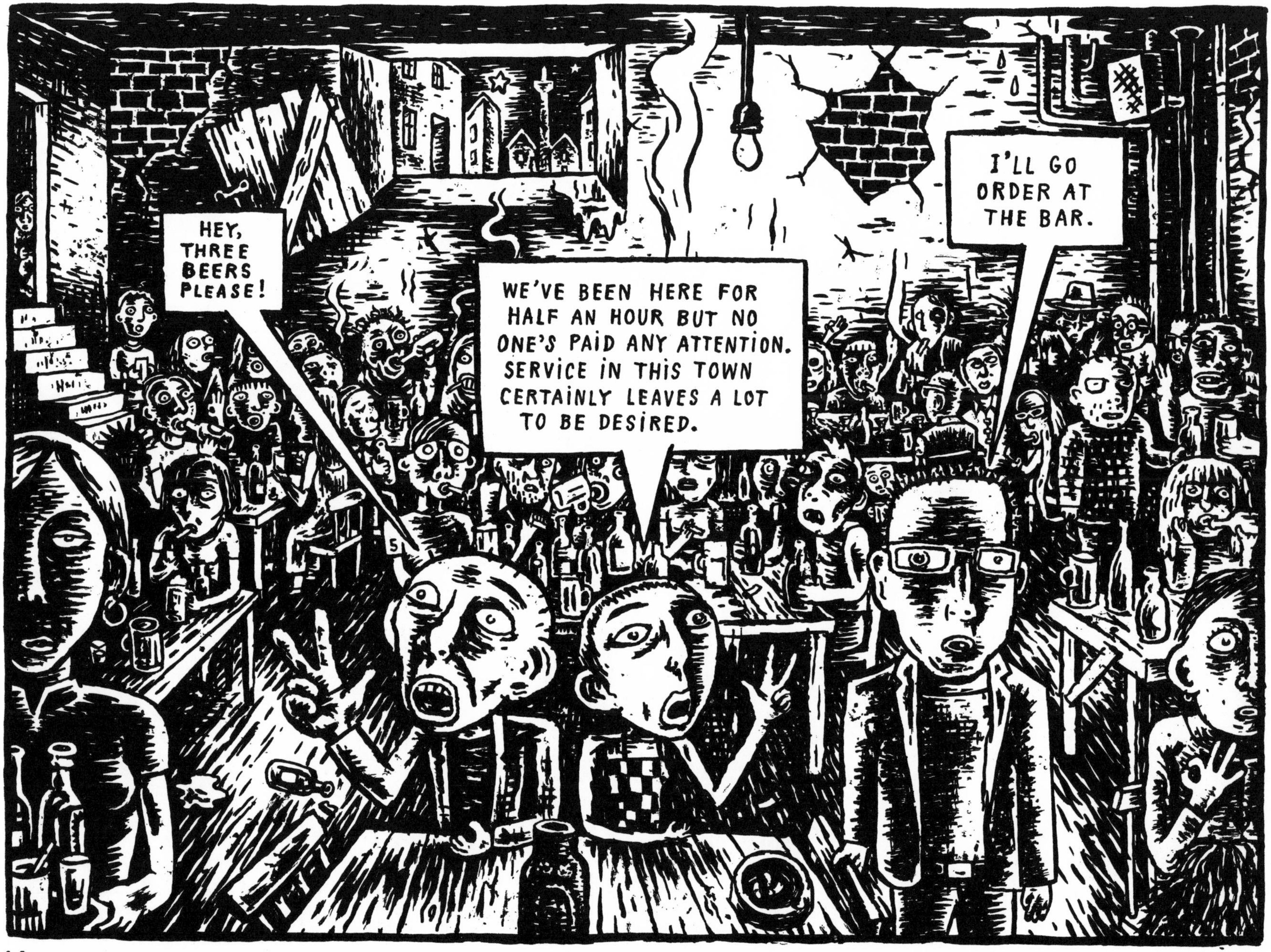
HEY, THREE BEERS PLEASE!
WE'VE BEEN HERE FOR HALF AN HOUR BUT NO ONE'S PAID ANY ATTENTION. SERVICE IN THIS TOWN CERTAINLY LEAVES A LOT TO BE DESIRED.
I'LL GO ORDER AT THE BAR.

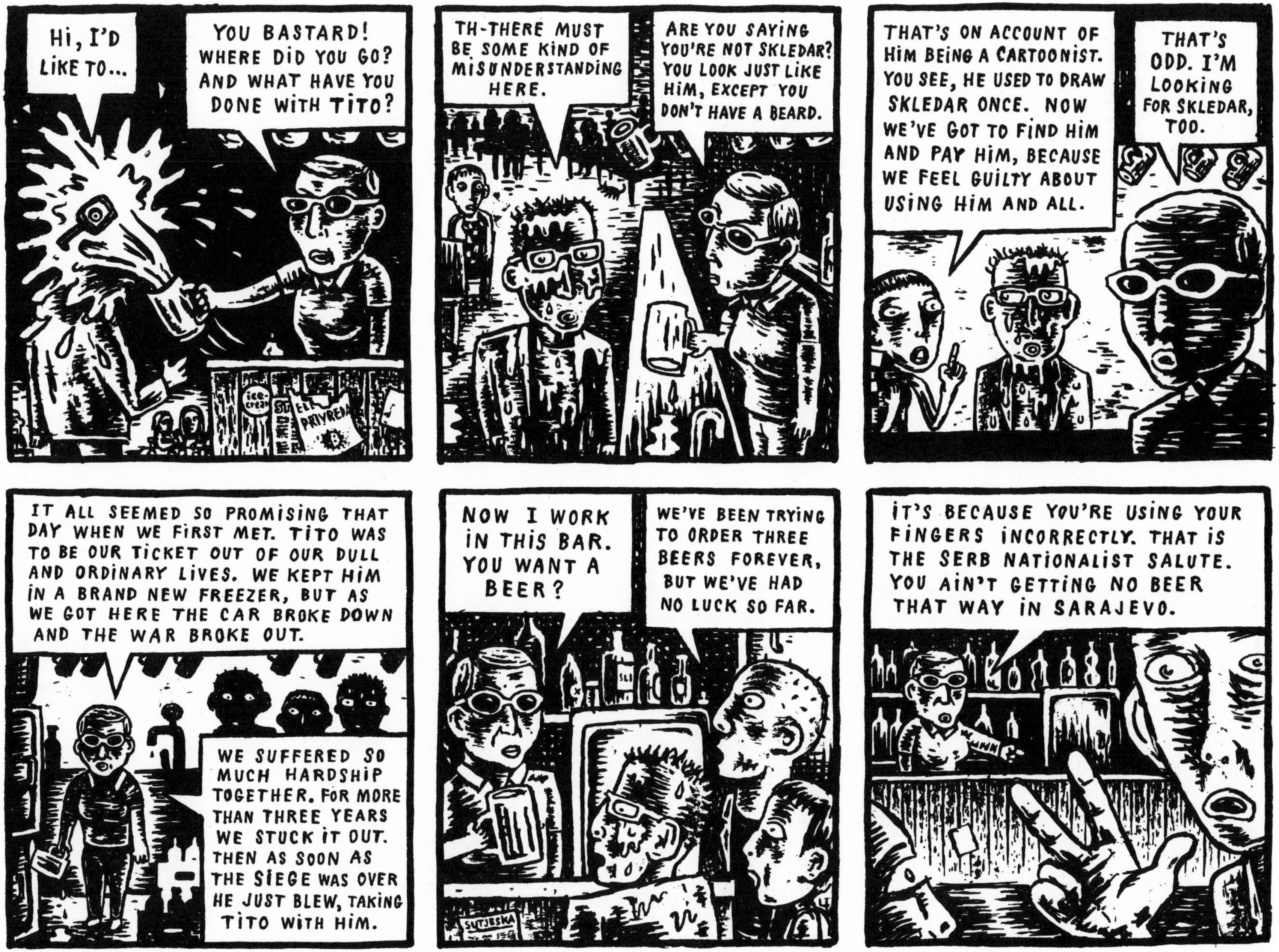
Hi, I'D LIKE TO...
YOU BASTARD! WHERE DID YOU GO? AND WHAT HAVE YOU DONE WITH TITO?
TH-THERE MUST BE SOME KIND OF MISUNDERSTANDING HERE.
ARE YOU SAYING YOU'RE NOT SKLEDAR? YOU LOOK JUST LIKE HIM, EXCEPT YOU DON'T HAVE A BEARD.
THAT'S ON ACCOUNT OF HIM BEING A CARTOONIST. YOU SEE, HE USED TO DRAW SKLEDAR ONCE. NOW WE'VE GOT TO FIND HIM AND PAY HIM, BECAUSE WE FEEL GUILTY ABOUT USING HIM AND ALL.
THAT'S ODD. I'M LOOKING FOR SKLEDAR, TOO.
IT ALL SEEMED SO PROMISING THAT DAY WHEN WE FIRST MET. TITO WAS TO BE OUR TICKET OUT OF OUR DULL AND ORDINARY LIVES. WE KEPT HIM IN A BRAND NEW FREEZER, BUT AS WE GOT HERE THE CAR BROKE DOWN AND THE WAR BROKE OUT.
WE SUFFERED SO MUCH HARDSHIP TOGETHER. FOR MORE THAN THREE YEARS WE STUCK IT OUT. THEN AS SOON AS THE SIEGE WAS OVER HE JUST BLEW, TAKING TITO WITH HIM.
NOW I WORK IN THIS BAR. YOU WANT A BEER?
WE'VE BEEN TRYING TO ORDER THREE BEERS FOREVER, BUT WE'VE HAD NO LUCK SO FAR.
IT'S BECAUSE YOU'RE USING YOUR FINGERS INCORRECTLY. THAT IS THE SERB NATIONALIST SALUTE. YOU AIN'T GETTING NO BEER THAT WAY IN SARAJEVO.

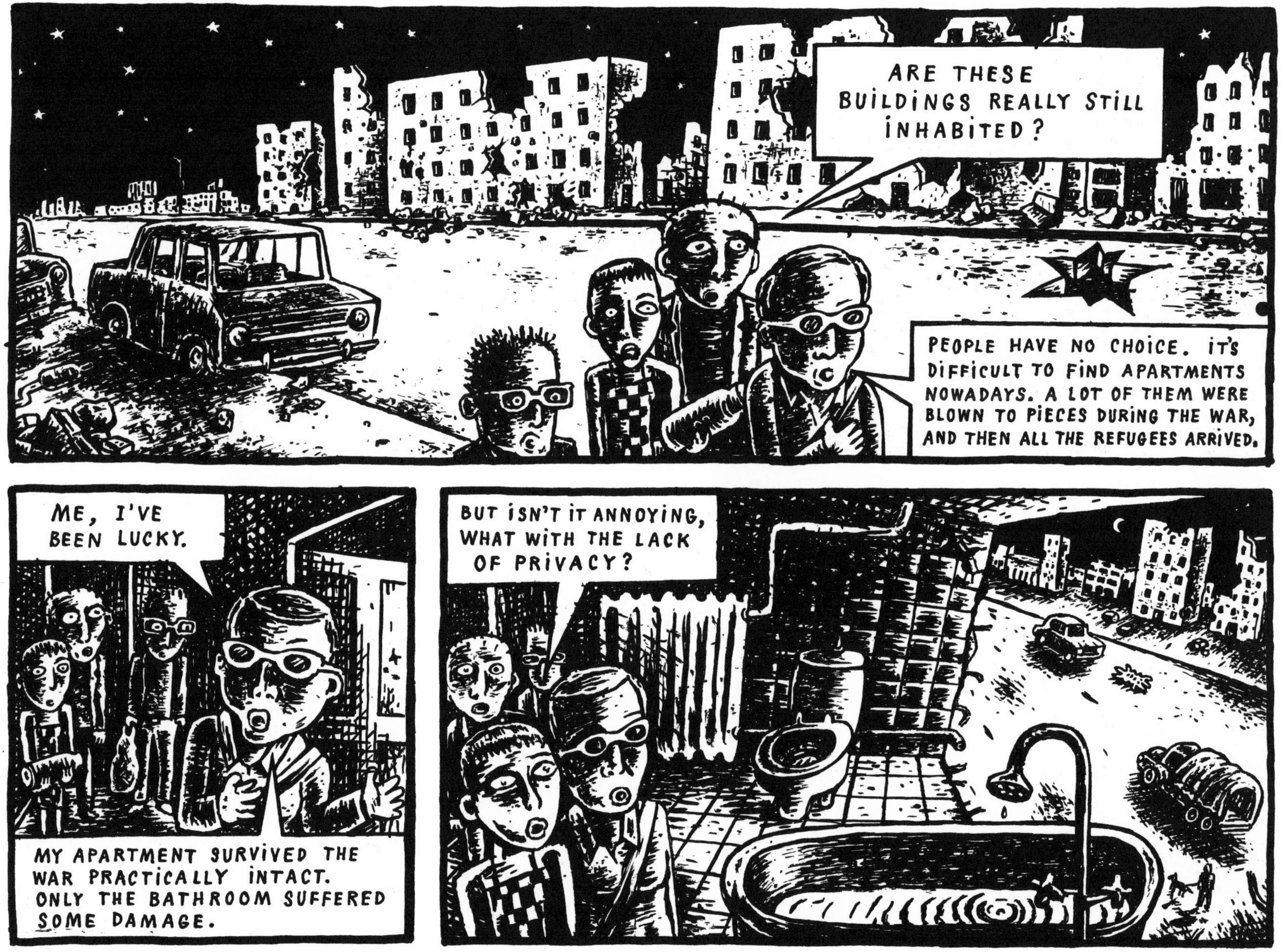
ARE THESE BUILDINGS REALLY STILL INHABITED?
PEOPLE HAVE NO CHOICE. IT'S DIFFICULT TO FIND APARTMENTS NOWADAYS. A LOT OF THEM WERE BLOWN TO PIECES DURING THE WAR, AND THEN ALL THE REFUGEES ARRIVED.
ME, I'VE BEEN LUCKY.
MY APARTMENT SURVIVED THE WAR PRACTICALLY INTACT. ONLY THE BATHROOM SUFFERED SOME DAMAGE.
BUT ISN'T IT ANNOYING, WHAT WITH THE LACK OF PRIVACY?

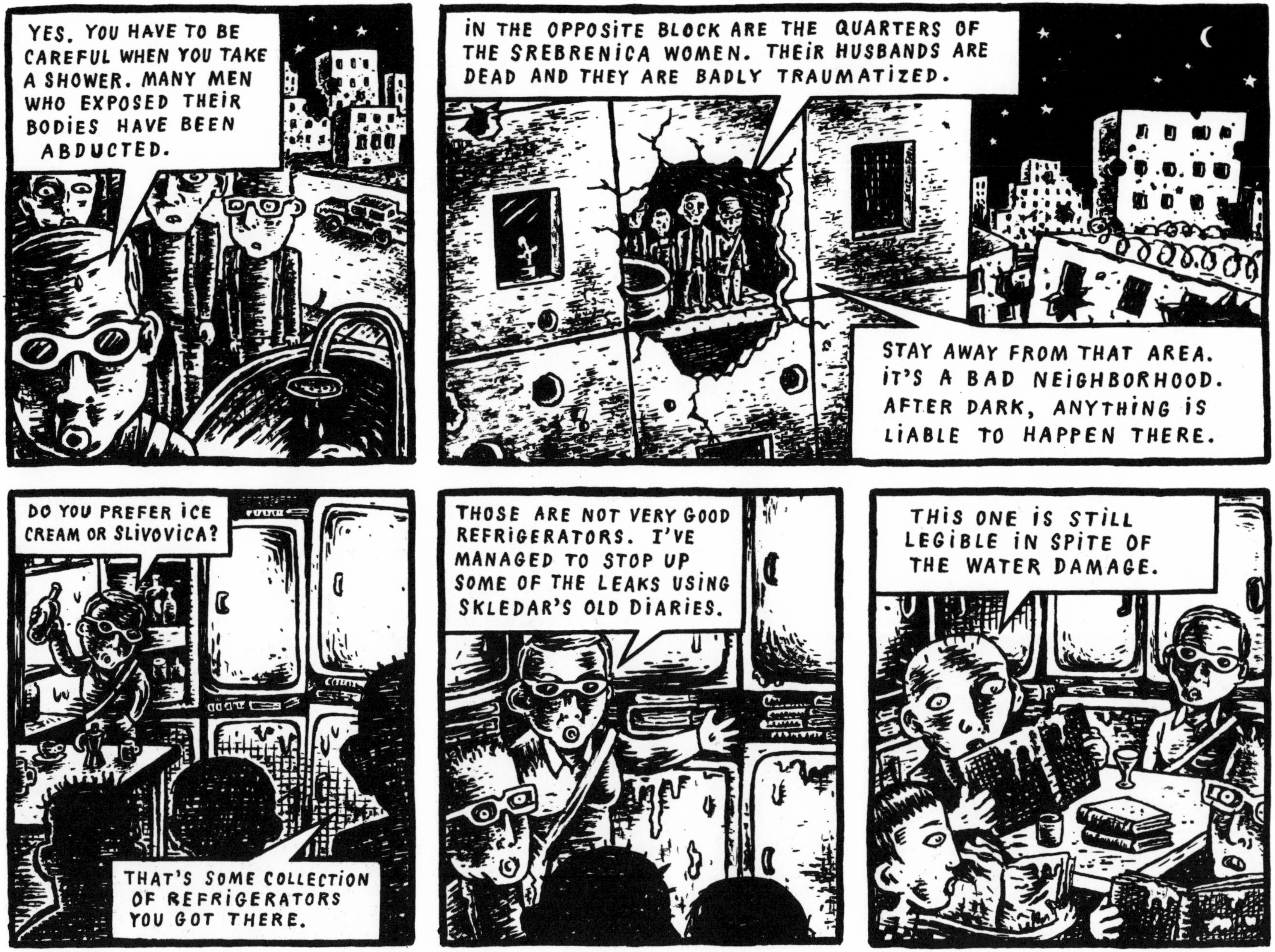
YES. YOU HAVE TO BE CAREFUL WHEN YOU TAKE A SHOWER. MANY MEN WHO EXPOSED THEIR BODIES HAVE BEEN ABDUCTED.
IN THE OPPOSITE BLOCK ARE THE QUARTERS OF THE SREBRENICA WOMEN. THEIR HUSBANDS ARE DEAD AND THEY ARE BADLY TRAUMATIZED.
STAY AWAY FROM THAT AREA. IT'S A BAD NEIGHBORHOOD. AFTER DARK, ANYTHING IS LIABLE TO HAPPEN THERE.
DO YOU PREFER ICE CREAM OR SLIVOVICA?
THAT'S SOME COLLECTION OF REFRIGERATORS YOU GOT THERE.
THOSE ARE NOT VERY GOOD REFRIGERATORS. I'VE MANAGED TO STOP UP SOME OF THE LEAKS USING SKLEDAR'S OLD DIARIES.
THIS ONE IS STILL LEGIBLE IN SPITE OF THE WATER DAMAGE.

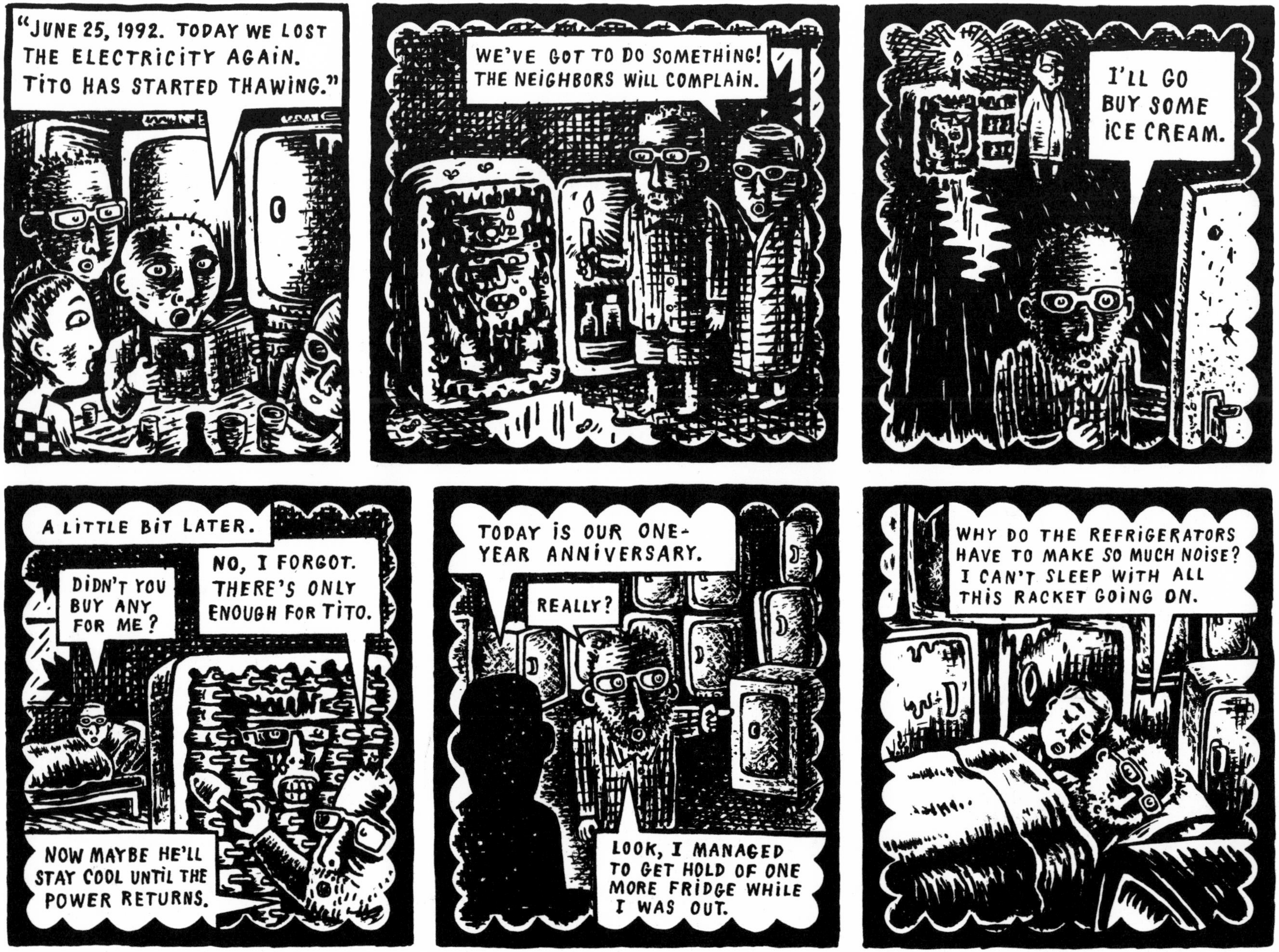
"JUNE 25, 1992. TODAY WE LOST THE ELECTRICITY AGAIN. TITO HAS STARTED THAWING."
WE'VE GOT TO DO SOMETHING! THE NEIGHBORS WILL COMPLAIN.
I'LL GO BUY SOME ICE CREAM.
A LITTLE BIT LATER.
DIDN'T YOU BUY ANY FOR ME?
NO, I FORGOT. THERE'S ONLY ENOUGH FOR TITO.
NOW MAYBE HE'LL STAY COOL UNTIL THE POWER RETURNS.
TODAY IS OUR ONE-YEAR ANNIVERSARY.
REALLY?
LOOK, I MANAGED TO GET HOLD OF ONE MORE FRIDGE WHILE I WAS OUT.
WHY DO THE REFRIGERATORS HAVE TO MAKE SO MUCH NOISE? I CAN'T SLEEP WITH ALL THIS RACKET GOING ON.

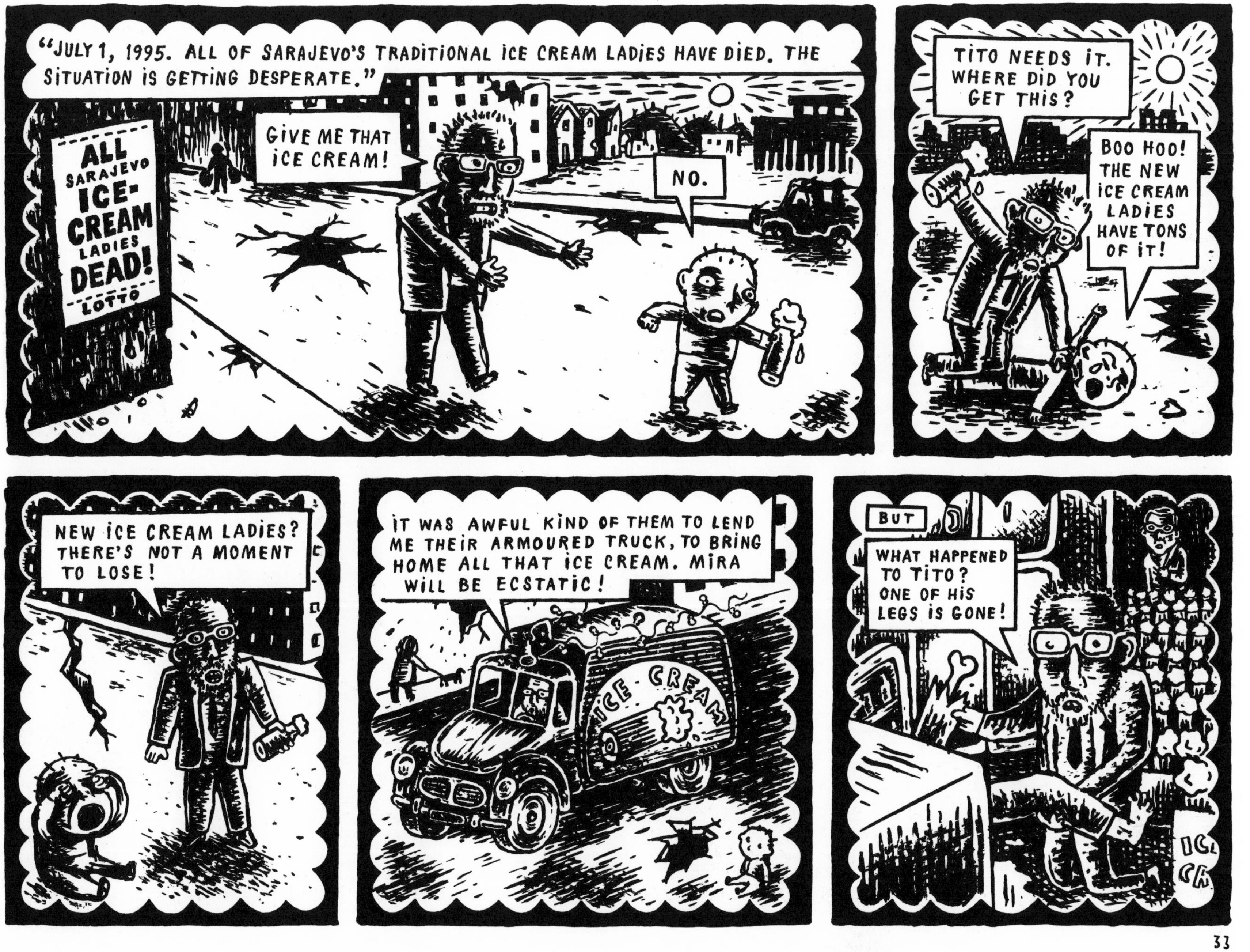
"JULY 1, 1995. ALL OF SARAJEVO'S TRADITIONAL ICE CREAM LADIES HAVE DIED. THE SITUATION IS GETTING DESPERATE."
ALL SARAJEVO ICE-CREAM LADIES DEAD!
LOTTO
GIVE ME THAT ICE CREAM!
NO.
TITO NEEDS IT. WHERE DID YOU GET THIS?
BOO HOO! THE NEW ICE CREAM LADIES HAVE TONS OF IT!
NEW ICE CREAM LADIES? THERE'S NOT A MOMENT TO LOSE!
IT WAS AWFUL KIND OF THEM TO LEND ME THEIR ARMOURED TRUCK, TO BRING HOME ALL THAT ICE CREAM. MIRA WILL BE ECSTATIC!
ICE CREAM
BUT
WHAT HAPPENED TO TITO? ONE OF HIS LEGS IS GONE!

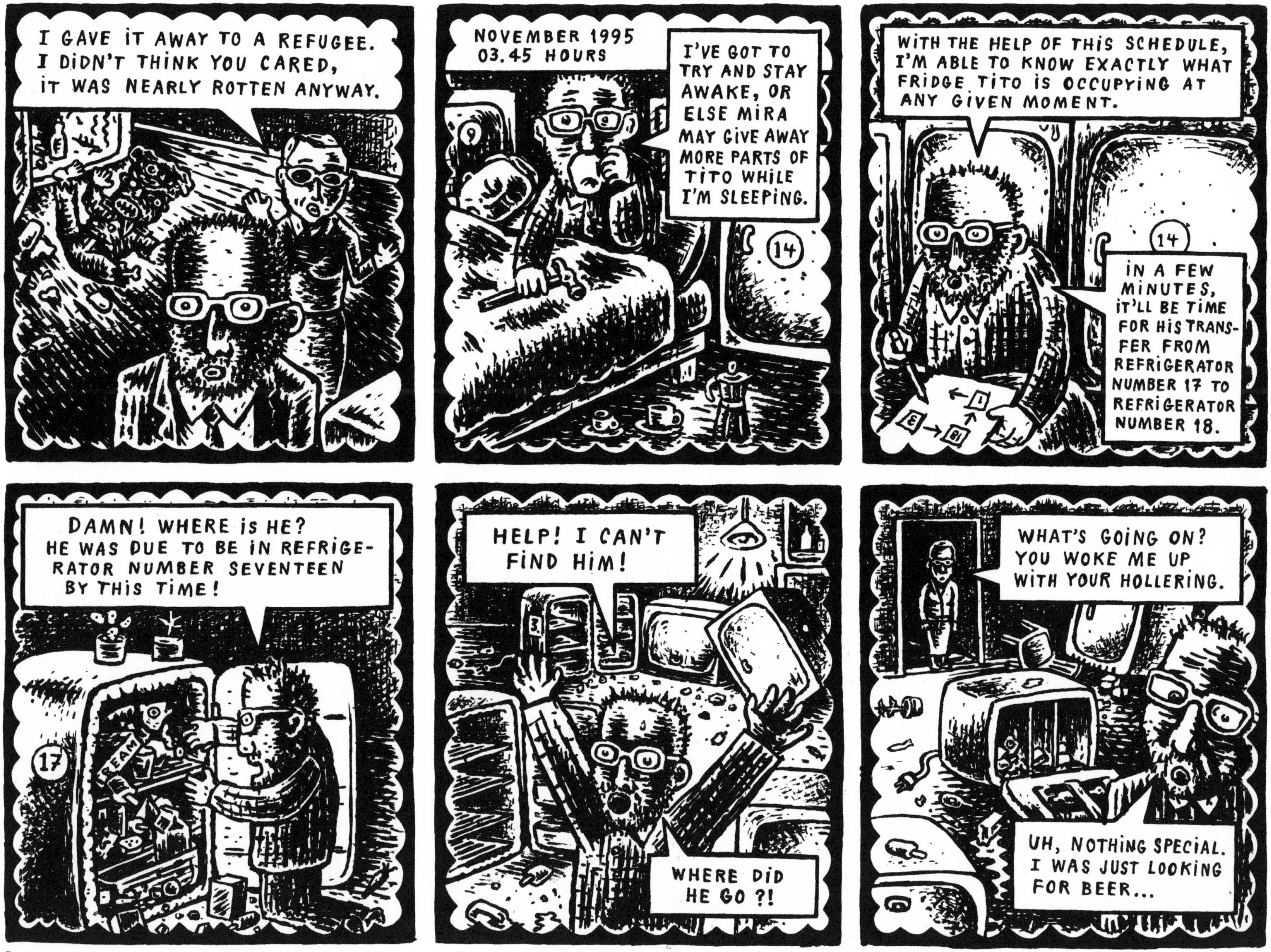
I GAVE IT AWAY TO A REFUGEE. I DIDN'T THINK YOU CARED, IT WAS NEARLY ROTTEN ANYWAY.
NOVEMBER 1995 03.45 HOURS
I'VE GOT TO TRY AND STAY AWAKE, OR ELSE MIRA MAY GIVE AWAY MORE PARTS OF TITO WHILE I'M SLEEPING.
14
WITH THE HELP OF THIS SCHEDULE, I'M ABLE TO KNOW EXACTLY WHAT FRIDGE TITO IS OCCUPYING AT ANY GIVEN MOMENT.
14
IN A FEW MINUTES, IT'LL BE TIME FOR HIS TRANSFER FROM REFRIGERATOR NUMBER 17 TO REFRIGERATOR NUMBER 18.
DAMN! WHERE IS HE? HE WAS DUE TO BE IN REFRIGERATOR NUMBER SEVENTEEN BY THIS TIME!
17
HELP! I CAN'T FIND HIM!
WHERE DID HE GO ?!
WHAT'S GOING ON? YOU WOKE ME UP WITH YOUR HOLLERING.
UH, NOTHING SPECIAL. I WAS JUST LOOKING FOR BEER...

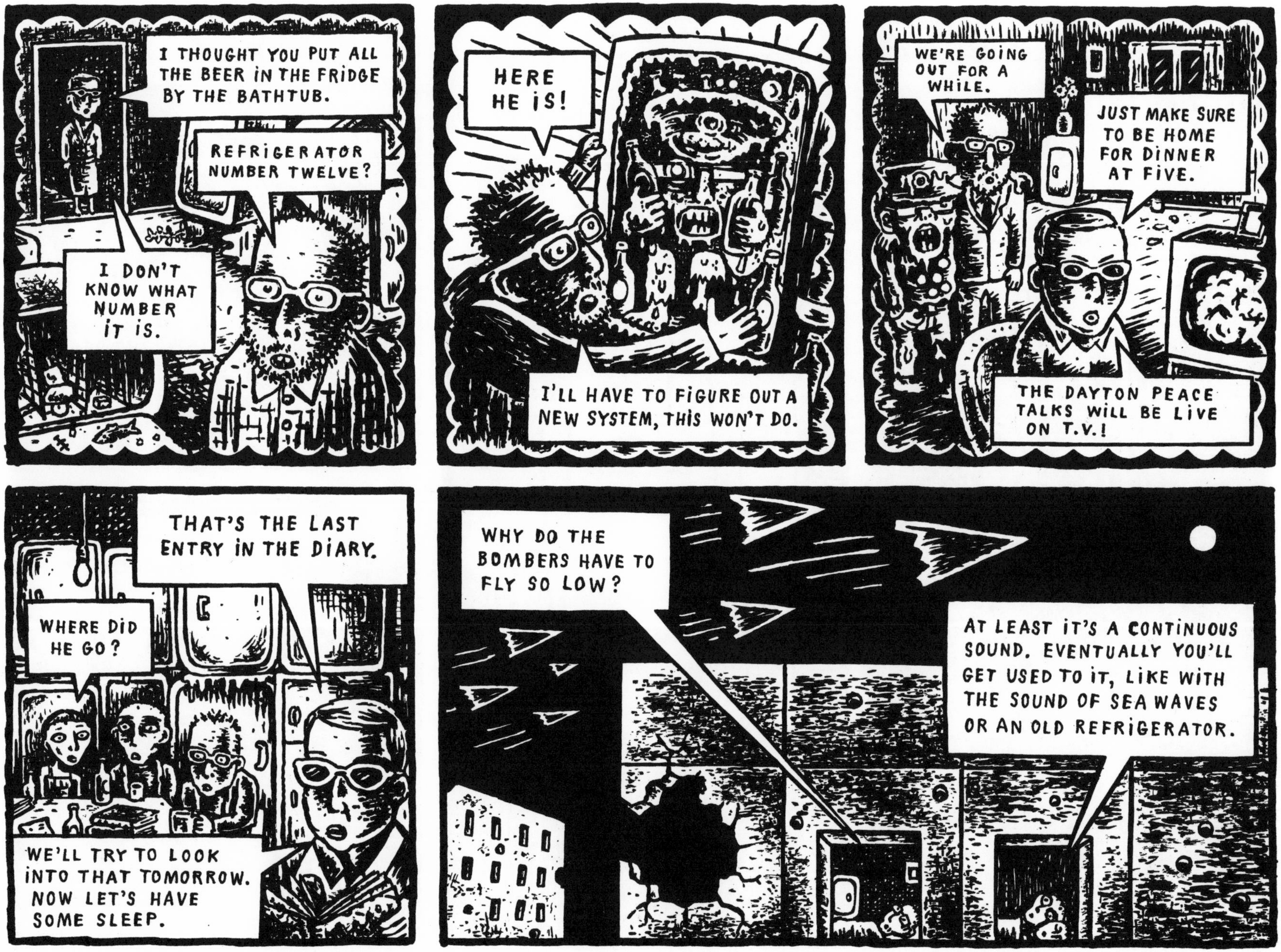
I THOUGHT YOU PUT ALL THE BEER IN THE FRIDGE BY THE BATHTUB.
REFRIGERATOR NUMBER TWELVE?
I DON'T KNOW WHAT NUMBER IT IS.
HERE HE IS!
I'LL HAVE TO FIGURE OUT A NEW SYSTEM, THIS WON'T DO.
WE'RE GOING OUT FOR A WHILE.
JUST MAKE SURE TO BE HOME FOR DINNER AT FIVE.
THE DAYTON PEACE TALKS WILL BE LIVE ON T.V.!
THAT'S THE LAST ENTRY IN THE DIARY.
WHERE DID HE GO?
WE'LL TRY TO LOOK INTO THAT TOMORROW. NOW LET'S HAVE SOME SLEEP.
WHY DO THE BOMBERS HAVE TO FLY SO LOW?
AT LEAST IT'S A CONTINUOUS SOUND. EVENTUALLY YOU'LL GET USED TO IT, LIKE WITH THE SOUND OF SEA WAVES OR AN OLD REFRIGERATOR.

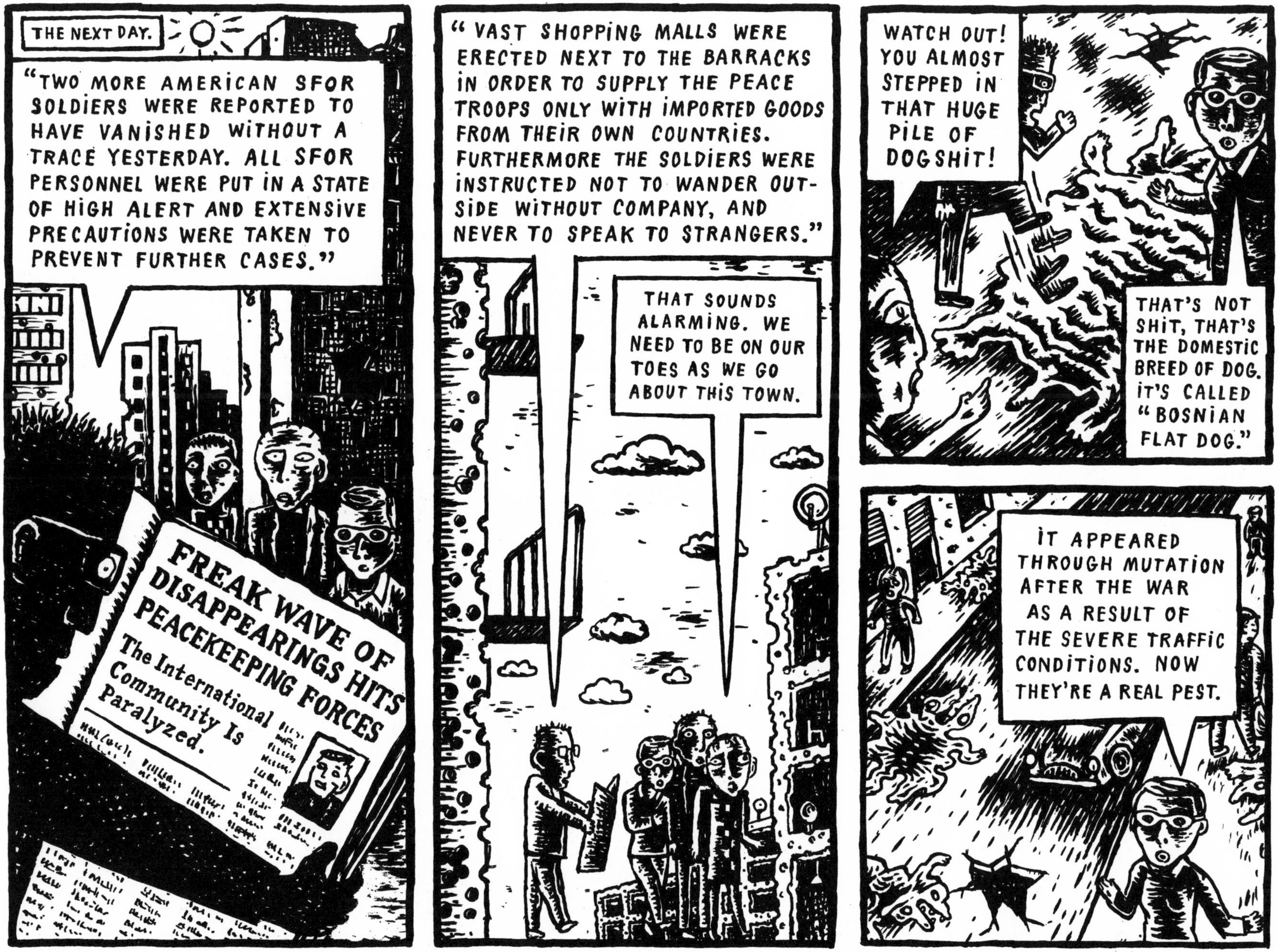
THE NEXT DAY.
"TWO MORE AMERICAN SFOR SOLDIERS WERE REPORTED TO HAVE VANISHED WITHOUT A TRACE YESTERDAY. ALL SFOR PERSONNEL WERE PUT IN A STATE OF HIGH ALERT AND EXTENSIVE PRECAUTIONS WERE TAKEN TO PREVENT FURTHER CASES."
FREAK WAVE OF DISAPPEARINGS HITS PEACEKEEPING FORCES
The International Community Is Paralyzed.
"VAST SHOPPING MALLS WERE ERECTED NEXT TO THE BARRACKS IN ORDER TO SUPPLY THE PEACE TROOPS ONLY WITH IMPORTED GOODS FROM THEIR OWN COUNTRIES. FURTHERMORE THE SOLDIERS WERE INSTRUCTED NOT TO WANDER OUTSIDE WITHOUT COMPANY, AND NEVER TO SPEAK TO STRANGERS."
THAT SOUNDS ALARMING. WE NEED TO BE ON OUR TOES AS WE GO ABOUT THIS TOWN.
WATCH OUT! YOU ALMOST STEPPED IN THAT HUGE PILE OF DOGSHIT!
THAT'S NOT SHIT, THAT'S THE DOMESTIC BREED OF DOG. IT'S CALLED "BOSNIAN FLAT DOG."
IT APPEARED THROUGH MUTATION AFTER THE WAR AS A RESULT OF THE SEVERE TRAFFIC CONDITIONS. NOW THEY'RE A REAL PEST.

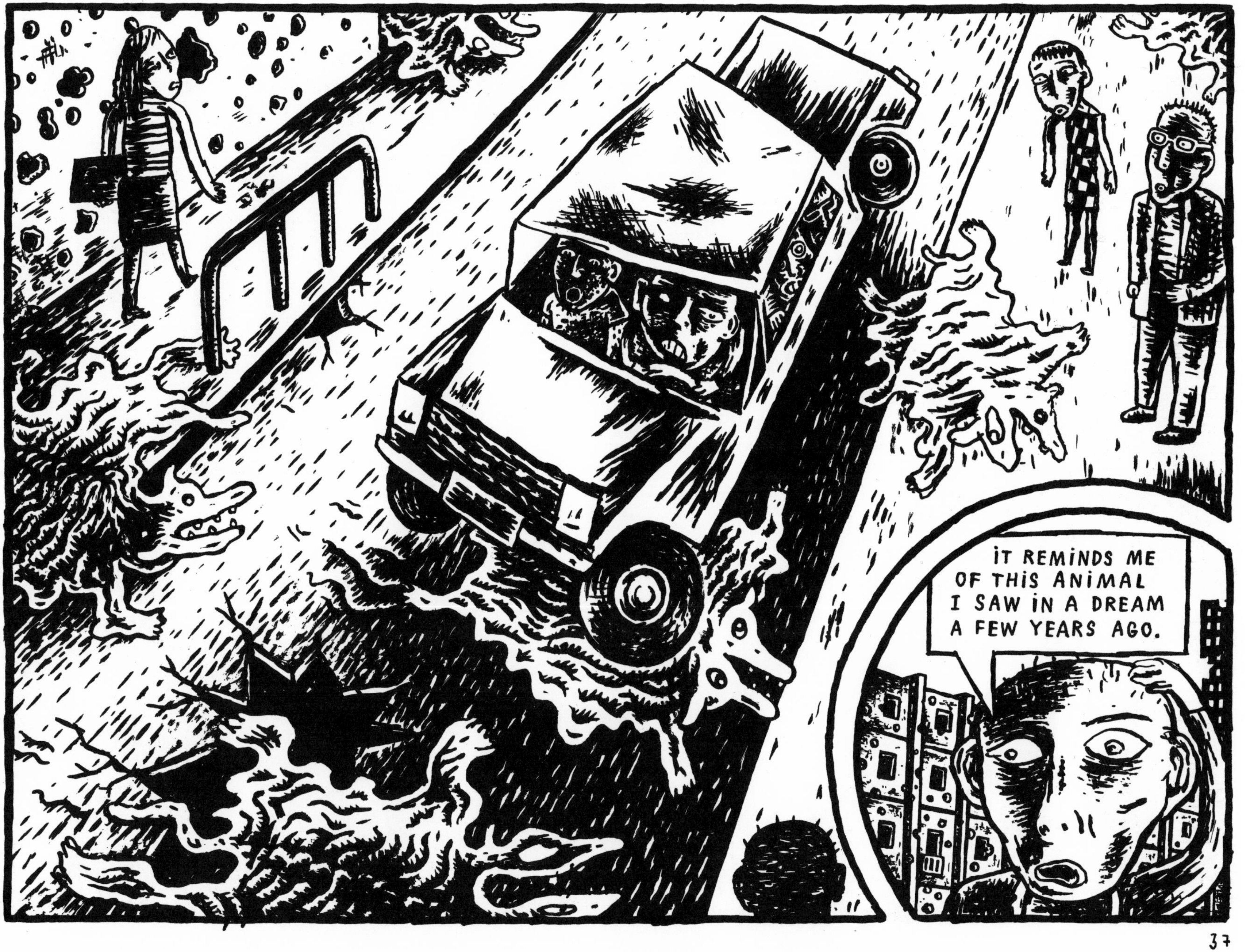
IT REMINDS ME OF THIS ANIMAL I SAW IN A DREAM A FEW YEARS AGO.

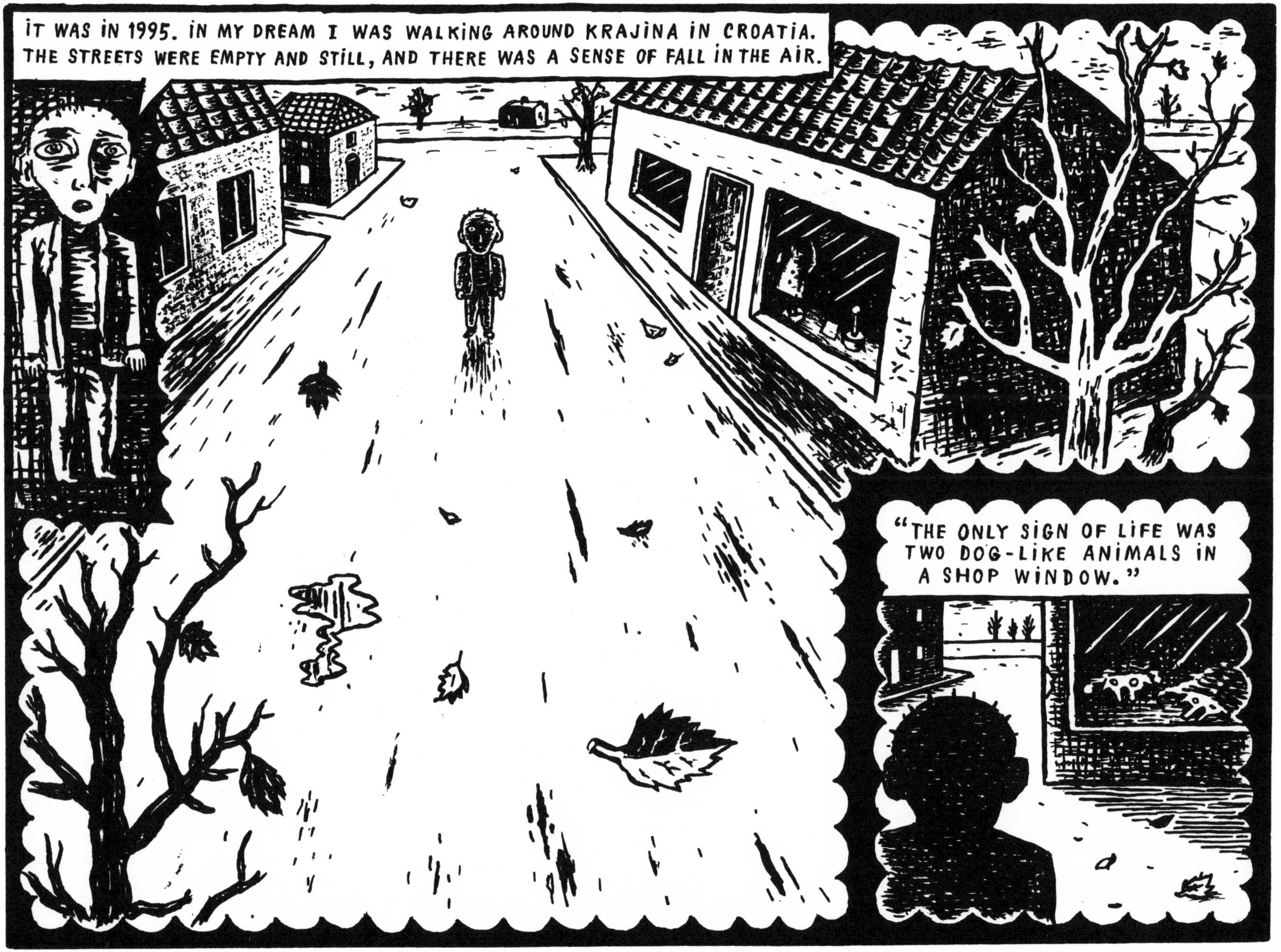
IT WAS IN 1995. IN MY DREAM I WAS WALKING AROUND KRAJINA IN CROATIA.
THE STREETS WERE EMPTY AND STILL, AND THERE WAS A SENSE OF FALL IN THE AIR.
"THE ONLY SIGN OF LIFE WAS TWO DOG-LIKE ANIMALS IN A SHOP WINDOW."

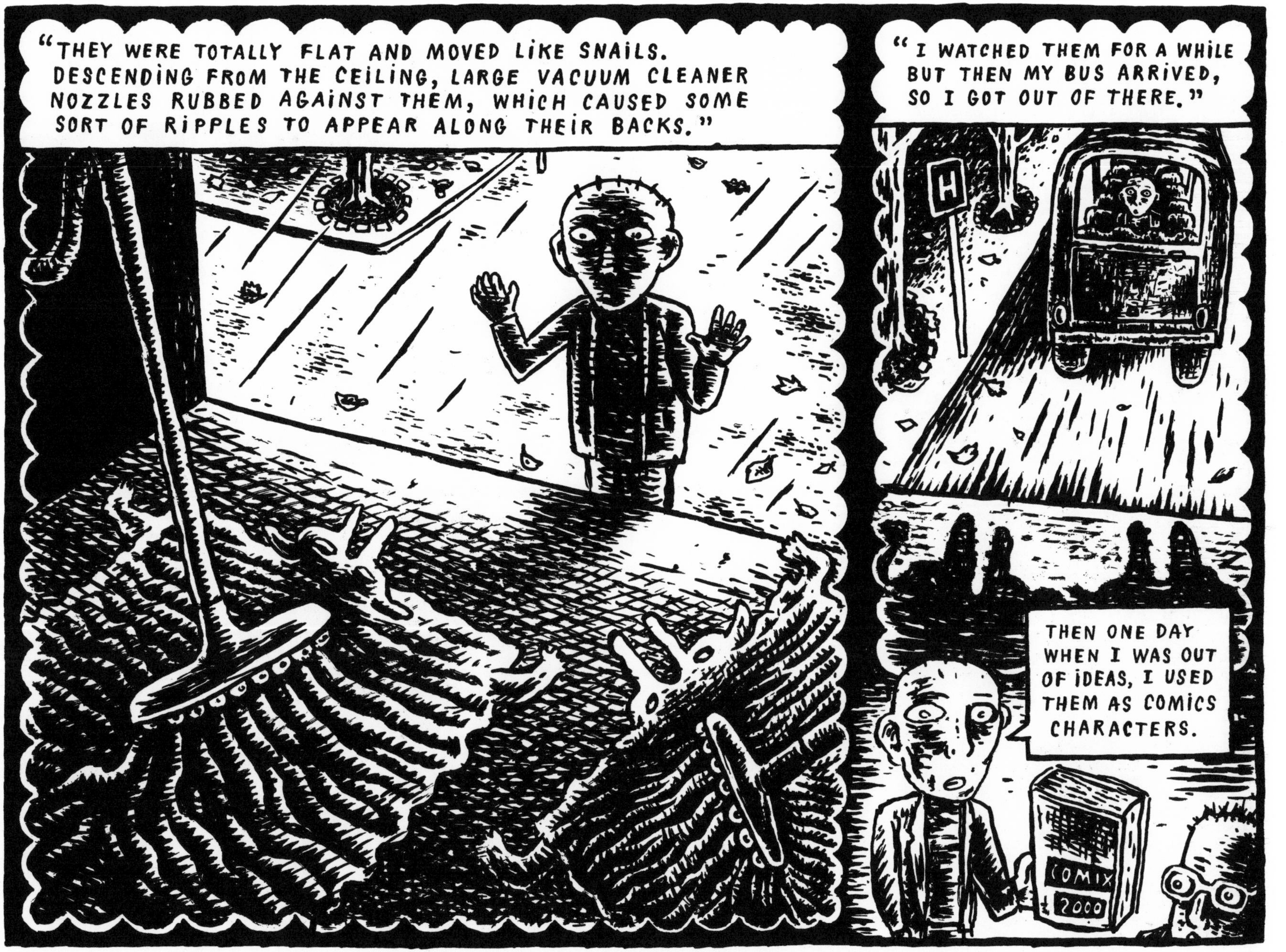
"THEY WERE TOTALLY FLAT AND MOVED LIKE SNAILS. DESCENDING FROM THE CEILING, LARGE VACUUM CLEANER NOZZLES RUBBED AGAINST THEM, WHICH CAUSED SOME SORT OF RIPPLES TO APPEAR ALONG THEIR BACKS."
"I WATCHED THEM FOR A WHILE BUT THEN MY BUS ARRIVED, SO I GOT OUT OF THERE."
H
THEN ONE DAY WHEN I WAS OUT OF IDEAS, I USED THEM AS COMICS CHARACTERS.
COMIX 2000

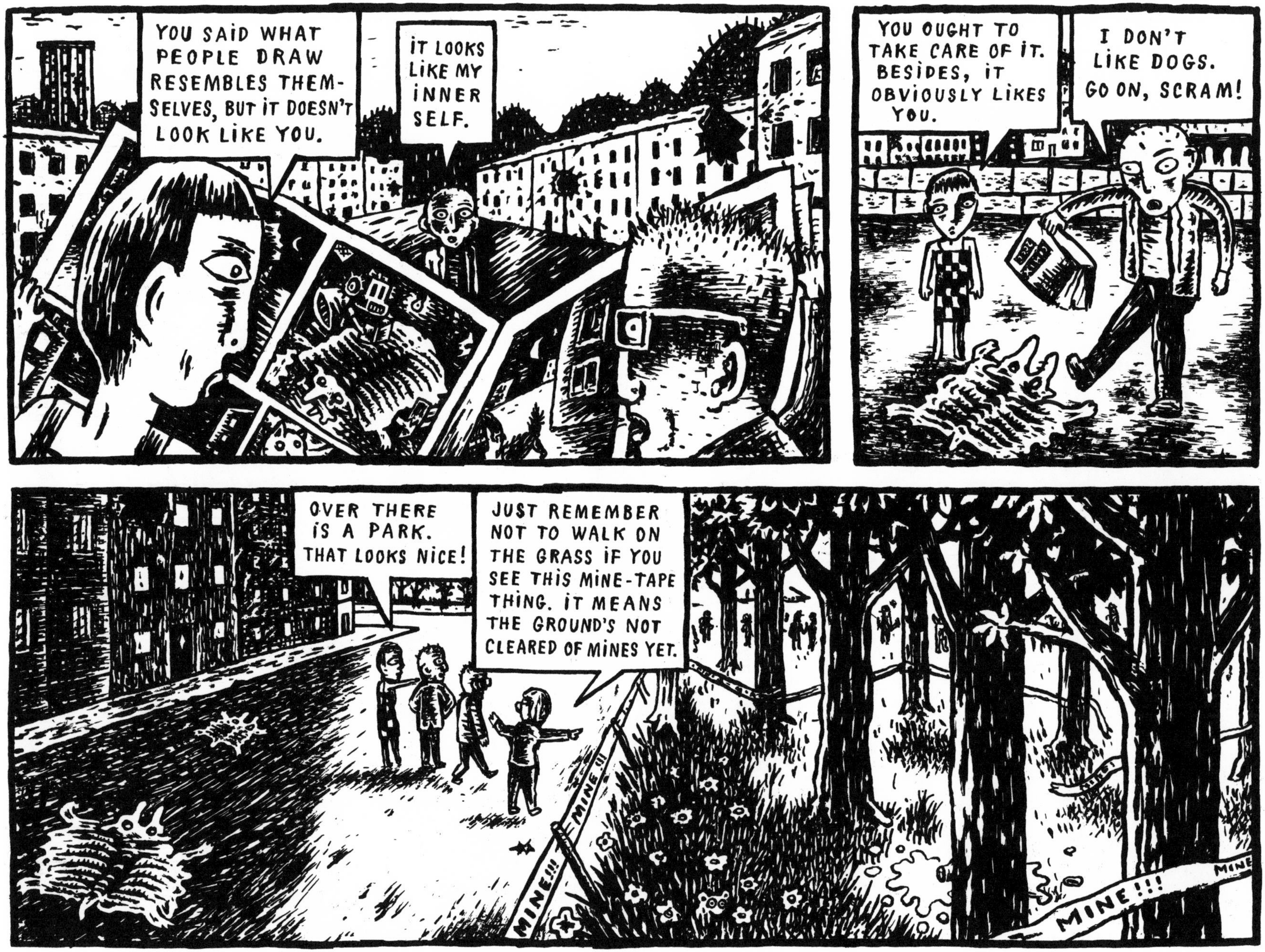
YOU SAID WHAT PEOPLE DRAW RESEMBLES THEMSELVES, BUT IT DOESN'T LOOK LIKE YOU.
IT LOOKS LIKE MY INNER SELF.
YOU OUGHT TO TAKE CARE OF IT. BESIDES, IT OBVIOUSLY LIKES YOU.
I DON'T LIKE DOGS. GO ON, SCRAM!
OVER THERE IS A PARK. THAT LOOKS NICE!
JUST REMEMBER NOT TO WALK ON THE GRASS IF YOU SEE THIS MINE-TAPE THING. IT MEANS THE GROUND'S NOT CLEARED OF MINES YET.
MINE!!!
MINE!!!
MINE!!!
MINE!!!

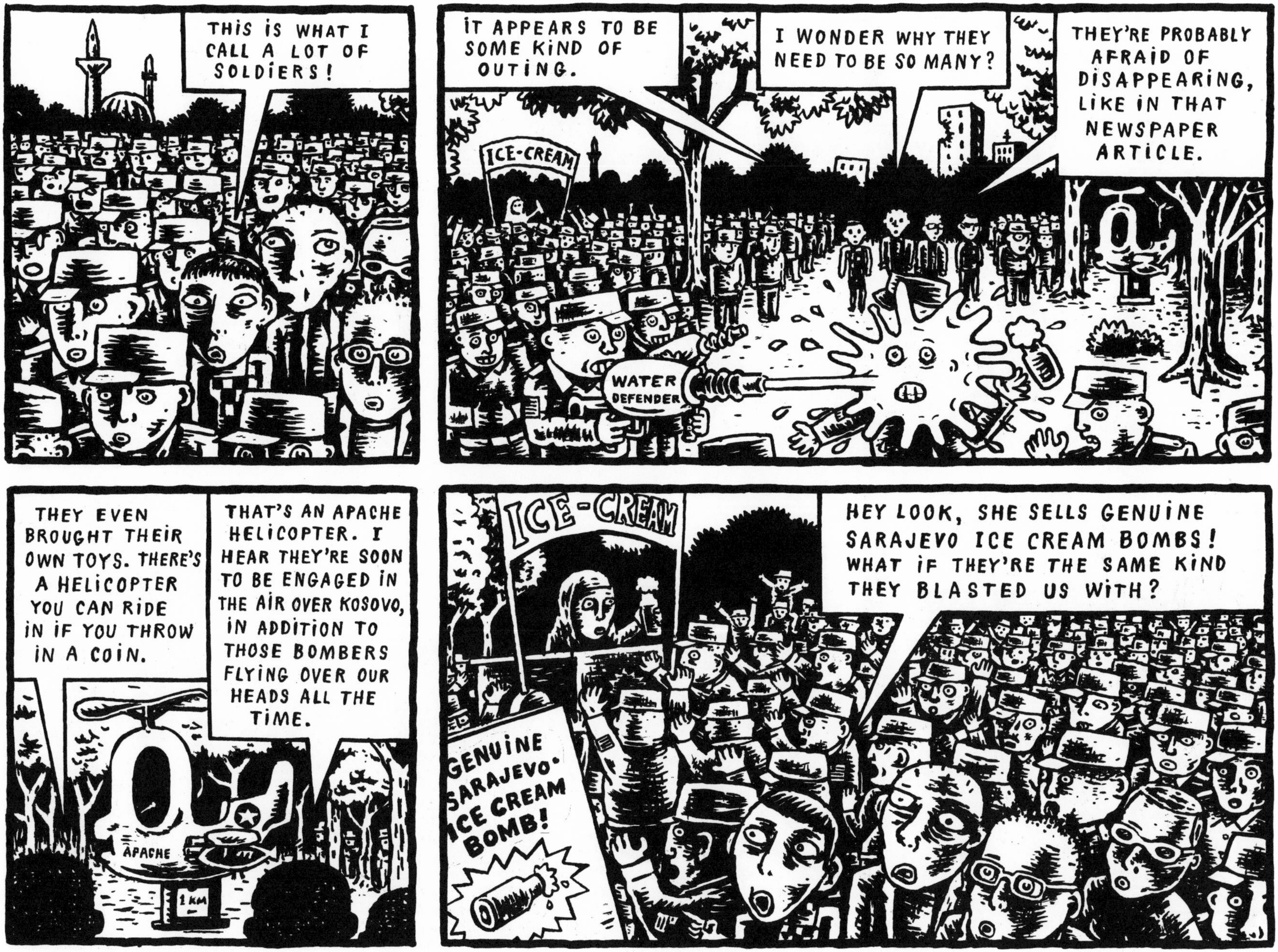
THIS IS WHAT I CALL A LOT OF SOLDIERS!
IT APPEARS TO BE SOME KIND OF OUTING.
I WONDER WHY THEY NEED TO BE SO MANY?
THEY'RE PROBABLY AFRAID OF DISAPPEARING, LIKE IN THAT NEWSPAPER ARTICLE.
ICE-CREAM
WATER DEFENDER
THEY EVEN BROUGHT THEIR OWN TOYS. THERE'S A HELICOPTER YOU CAN RIDE IN IF YOU THROW IN A COIN.
THAT'S AN APACHE HELICOPTER. I HEAR THEY'RE SOON TO BE ENGAGED IN THE AIR OVER KOSOVO, IN ADDITION TO THOSE BOMBERS FLYING OVER OUR HEADS ALL THE TIME.
APACHE
1 KM
ICE-CREAM
HEY LOOK, SHE SELLS GENUINE SARAJEVO ICE CREAM BOMBS! WHAT IF THEY'RE THE SAME KIND THEY BLASTED US WITH?
GENUINE SARAJEVO ICE CREAM BOMB!

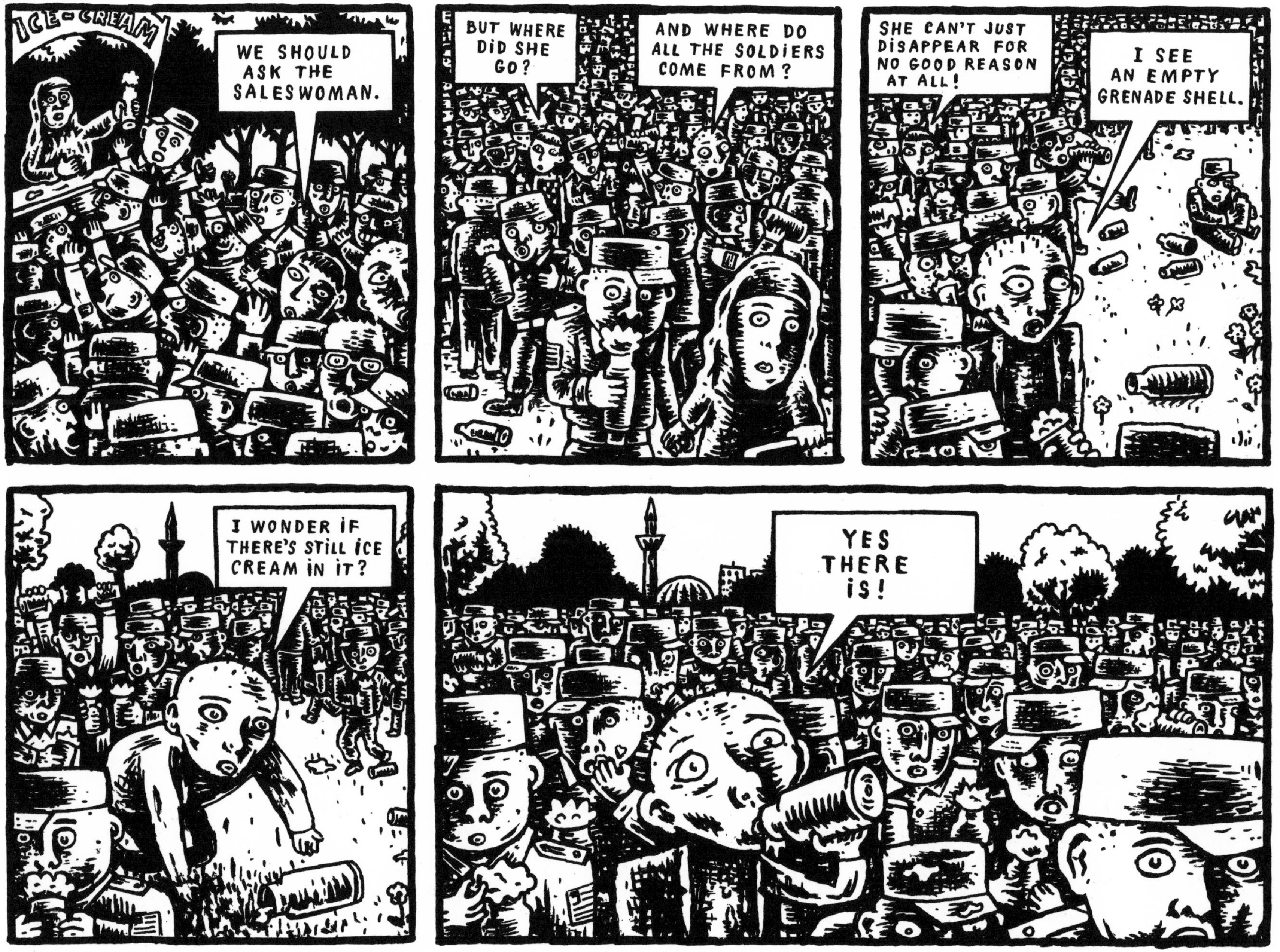
ICE-CREAM
WE SHOULD ASK THE SALESWOMAN.
BUT WHERE DID SHE GO?
AND WHERE DO ALL THE SOLDIERS COME FROM?
SHE CAN'T JUST DISAPPEAR FOR NO GOOD REASON AT ALL!
I SEE AN EMPTY GRENADE SHELL.
I WONDER IF THERE'S STILL ICE CREAM IN IT?
YES THERE IS!

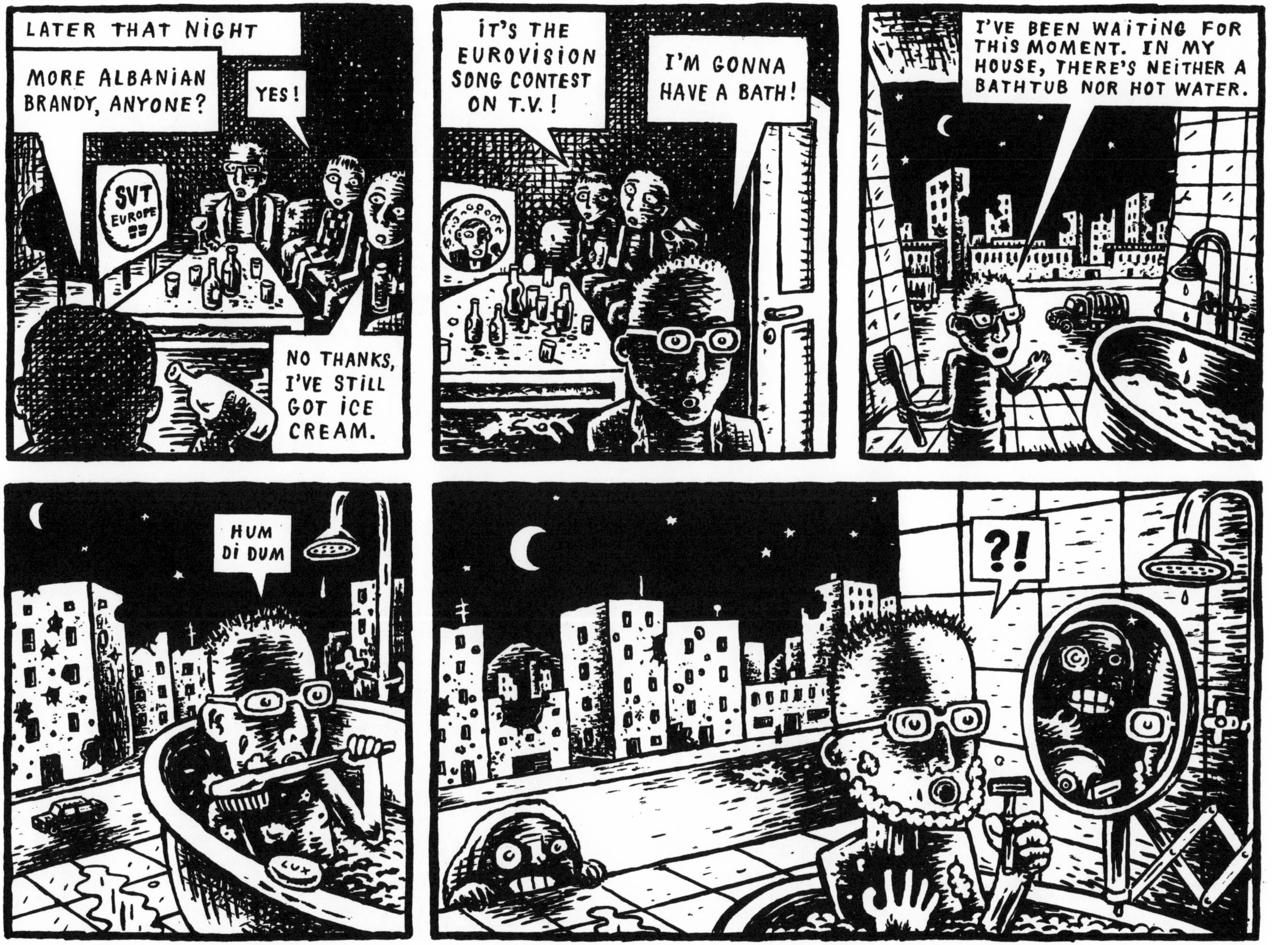
LATER THAT NIGHT
MORE ALBANIAN BRANDY, ANYONE?
YES!
SVT EUROPE
NO THANKS, I'VE STILL GOT ICE CREAM.
IT'S THE EUROVISION SONG CONTEST ON T.V.!
I'M GONNA HAVE A BATH!
I'VE BEEN WAITING FOR THIS MOMENT. IN MY HOUSE, THERE'S NEITHER A BATHTUB NOR HOT WATER.
HUM DI DUM
LUX
?!

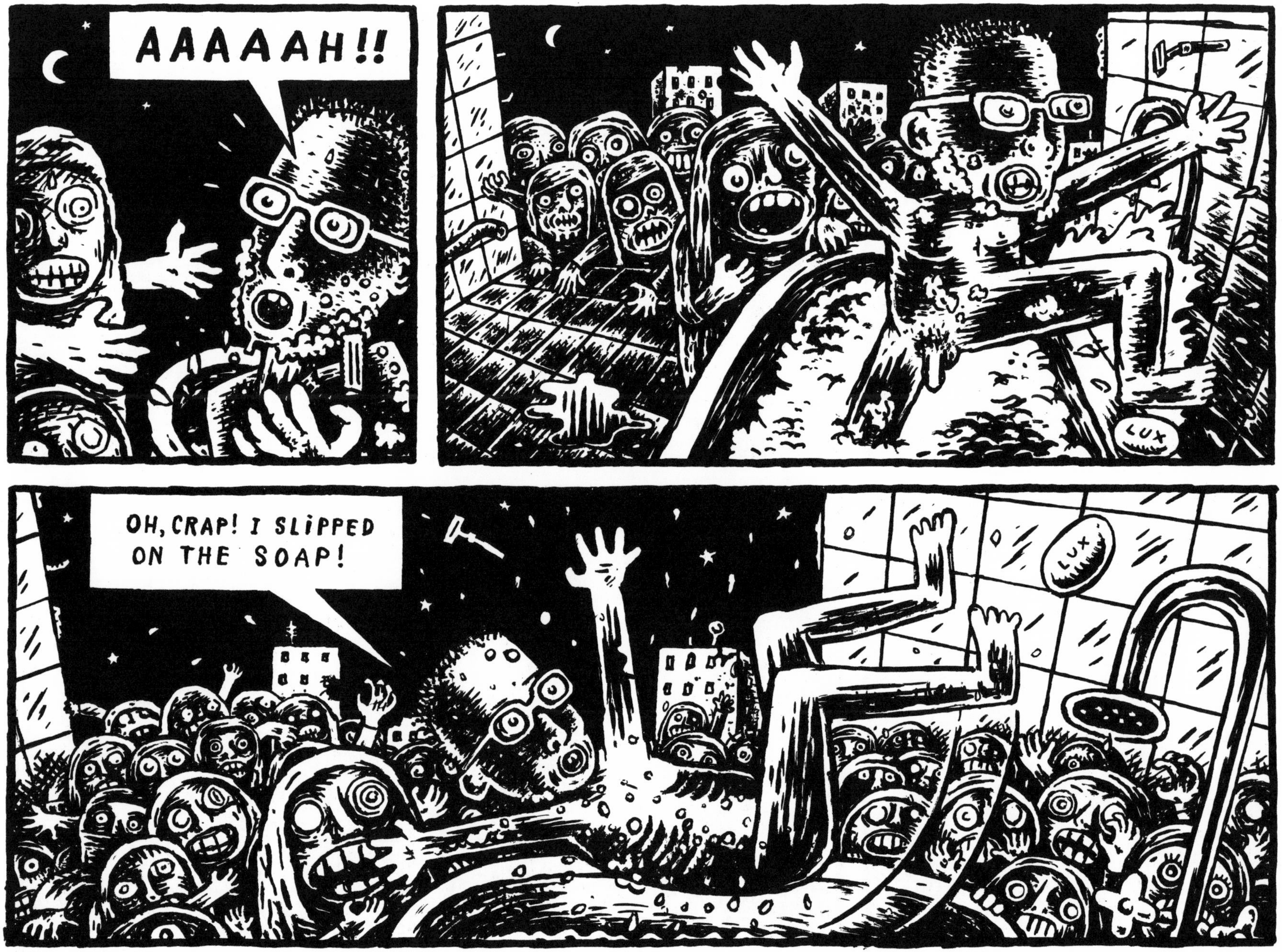
AAAAAH!!
LUX
OH, CRAP! I SLIPPED ON THE SOAP!
LUX

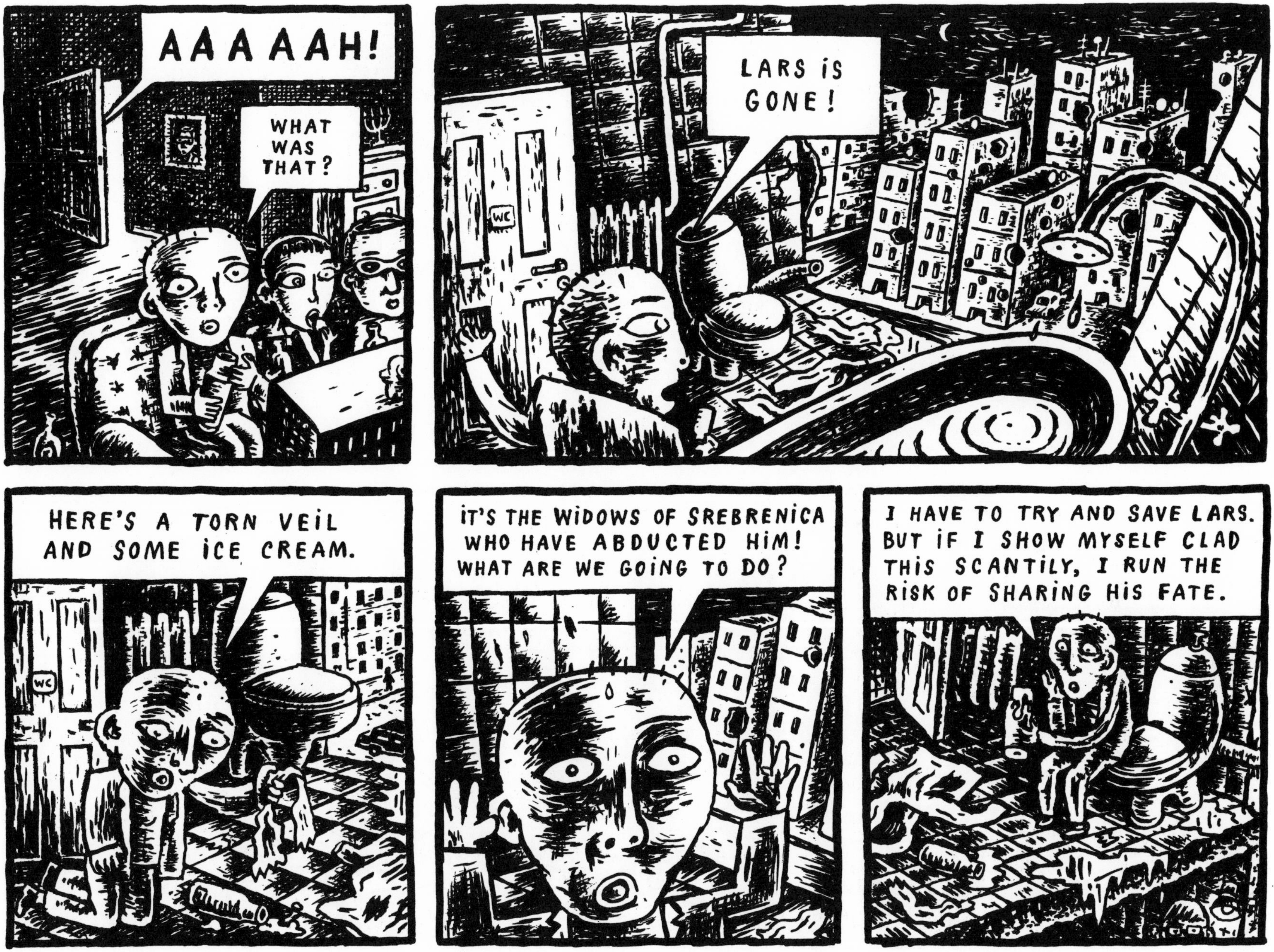
AAAAAH!
WHAT WAS THAT?
LARS IS GONE!
HERE'S A TORN VEIL AND SOME ICE CREAM.
IT'S THE WIDOWS OF SREBRENICA WHO HAVE ABDUCTED HIM! WHAT ARE WE GOING TO DO?
I HAVE TO TRY AND SAVE LARS. BUT IF I SHOW MYSELF CLAD THIS SCANTILY, I RUN THE RISK OF SHARING HIS FATE.

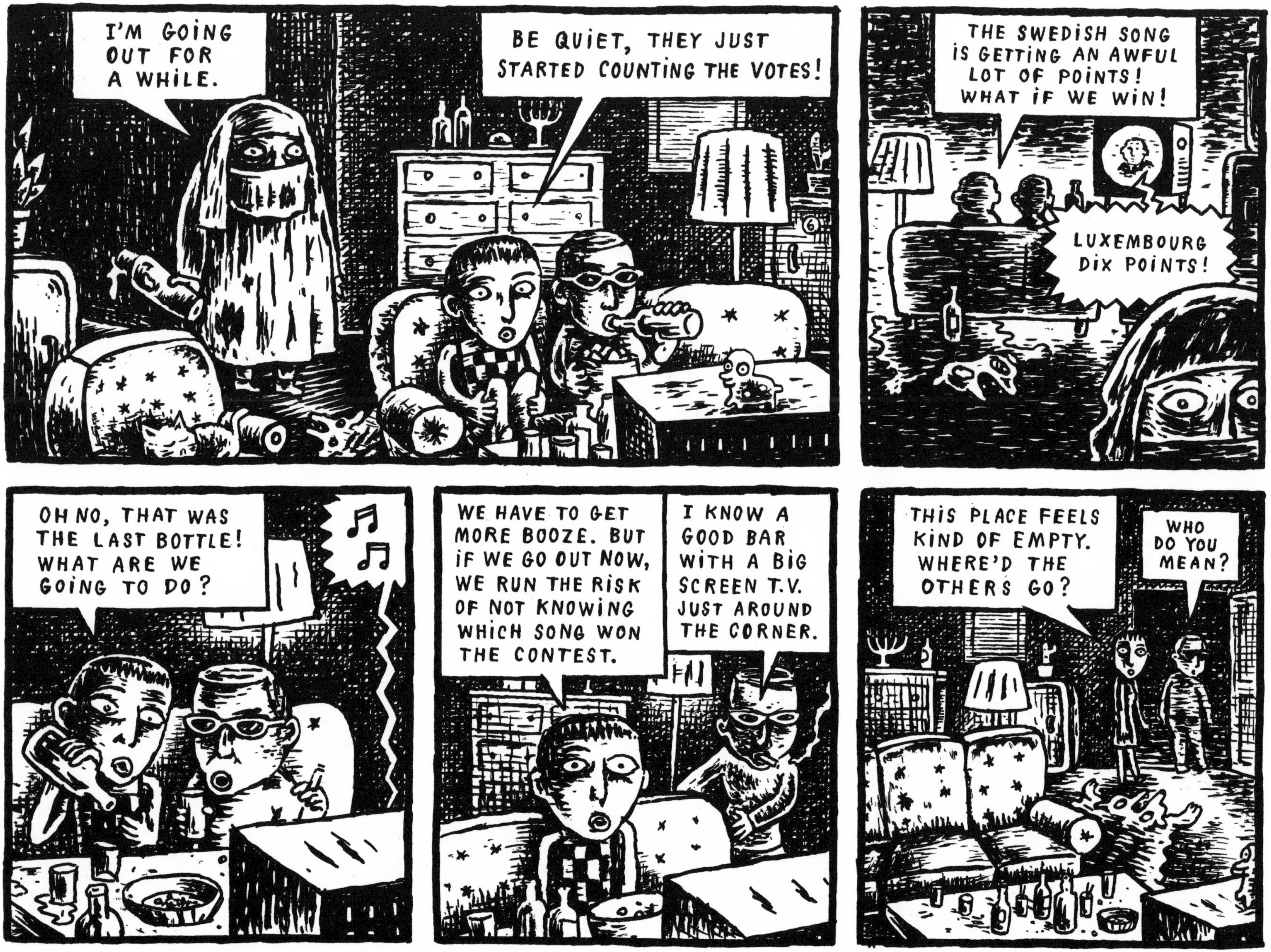
I'M GOING OUT FOR A WHILE.
BE QUIET, THEY JUST STARTED COUNTING THE VOTES!
THE SWEDISH SONG IS GETTING AN AWFUL LOT OF POINTS! WHAT IF WE WIN!
LUXEMBOURG DIX POINTS!
OH NO, THAT WAS THE LAST BOTTLE! WHAT ARE WE GOING TO DO?
WE HAVE TO GET MORE BOOZE. BUT IF WE GO OUT NOW, WE RUN THE RISK OF NOT KNOWING WHICH SONG WON THE CONTEST.
I KNOW A GOOD BAR WITH A BIG SCREEN T.V. JUST AROUND THE CORNER.
THIS PLACE FEELS KIND OF EMPTY. WHERE'D THE OTHERS GO?
WHO DO YOU MEAN?

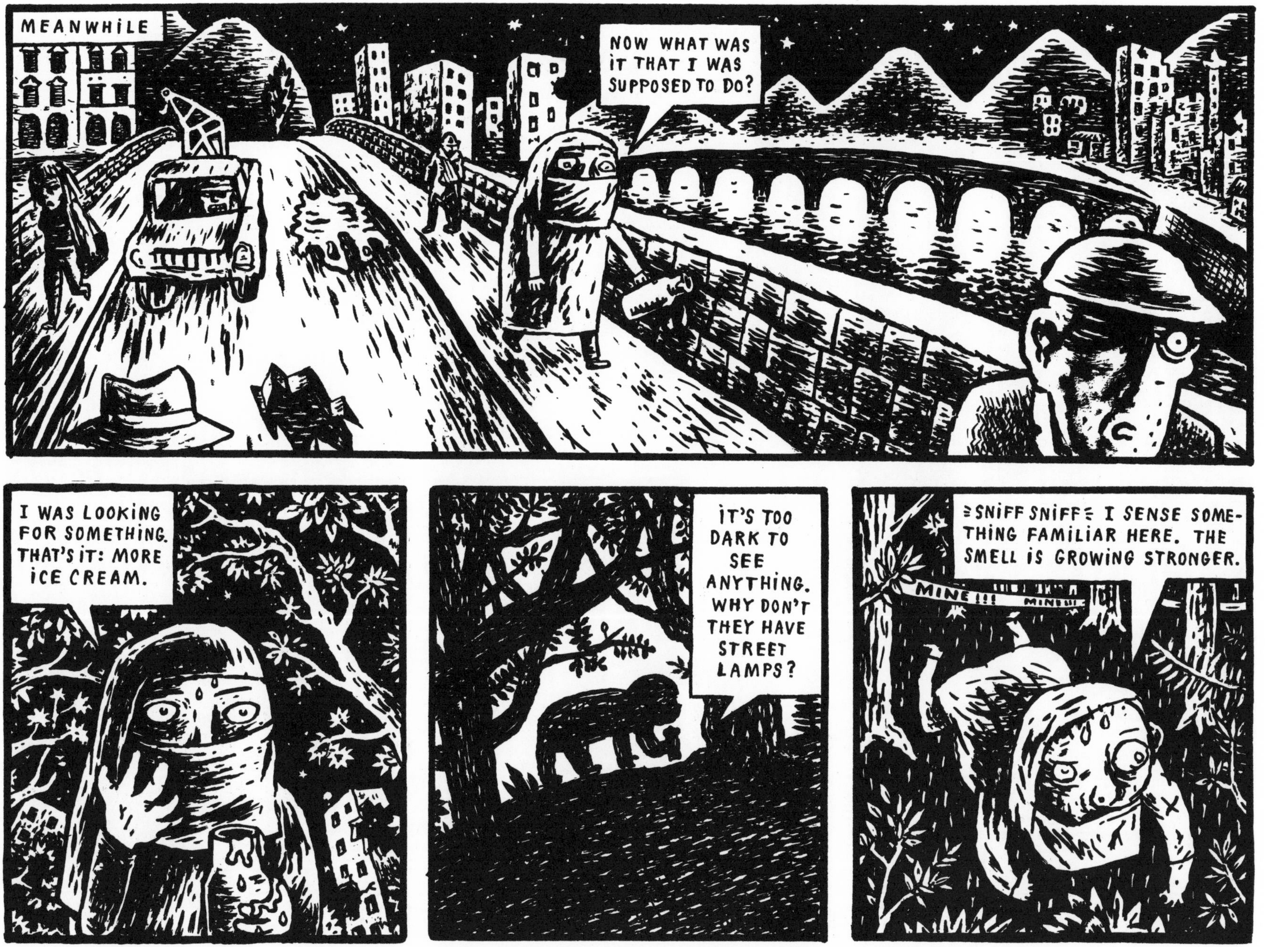
MEANWHILE
NOW WHAT WAS IT THAT I WAS SUPPOSED TO DO?
I WAS LOOKING FOR SOMETHING. THAT'S IT: MORE ICE CREAM.
IT'S TOO DARK TO SEE ANYTHING. WHY DON'T THEY HAVE STREET LAMPS?
≡SNIFF SNIFF≡ I SENSE SOMETHING FAMILIAR HERE. THE SMELL IS GROWING STRONGER.
MINE!!!

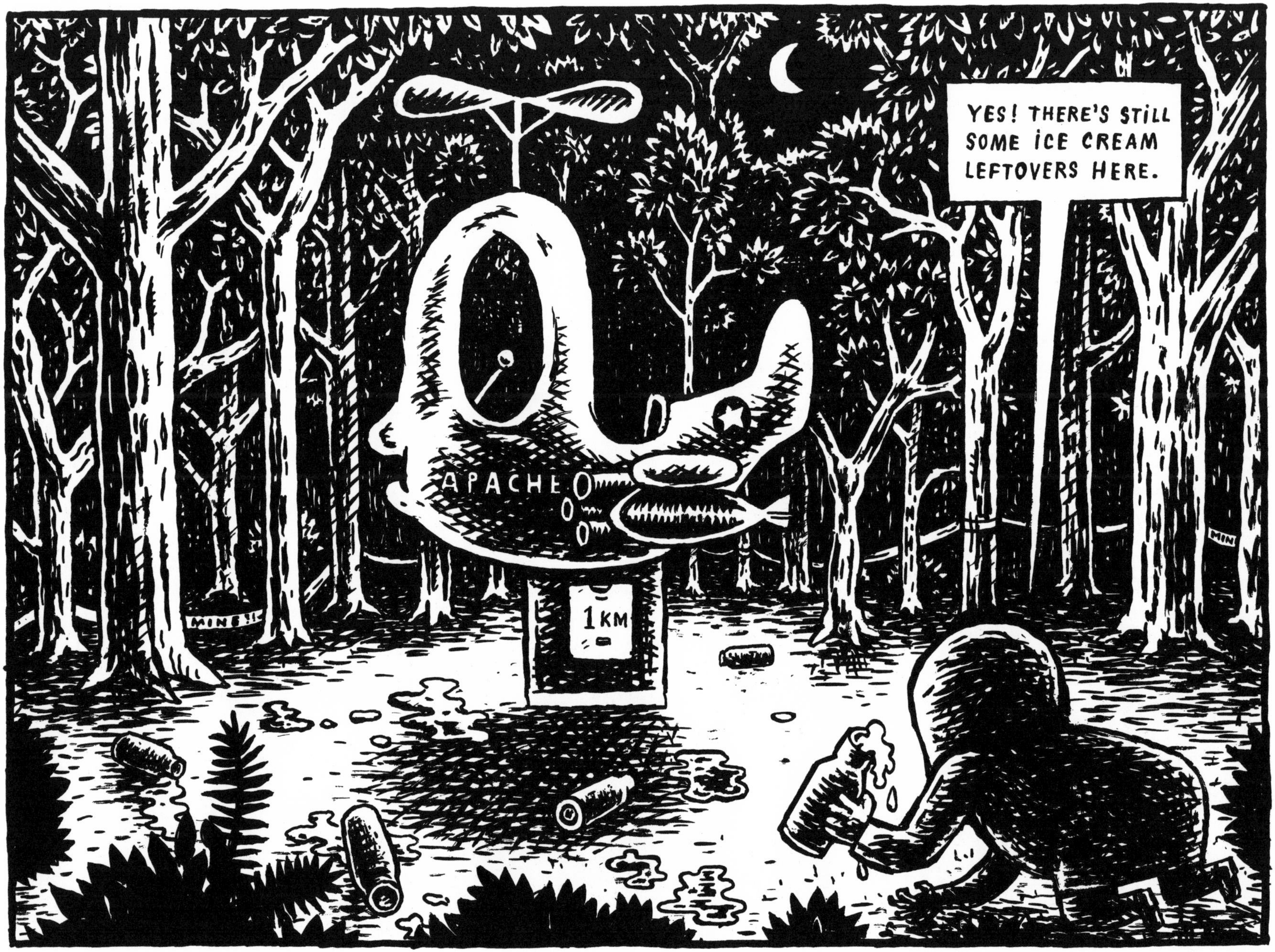
YES! THERE'S STILL SOME ICE CREAM LEFTOVERS HERE.
APACHE
1KM

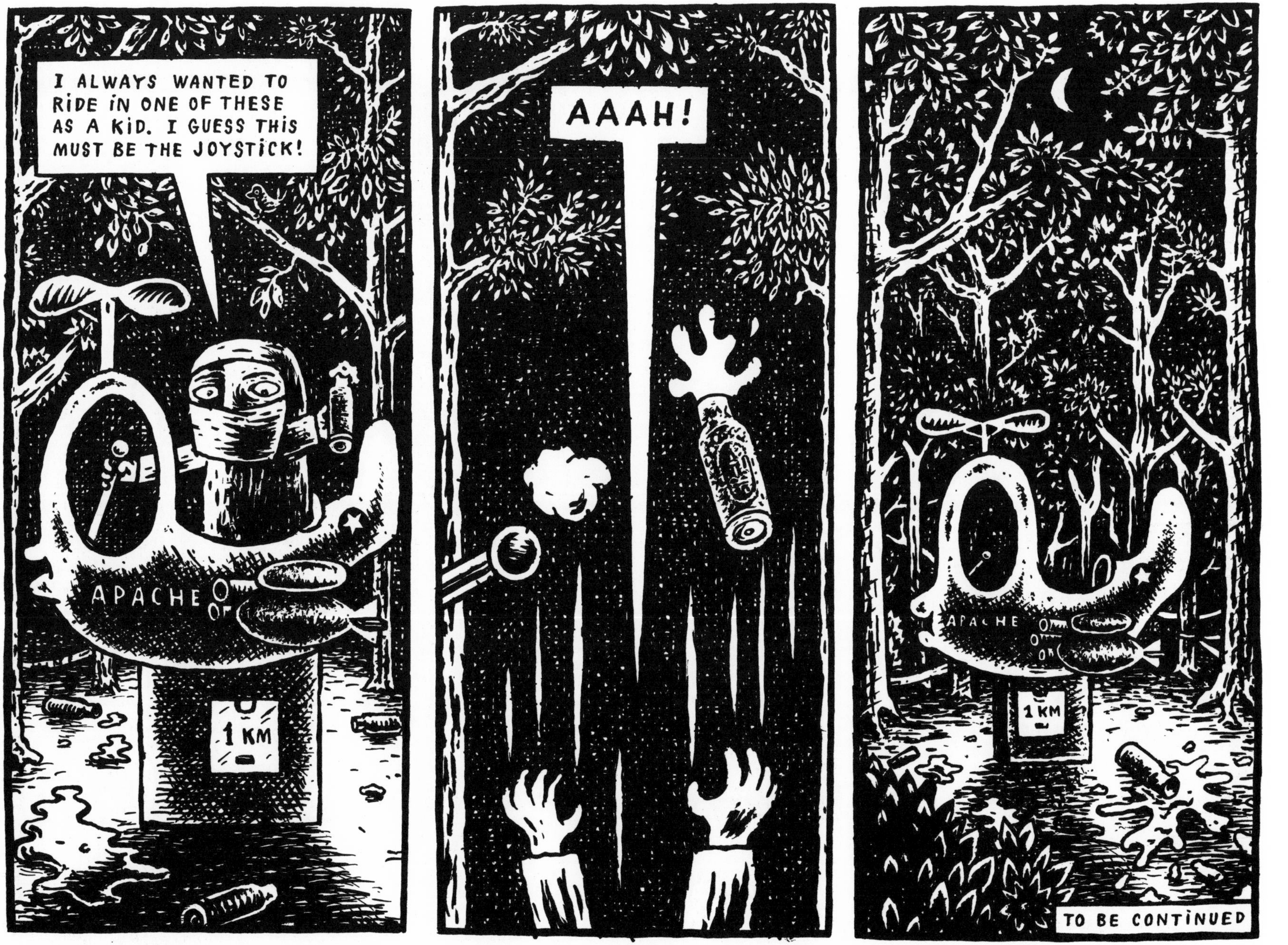
I ALWAYS WANTED TO RIDE IN ONE OF THESE AS A KID. I GUESS THIS MUST BE THE JOYSTICK!
APACHE
1 KM
AAAH!
APACHE
1 KM
TO BE CONTINUED

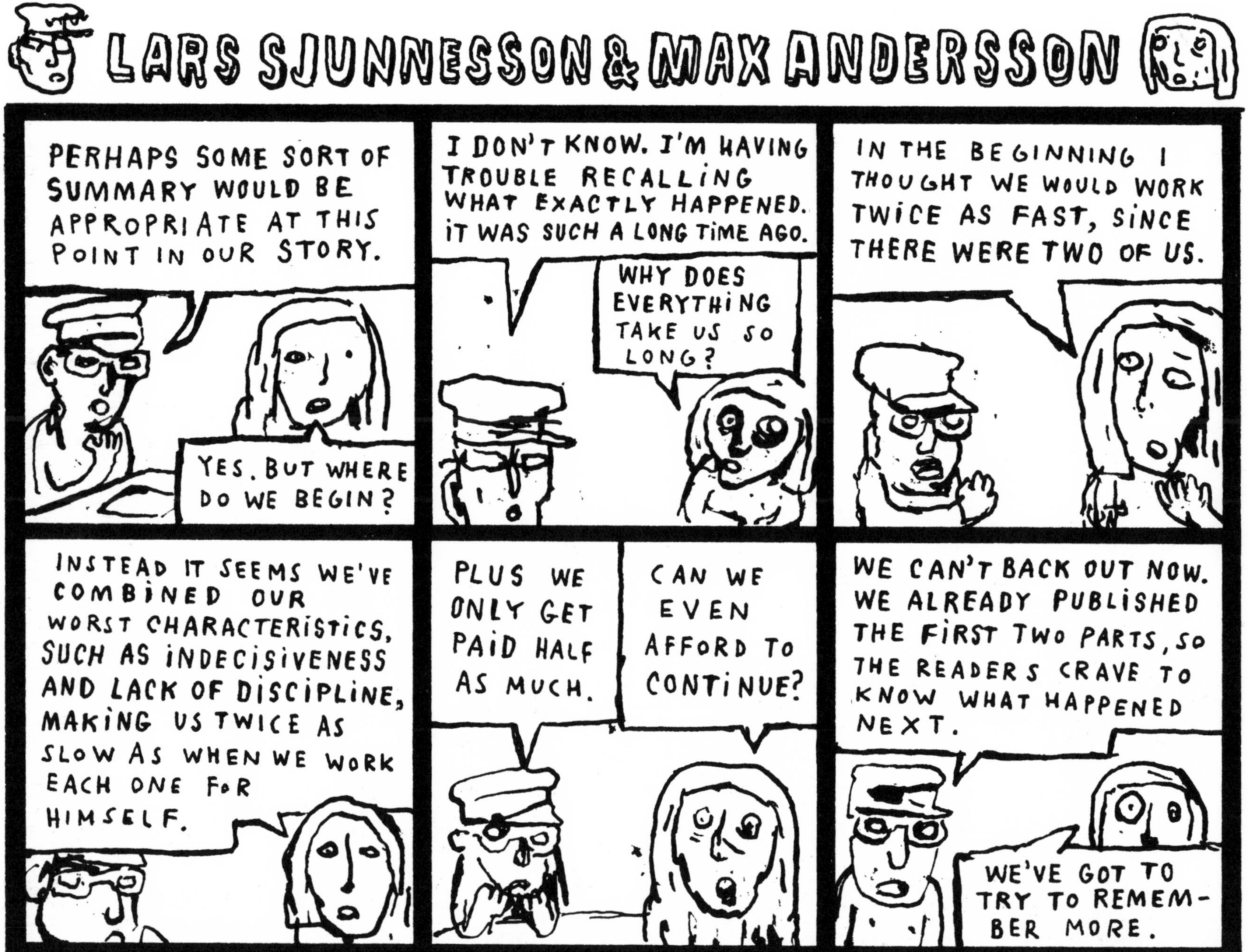
LARS SJUNNESSON & MAX ANDERSSON
PERHAPS SOME SORT OF SUMMARY WOULD BE APPROPRIATE AT THIS POINT IN OUR STORY.
YES. BUT WHERE DO WE BEGIN?
I DON'T KNOW. I'M HAVING TROUBLE RECALLING WHAT EXACTLY HAPPENED. IT WAS SUCH A LONG TIME AGO.
WHY DOES EVERYTHING TAKE US SO LONG?
IN THE BEGINNING I THOUGHT WE WOULD WORK TWICE AS FAST, SINCE THERE WERE TWO OF US.
INSTEAD IT SEEMS WE'VE COMBINED OUR WORST CHARACTERISTICS, SUCH AS INDECISIVENESS AND LACK OF DISCIPLINE, MAKING US TWICE AS SLOW AS WHEN WE WORK EACH ONE FOR HIMSELF.
PLUS WE ONLY GET PAID HALF AS MUCH.
CAN WE EVEN AFFORD TO CONTINUE?
WE CAN'T BACK OUT NOW. WE ALREADY PUBLISHED THE FIRST TWO PARTS, SO THE READERS CRAVE TO KNOW WHAT HAPPENED NEXT.
WE'VE GOT TO TRY TO REMEMBER MORE.

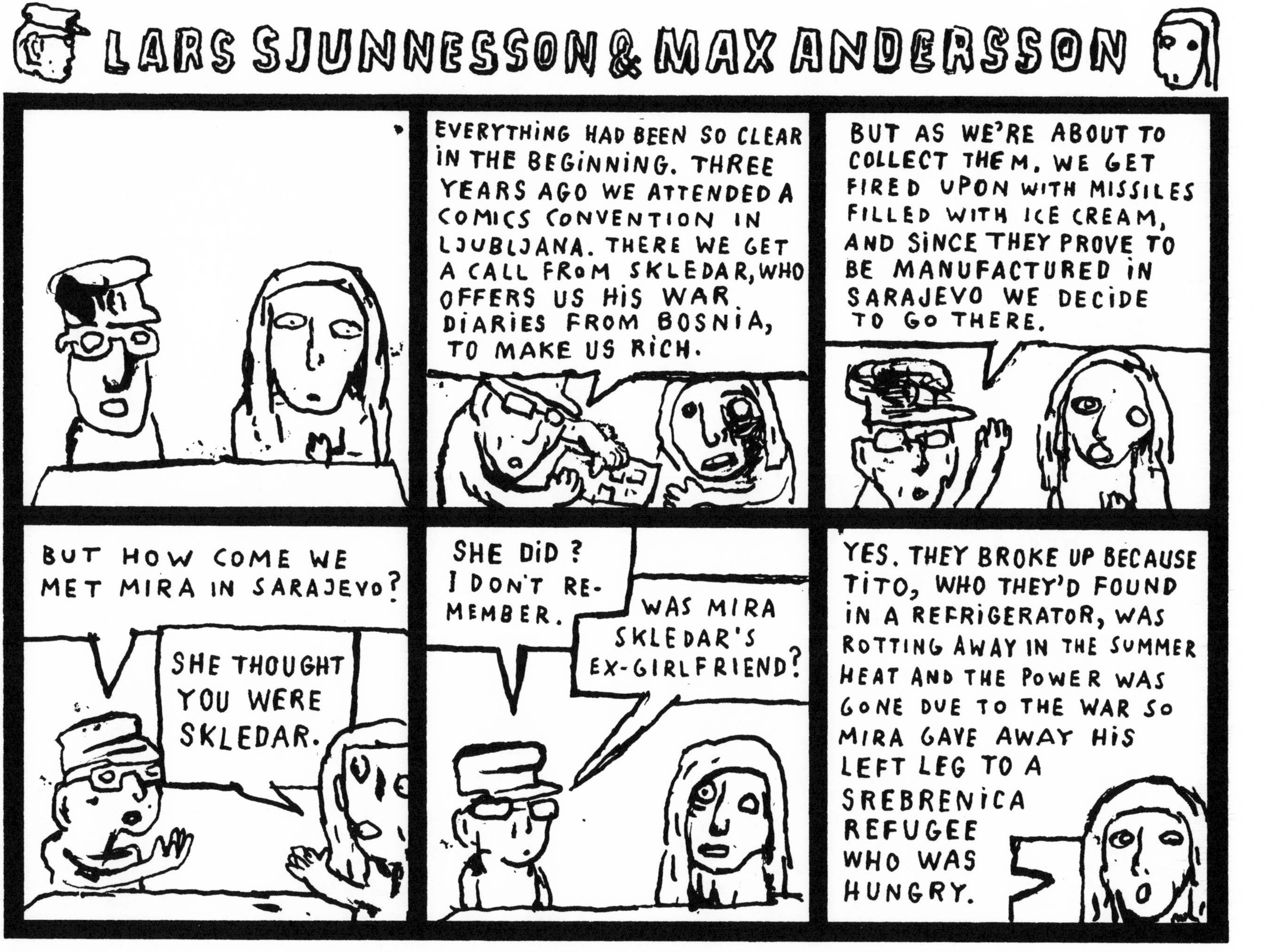
LARS SJUNNESSON & MAX ANDERSSON
EVERYTHING HAD BEEN SO CLEAR IN THE BEGINNING. THREE YEARS AGO WE ATTENDED A COMICS CONVENTION IN LJUBLJANA. THERE WE GET A CALL FROM SKLEDAR, WHO OFFERS US HIS WAR DIARIES FROM BOSNIA, TO MAKE US RICH.
BUT AS WE'RE ABOUT TO COLLECT THEM, WE GET FIRED UPON WITH MISSILES FILLED WITH ICE CREAM, AND SINCE THEY PROVE TO BE MANUFACTURED IN SARAJEVO WE DECIDE TO GO THERE.
BUT HOW COME WE MET MIRA IN SARAJEVO?
SHE THOUGHT YOU WERE SKLEDAR.
SHE DID? I DON'T RE-MEMBER.
WAS MIRA SKLEDAR'S EX-GIRLFRIEND?
YES. THEY BROKE UP BECAUSE TITO, WHO THEY'D FOUND IN A REFRIGERATOR, WAS ROTTING AWAY IN THE SUMMER HEAT AND THE POWER WAS GONE DUE TO THE WAR SO MIRA GAVE AWAY HIS LEFT LEG TO A SREBRENICA REFUGEE WHO WAS HUNGRY.

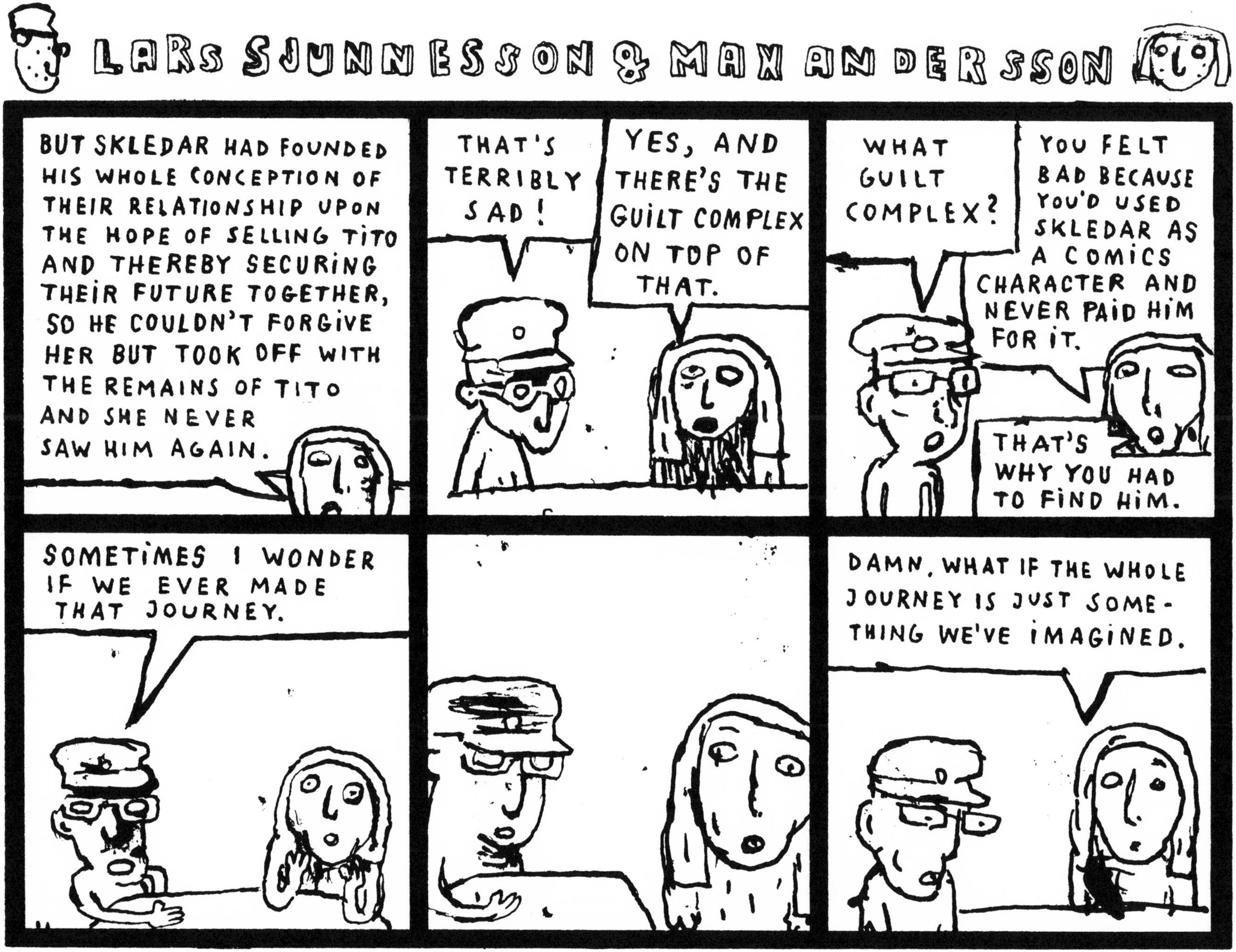
LARS SJUNNESSON & MAX ANDERSSON
BUT SKLEDAR HAD FOUNDED HIS WHOLE CONCEPTION OF THEIR RELATIONSHIP UPON THE HOPE OF SELLING TITO AND THEREBY SECURING THEIR FUTURE TOGETHER, SO HE COULDN'T FORGIVE HER BUT TOOK OFF WITH THE REMAINS OF TITO AND SHE NEVER SAW HIM AGAIN.
THAT'S TERRIBLY SAD!
YES, AND THERE'S THE GUILT COMPLEX ON TOP OF THAT.
WHAT GUILT COMPLEX?
YOU FELT BAD BECAUSE YOU'D USED SKLEDAR AS A COMICS CHARACTER AND NEVER PAID HIM FOR IT.
THAT'S WHY YOU HAD TO FIND HIM.
SOMETIMES I WONDER IF WE EVER MADE THAT JOURNEY.
DAMN. WHAT IF THE WHOLE JOURNEY IS JUST SOMETHING WE'VE IMAGINED.

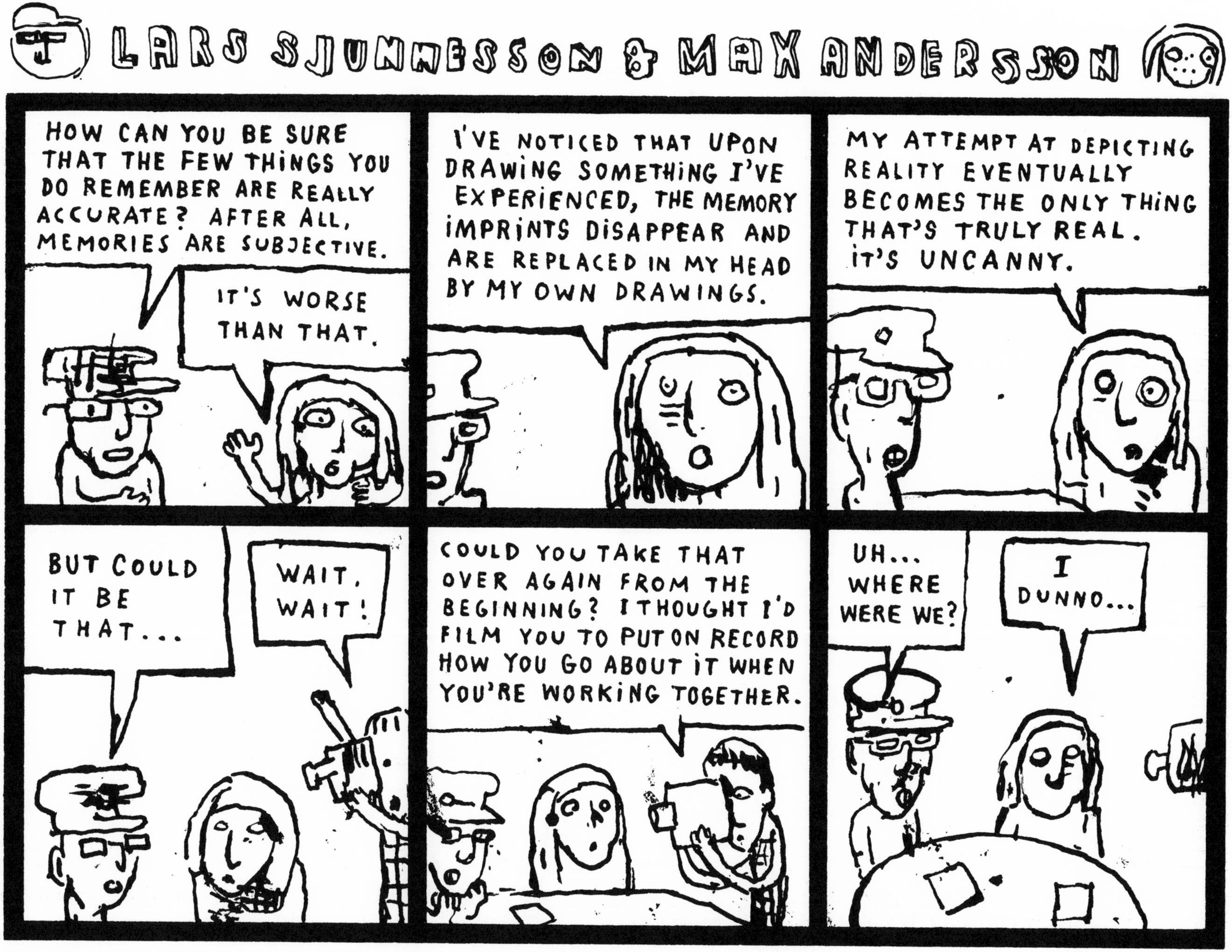
LARS SJUNNESSON & MAX ANDERSSON
HOW CAN YOU BE SURE THAT THE FEW THINGS YOU DO REMEMBER ARE REALLY ACCURATE? AFTER ALL, MEMORIES ARE SUBJECTIVE.
IT'S WORSE THAN THAT.
I'VE NOTICED THAT UPON DRAWING SOMETHING I'VE EXPERIENCED, THE MEMORY IMPRINTS DISAPPEAR AND ARE REPLACED IN MY HEAD BY MY OWN DRAWINGS.
MY ATTEMPT AT DEPICTING REALITY EVENTUALLY BECOMES THE ONLY THING THAT'S TRULY REAL. IT'S UNCANNY.
BUT COULD IT BE THAT...
WAIT. WAIT!
COULD YOU TAKE THAT OVER AGAIN FROM THE BEGINNING? I THOUGHT I'D FILM YOU TO PUT ON RECORD HOW YOU GO ABOUT IT WHEN YOU'RE WORKING TOGETHER.
UH... WHERE WERE WE?
I DUNNO...

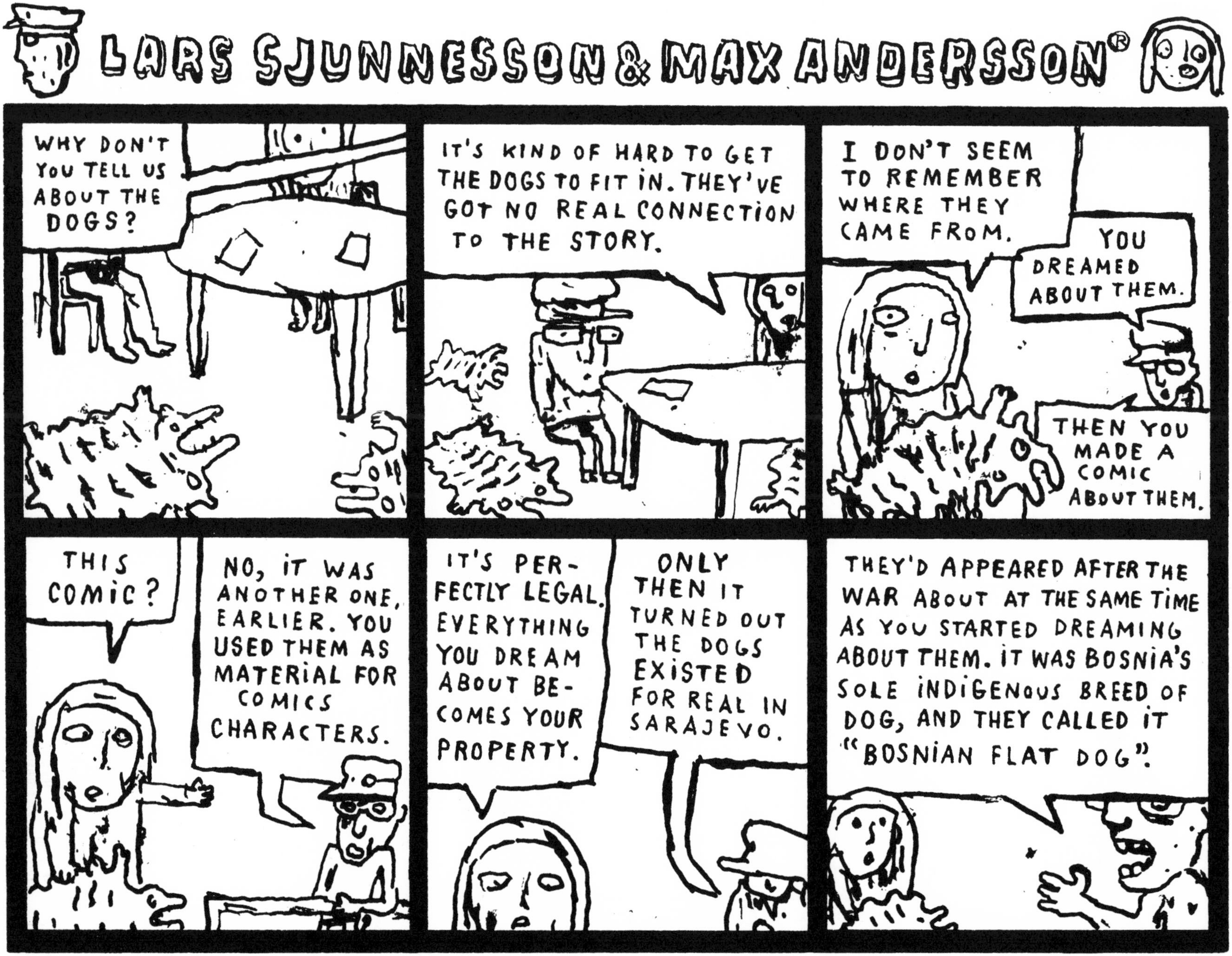
LARS SJUNNESSON & MAX ANDERSSON®
WHY DON'T YOU TELL US ABOUT THE DOGS?
IT'S KIND OF HARD TO GET THE DOGS TO FIT IN. THEY'VE GOT NO REAL CONNECTION TO THE STORY.
I DON'T SEEM TO REMEMBER WHERE THEY CAME FROM.
YOU DREAMED ABOUT THEM.
THEN YOU MADE A COMIC ABOUT THEM.
THIS COMIC?
NO, IT WAS ANOTHER ONE, EARLIER. YOU USED THEM AS MATERIAL FOR COMICS CHARACTERS.
IT'S PERFECTLY LEGAL. EVERYTHING YOU DREAM ABOUT BECOMES YOUR PROPERTY.
ONLY THEN IT TURNED OUT THE DOGS EXISTED FOR REAL IN SARAJEVO.
THEY'D APPEARED AFTER THE WAR ABOUT AT THE SAME TIME AS YOU STARTED DREAMING ABOUT THEM. IT WAS BOSNIA'S SOLE INDIGENOUS BREED OF DOG, AND THEY CALLED IT "BOSNIAN FLAT DOG".

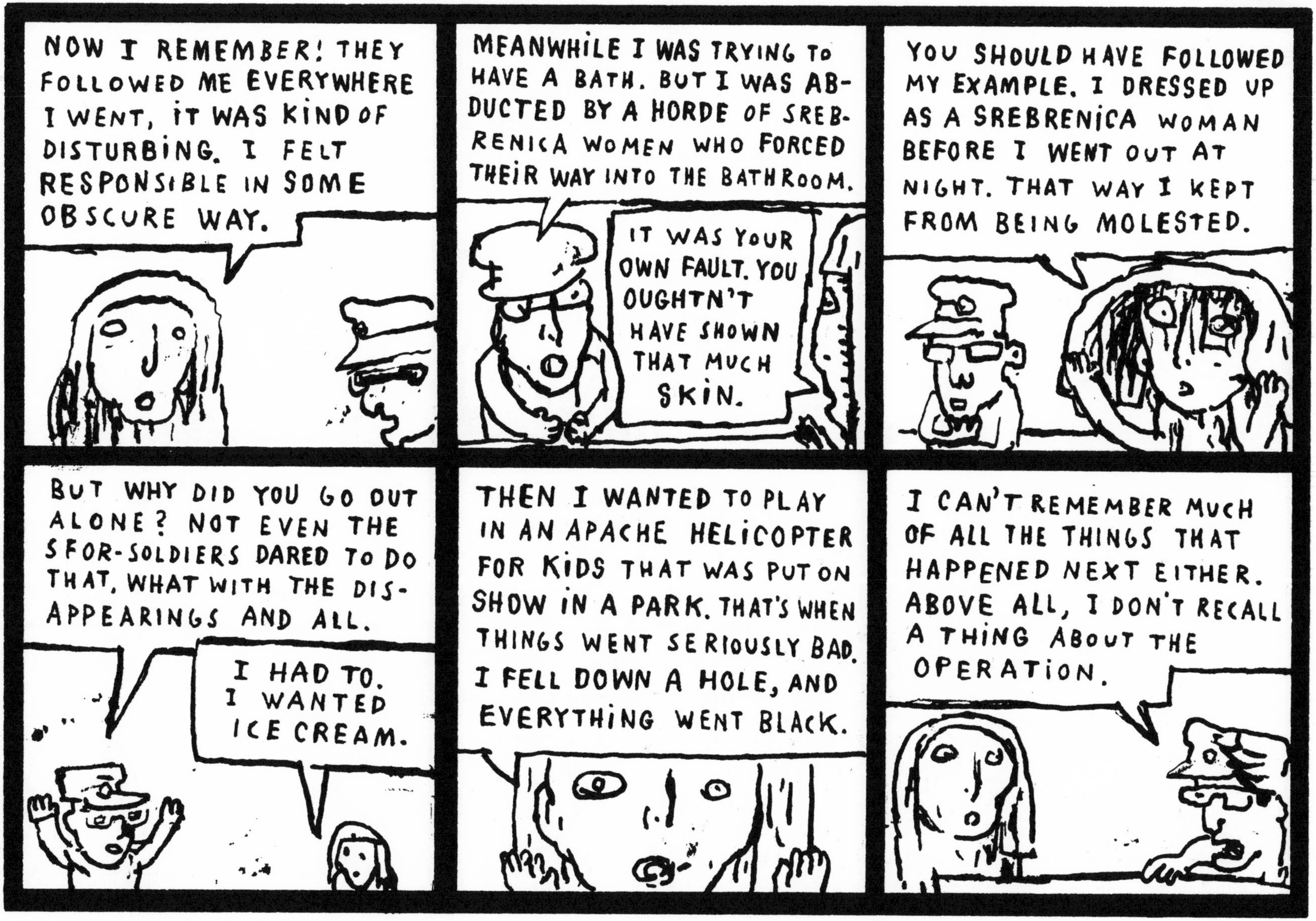
NOW I REMEMBER! THEY FOLLOWED ME EVERYWHERE I WENT, IT WAS KIND OF DISTURBING. I FELT RESPONSIBLE IN SOME OBSCURE WAY.
MEANWHILE I WAS TRYING TO HAVE A BATH. BUT I WAS ABDUCTED BY A HORDE OF SREBRENICA WOMEN WHO FORCED THEIR WAY INTO THE BATHROOM.
IT WAS YOUR OWN FAULT. YOU OUGHTN'T HAVE SHOWN THAT MUCH SKIN.
YOU SHOULD HAVE FOLLOWED MY EXAMPLE. I DRESSED UP AS A SREBRENICA WOMAN BEFORE I WENT OUT AT NIGHT. THAT WAY I KEPT FROM BEING MOLESTED.
BUT WHY DID YOU GO OUT ALONE? NOT EVEN THE SFOR-SOLDIERS DARED TO DO THAT, WHAT WITH THE DISAPPEARINGS AND ALL.
I HAD TO. I WANTED ICE CREAM.
THEN I WANTED TO PLAY IN AN APACHE HELICOPTER FOR KIDS THAT WAS PUT ON SHOW IN A PARK. THAT'S WHEN THINGS WENT SERIOUSLY BAD. I FELL DOWN A HOLE, AND EVERYTHING WENT BLACK.
I CAN'T REMEMBER MUCH OF ALL THE THINGS THAT HAPPENED NEXT EITHER. ABOVE ALL, I DON'T RECALL A THING ABOUT THE OPERATION.

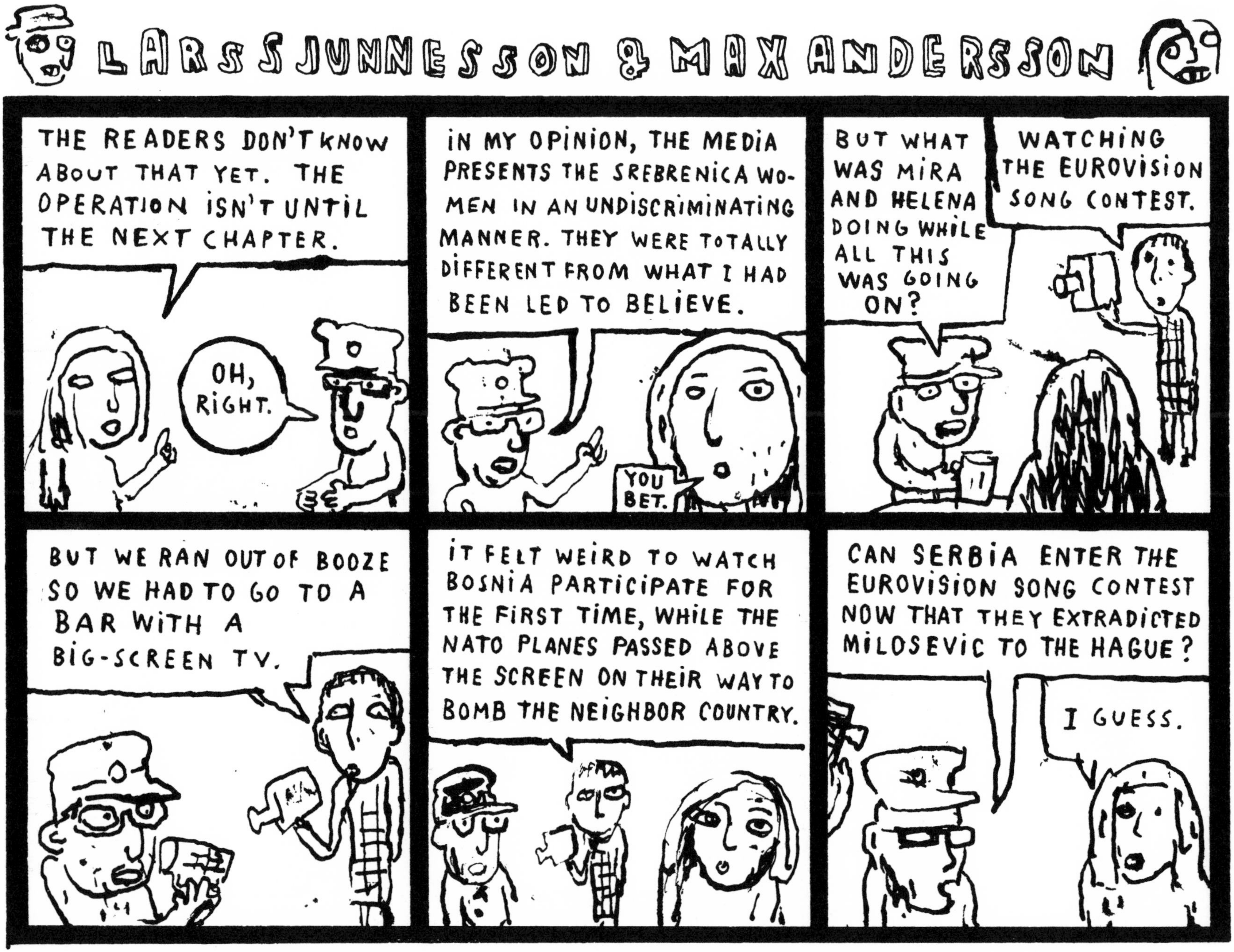
LARS SJUNNESSON & MAX ANDERSSON
THE READERS DON'T KNOW ABOUT THAT YET. THE OPERATION ISN'T UNTIL THE NEXT CHAPTER.
OH, RIGHT.
IN MY OPINION, THE MEDIA PRESENTS THE SREBRENICA WOMEN IN AN UNDISCRIMINATING MANNER. THEY WERE TOTALLY DIFFERENT FROM WHAT I HAD BEEN LED TO BELIEVE.
YOU BET.
BUT WHAT WAS MIRA AND HELENA DOING WHILE ALL THIS WAS GOING ON?
WATCHING THE EUROVISION SONG CONTEST.
BUT WE RAN OUT OF BOOZE SO WE HAD TO GO TO A BAR WITH A BIG-SCREEN TV.
IT FELT WEIRD TO WATCH BOSNIA PARTICIPATE FOR THE FIRST TIME, WHILE THE NATO PLANES PASSED ABOVE THE SCREEN ON THEIR WAY TO BOMB THE NEIGHBOR COUNTRY.
CAN SERBIA ENTER THE EUROVISION SONG CONTEST NOW THAT THEY EXTRADICTED MILOSEVIC TO THE HAGUE?
I GUESS.

LARS SJUNNESSON & MAX ANDERSSON

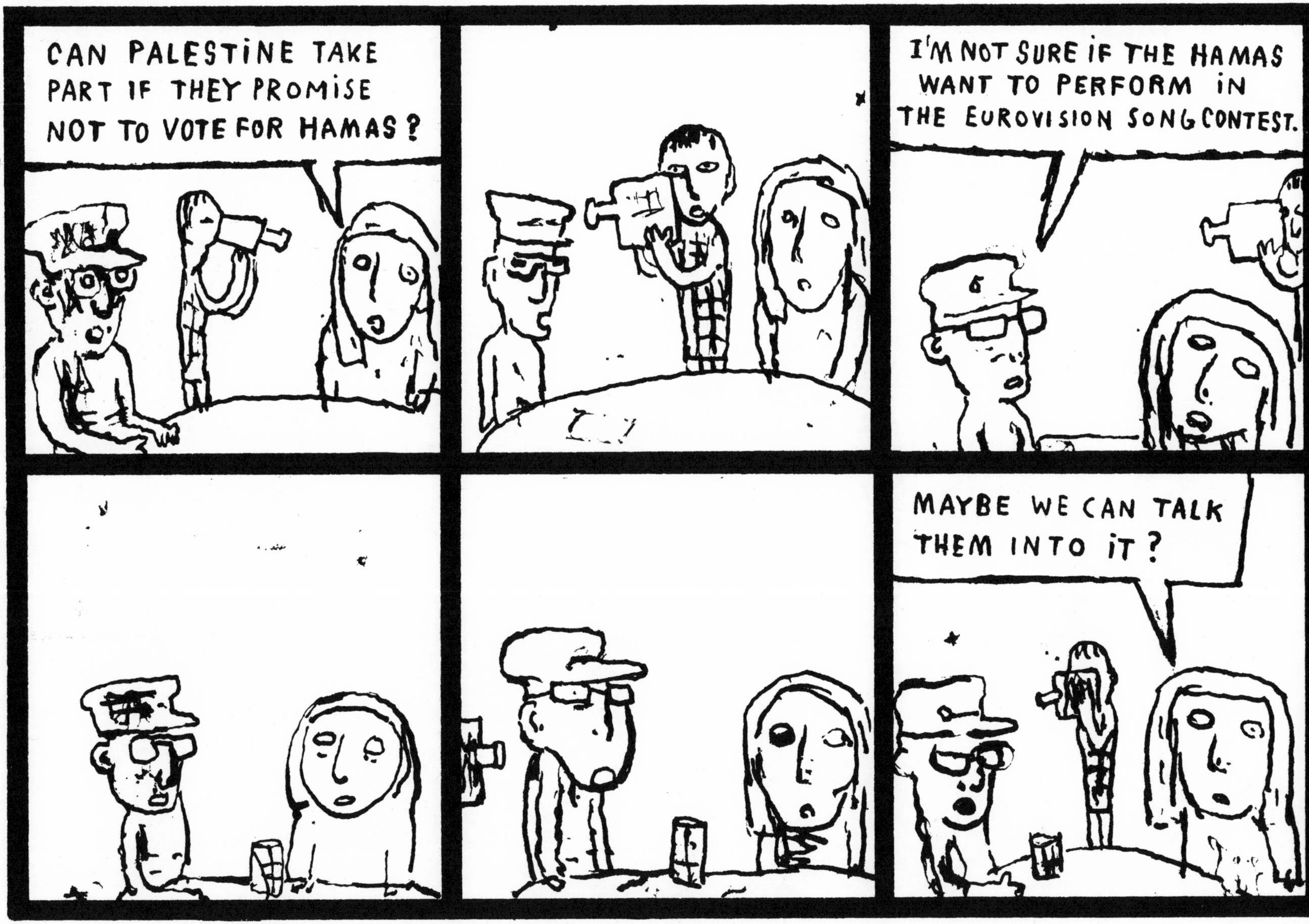
CAN PALESTINE TAKE PART IF THEY PROMISE NOT TO VOTE FOR HAMAS?
I'M NOT SURE IF THE HAMAS WANT TO PERFORM IN THE EUROVISION SONG CONTEST.
MAYBE WE CAN TALK THEM INTO IT?

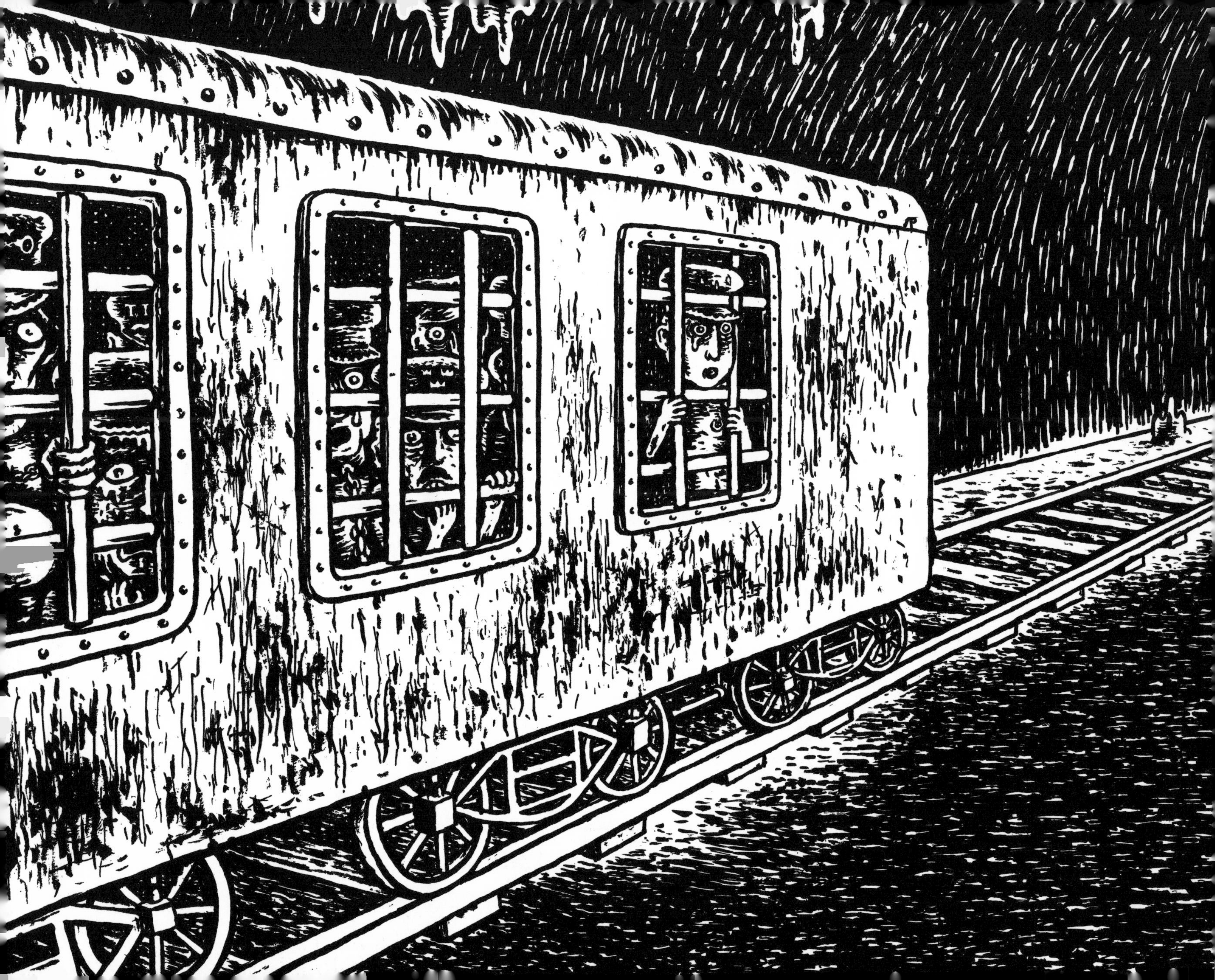

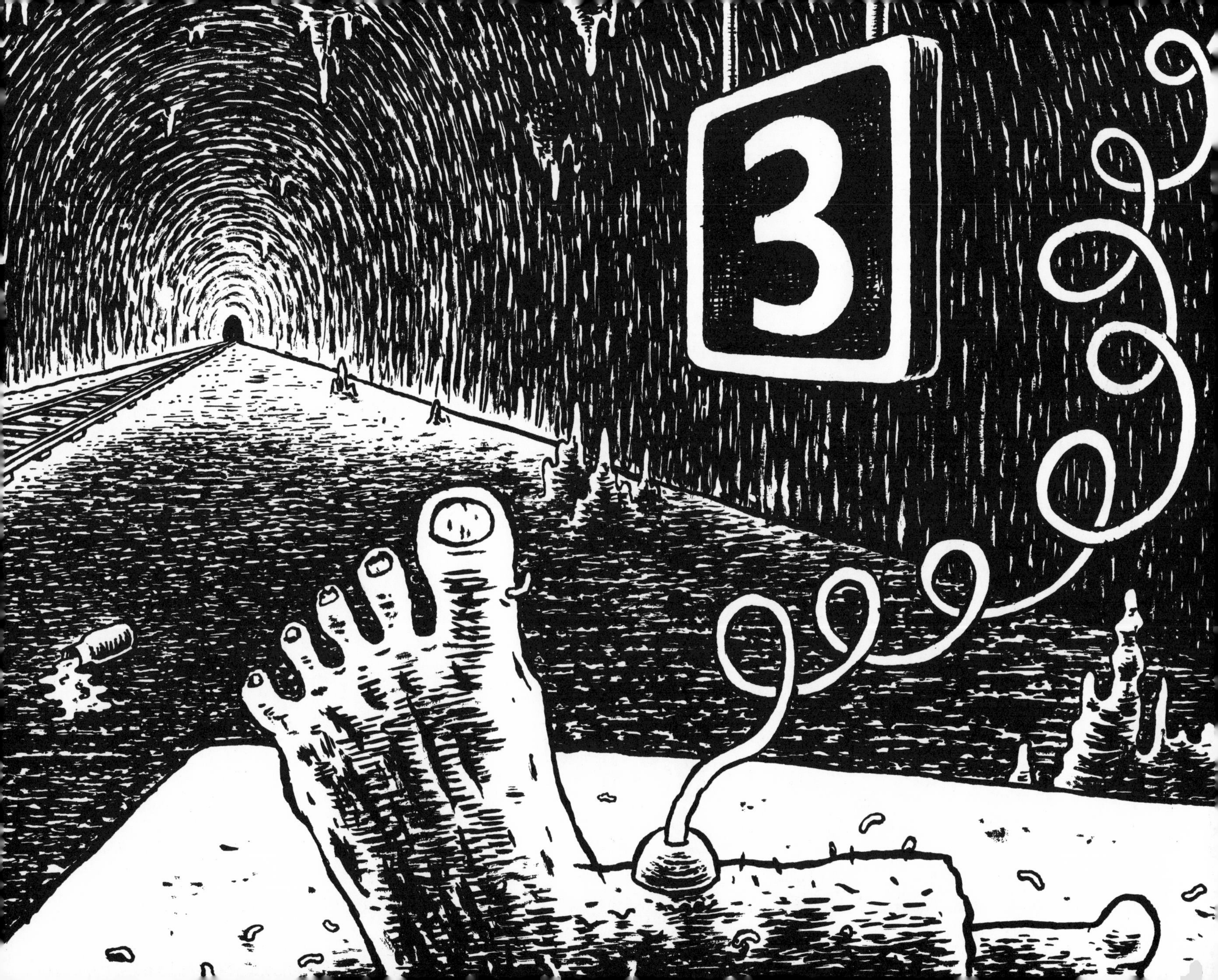
3

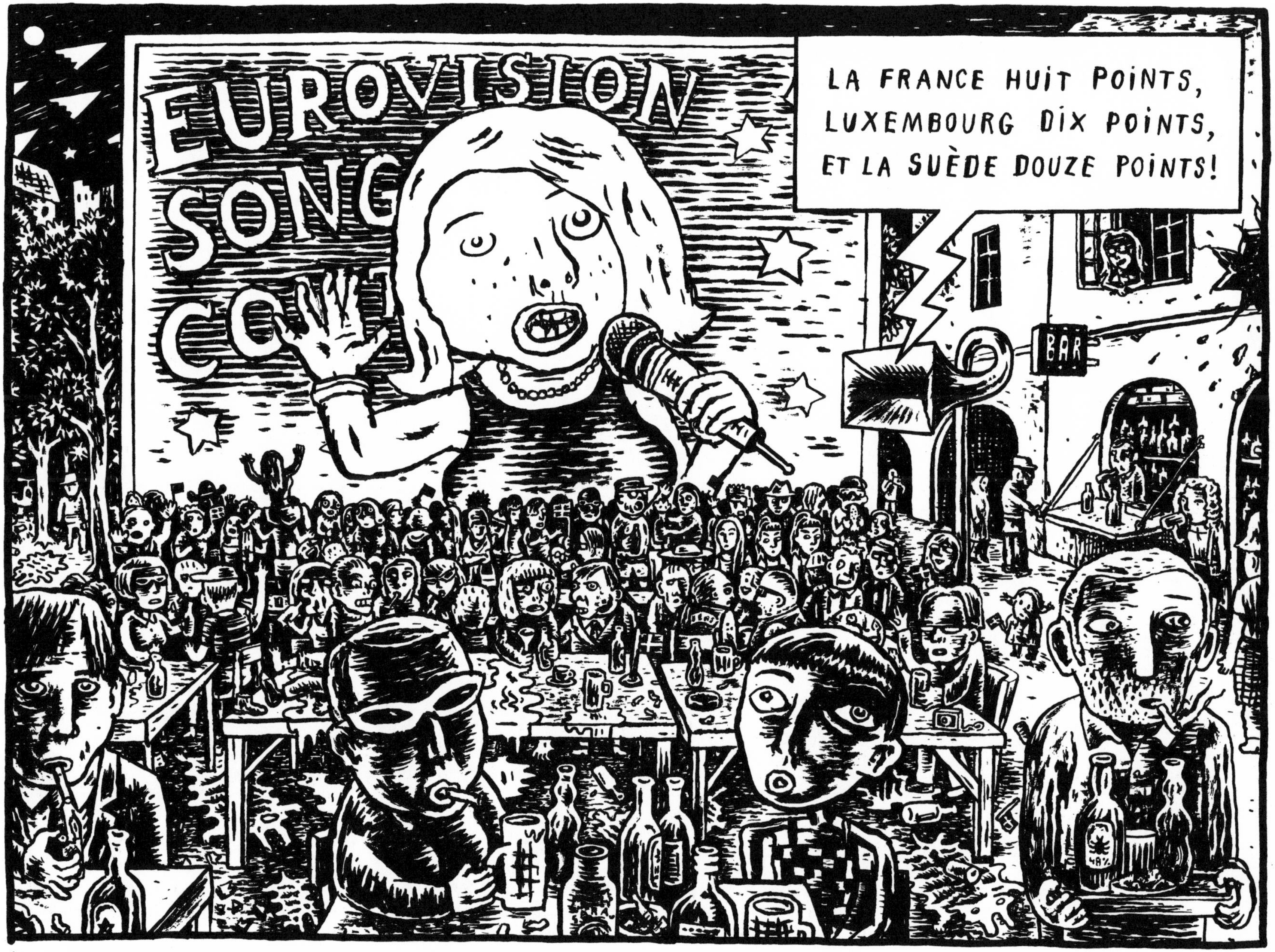
EUROVISION
SONG
CO
LA FRANCE HUIT POINTS, LUXEMBOURG DIX POINTS, ET LA SUÈDE DOUZE POINTS!
BAR

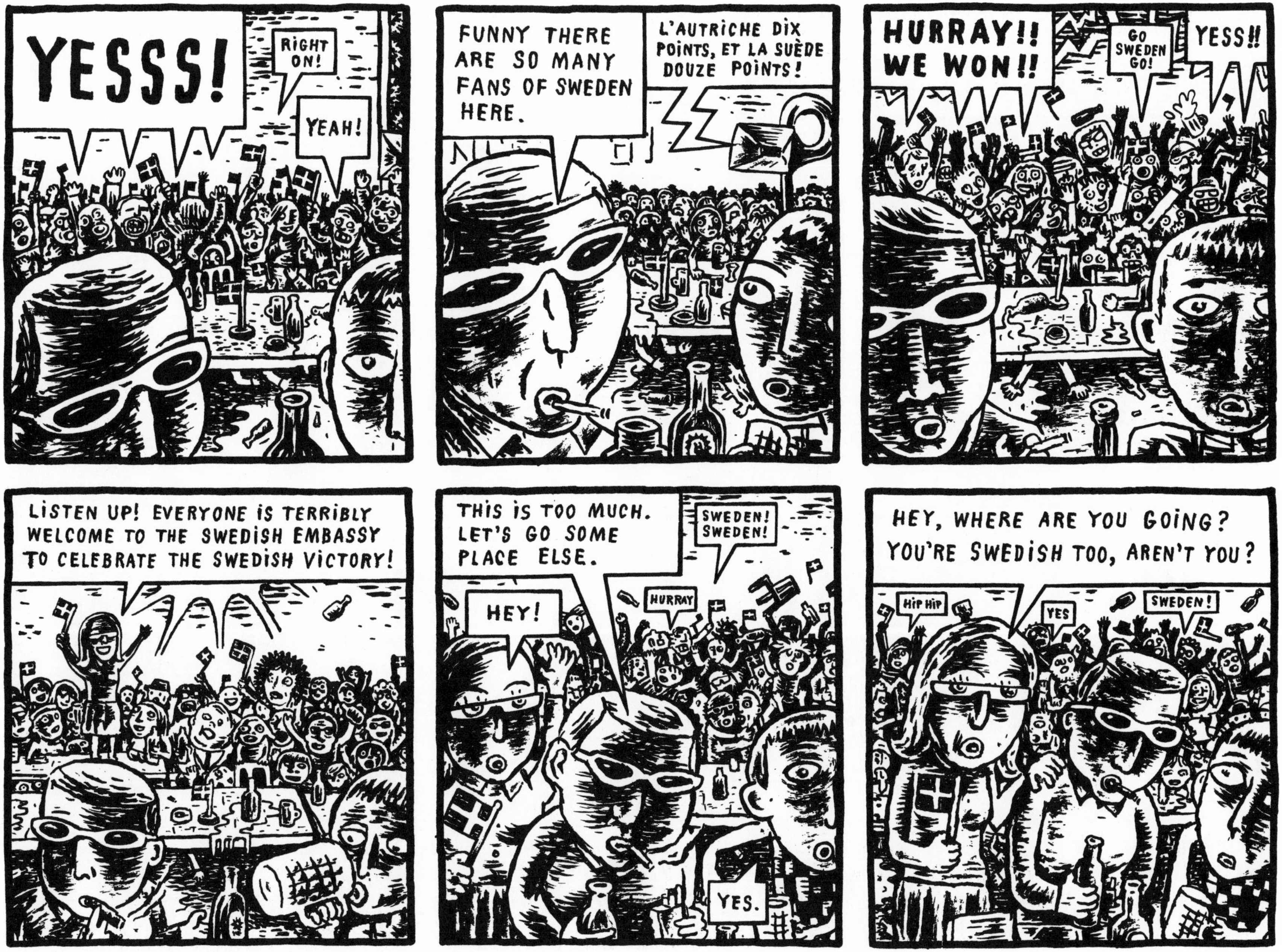
YESSS!
RIGHT ON!
YEAH!
FUNNY THERE ARE SO MANY FANS OF SWEDEN HERE.
L'AUTRICHE DIX POINTS, ET LA SUÈDE DOUZE POINTS!
HURRAY!! WE WON!!
GO SWEDEN GO!
YESS!!
LISTEN UP! EVERYONE IS TERRIBLY WELCOME TO THE SWEDISH EMBASSY TO CELEBRATE THE SWEDISH VICTORY!
THIS IS TOO MUCH. LET'S GO SOME PLACE ELSE.
SWEDEN! SWEDEN!
HEY!
HURRAY
YES.
HEY, WHERE ARE YOU GOING? YOU'RE SWEDISH TOO, AREN'T YOU?
HIP HIP
YES
SWEDEN!

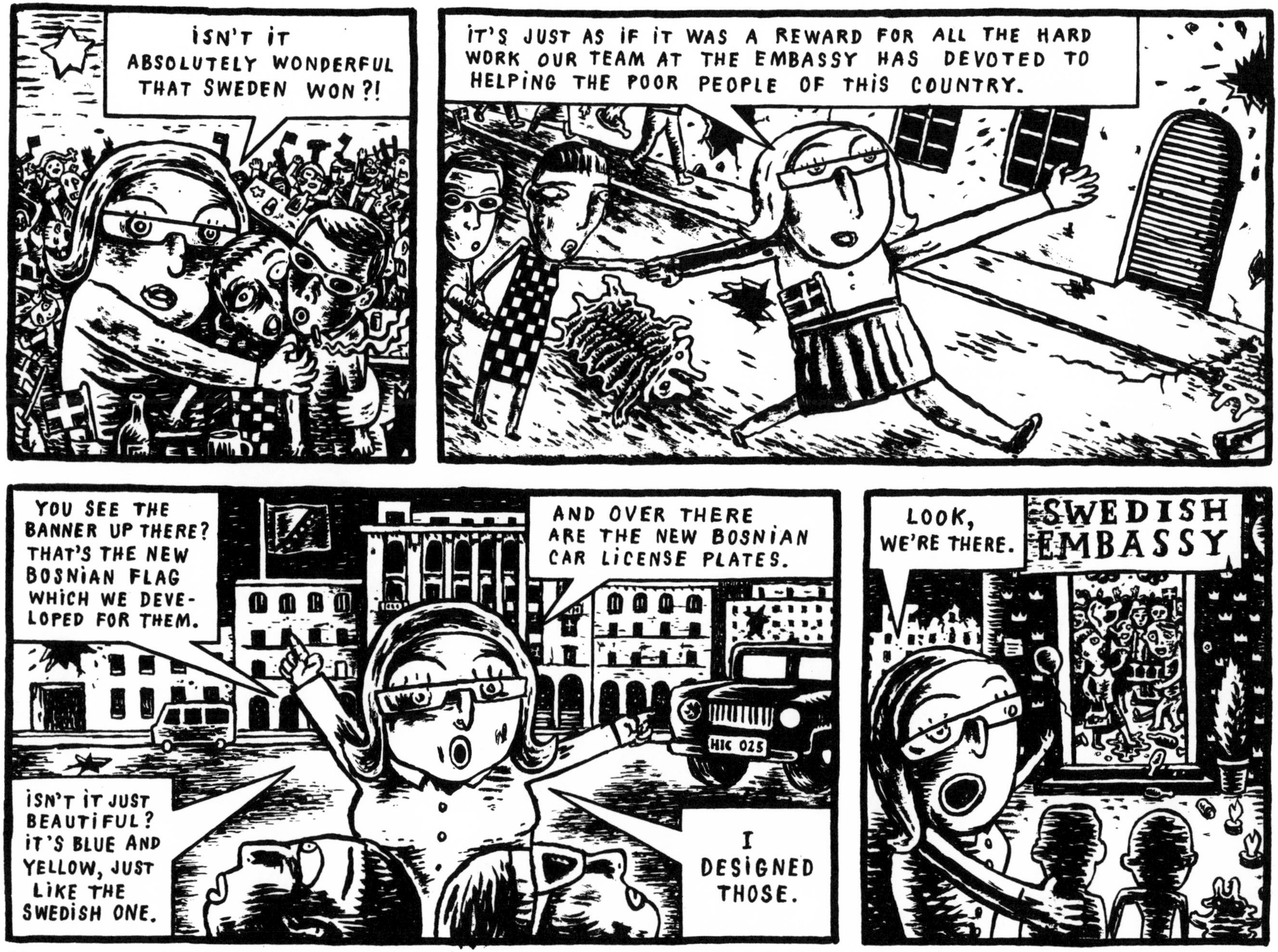
ISN'T IT ABSOLUTELY WONDERFUL THAT SWEDEN WON?!
IT'S JUST AS IF IT WAS A REWARD FOR ALL THE HARD WORK OUR TEAM AT THE EMBASSY HAS DEVOTED TO HELPING THE POOR PEOPLE OF THIS COUNTRY.
YOU SEE THE BANNER UP THERE? THAT'S THE NEW BOSNIAN FLAG WHICH WE DEVE-LOPED FOR THEM.
AND OVER THERE ARE THE NEW BOSNIAN CAR LICENSE PLATES.
HIC 025
ISN'T IT JUST BEAUTIFUL? IT'S BLUE AND YELLOW, JUST LIKE THE SWEDISH ONE.
I DESIGNED THOSE.
LOOK, WE'RE THERE.
SWEDISH EMBASSY

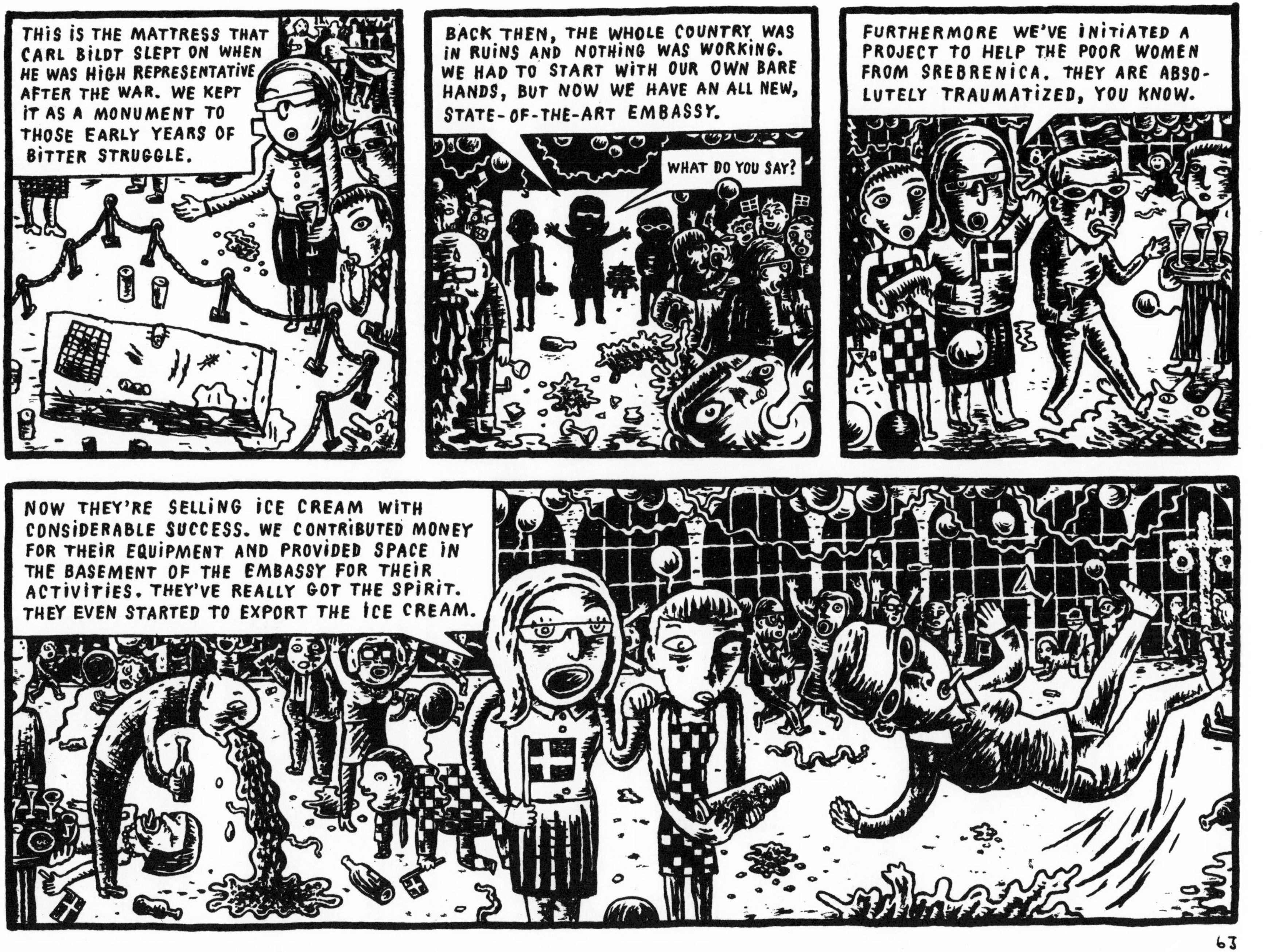
THIS IS THE MATTRESS THAT CARL BILDT SLEPT ON WHEN HE WAS HIGH REPRESENTATIVE AFTER THE WAR. WE KEPT IT AS A MONUMENT TO THOSE EARLY YEARS OF BITTER STRUGGLE.
BACK THEN, THE WHOLE COUNTRY WAS IN RUINS AND NOTHING WAS WORKING. WE HAD TO START WITH OUR OWN BARE HANDS, BUT NOW WE HAVE AN ALL NEW, STATE-OF-THE-ART EMBASSY.
WHAT DO YOU SAY?
FURTHERMORE WE'VE INITIATED A PROJECT TO HELP THE POOR WOMEN FROM SREBRENICA. THEY ARE ABSOLUTELY TRAUMATIZED, YOU KNOW.
NOW THEY'RE SELLING ICE CREAM WITH CONSIDERABLE SUCCESS. WE CONTRIBUTED MONEY FOR THEIR EQUIPMENT AND PROVIDED SPACE IN THE BASEMENT OF THE EMBASSY FOR THEIR ACTIVITIES. THEY'VE REALLY GOT THE SPIRIT. THEY EVEN STARTED TO EXPORT THE ICE CREAM.

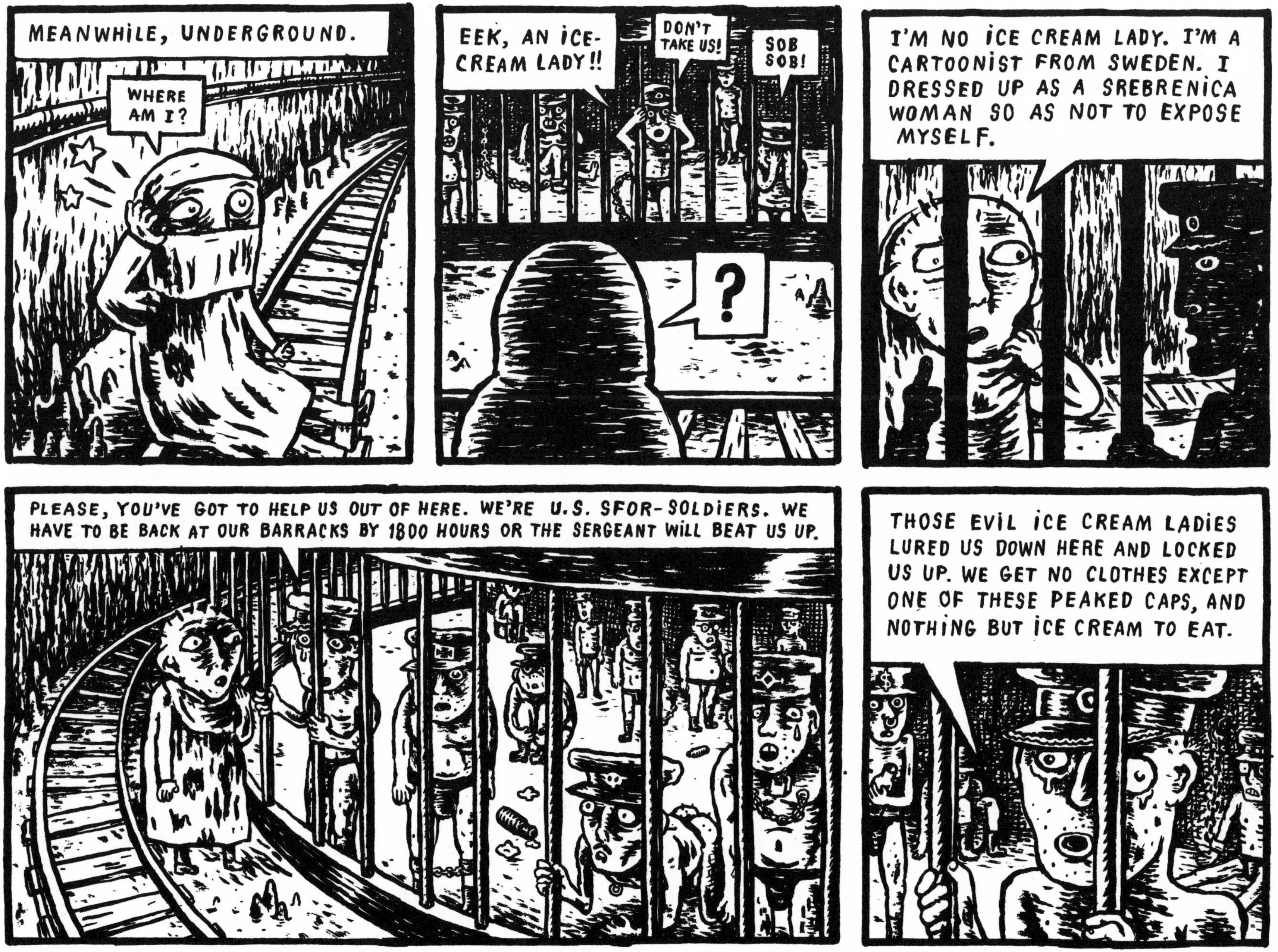
MEANWHILE, UNDERGROUND.
WHERE AM I?
EEK, AN ICE-CREAM LADY!!
DON'T TAKE US!
SOB SOB!
?
I'M NO ICE CREAM LADY. I'M A CARTOONIST FROM SWEDEN. I DRESSED UP AS A SREBRENICA WOMAN SO AS NOT TO EXPOSE MYSELF.
PLEASE, YOU'VE GOT TO HELP US OUT OF HERE. WE'RE U.S. SFOR-SOLDIERS. WE HAVE TO BE BACK AT OUR BARRACKS BY 1800 HOURS OR THE SERGEANT WILL BEAT US UP.
THOSE EVIL ICE CREAM LADIES LURED US DOWN HERE AND LOCKED US UP. WE GET NO CLOTHES EXCEPT ONE OF THESE PEAKED CAPS, AND NOTHING BUT ICE CREAM TO EAT.

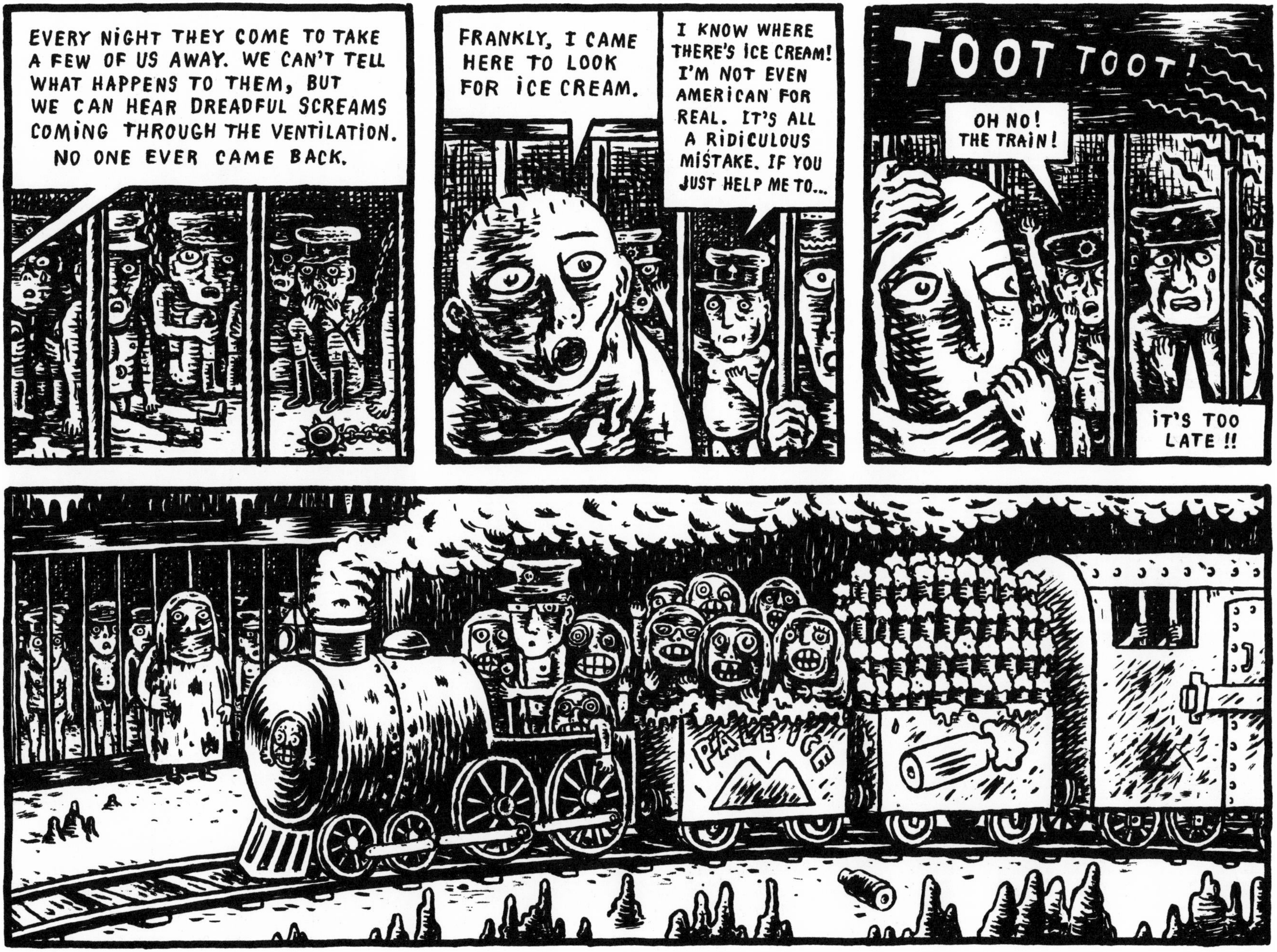
EVERY NIGHT THEY COME TO TAKE A FEW OF US AWAY. WE CAN'T TELL WHAT HAPPENS TO THEM, BUT WE CAN HEAR DREADFUL SCREAMS COMING THROUGH THE VENTILATION. NO ONE EVER CAME BACK.
FRANKLY, I CAME HERE TO LOOK FOR ICE CREAM.
I KNOW WHERE THERE'S ICE CREAM! I'M NOT EVEN AMERICAN FOR REAL. IT'S ALL A RIDICULOUS MISTAKE. IF YOU JUST HELP ME TO...
TOOT TOOT!
OH NO! THE TRAIN!
IT'S TOO LATE !!
PALE ICE

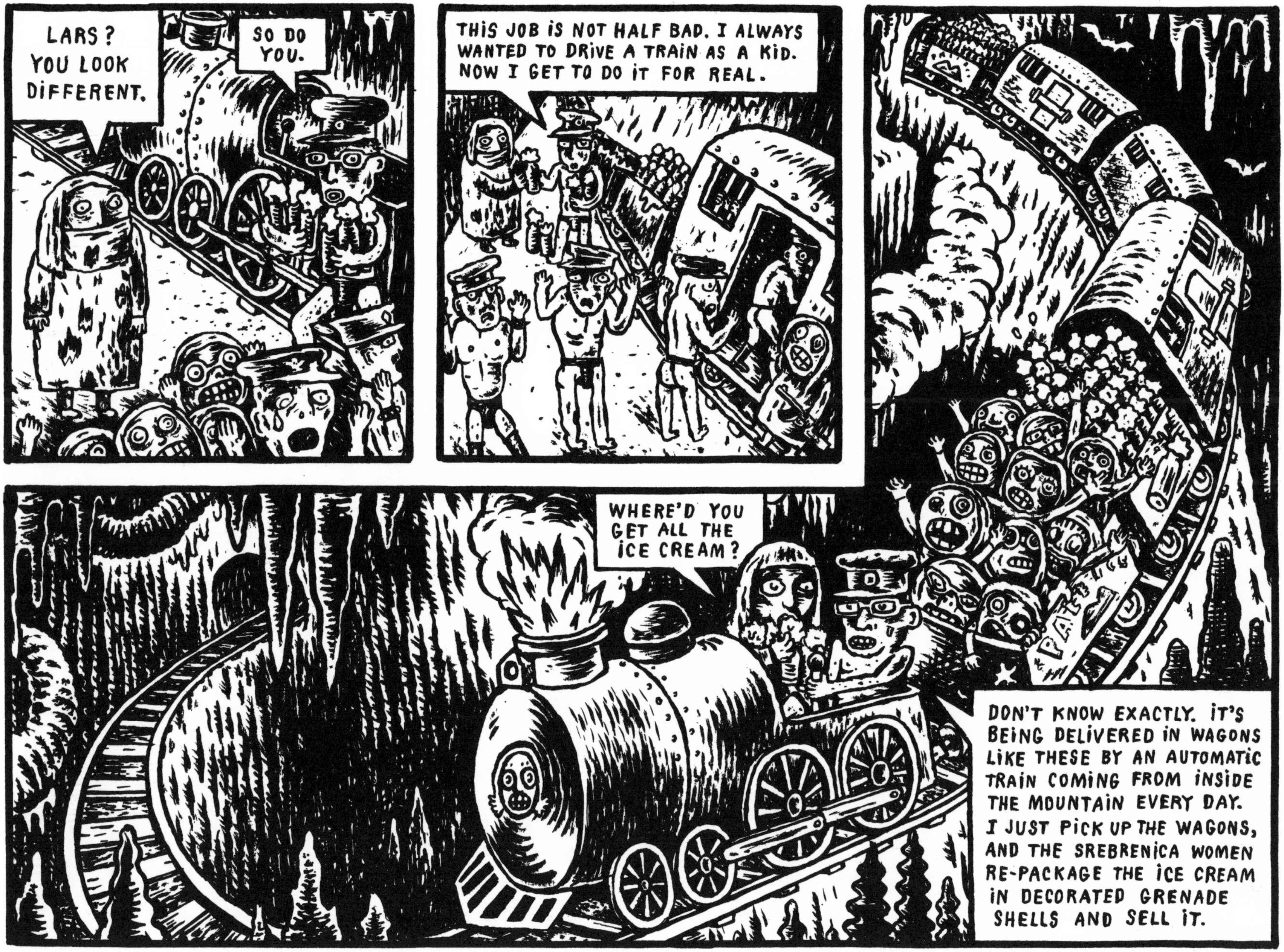
LARS? YOU LOOK DIFFERENT.
SO DO YOU.
THIS JOB IS NOT HALF BAD. I ALWAYS WANTED TO DRIVE A TRAIN AS A KID. NOW I GET TO DO IT FOR REAL.
WHERE'D YOU GET ALL THE ICE CREAM?
DON'T KNOW EXACTLY. IT'S BEING DELIVERED IN WAGONS LIKE THESE BY AN AUTOMATIC TRAIN COMING FROM INSIDE THE MOUNTAIN EVERY DAY. I JUST PICK UP THE WAGONS, AND THE SREBRENICA WOMEN RE-PACKAGE THE ICE CREAM IN DECORATED GRENADE SHELLS AND SELL IT.

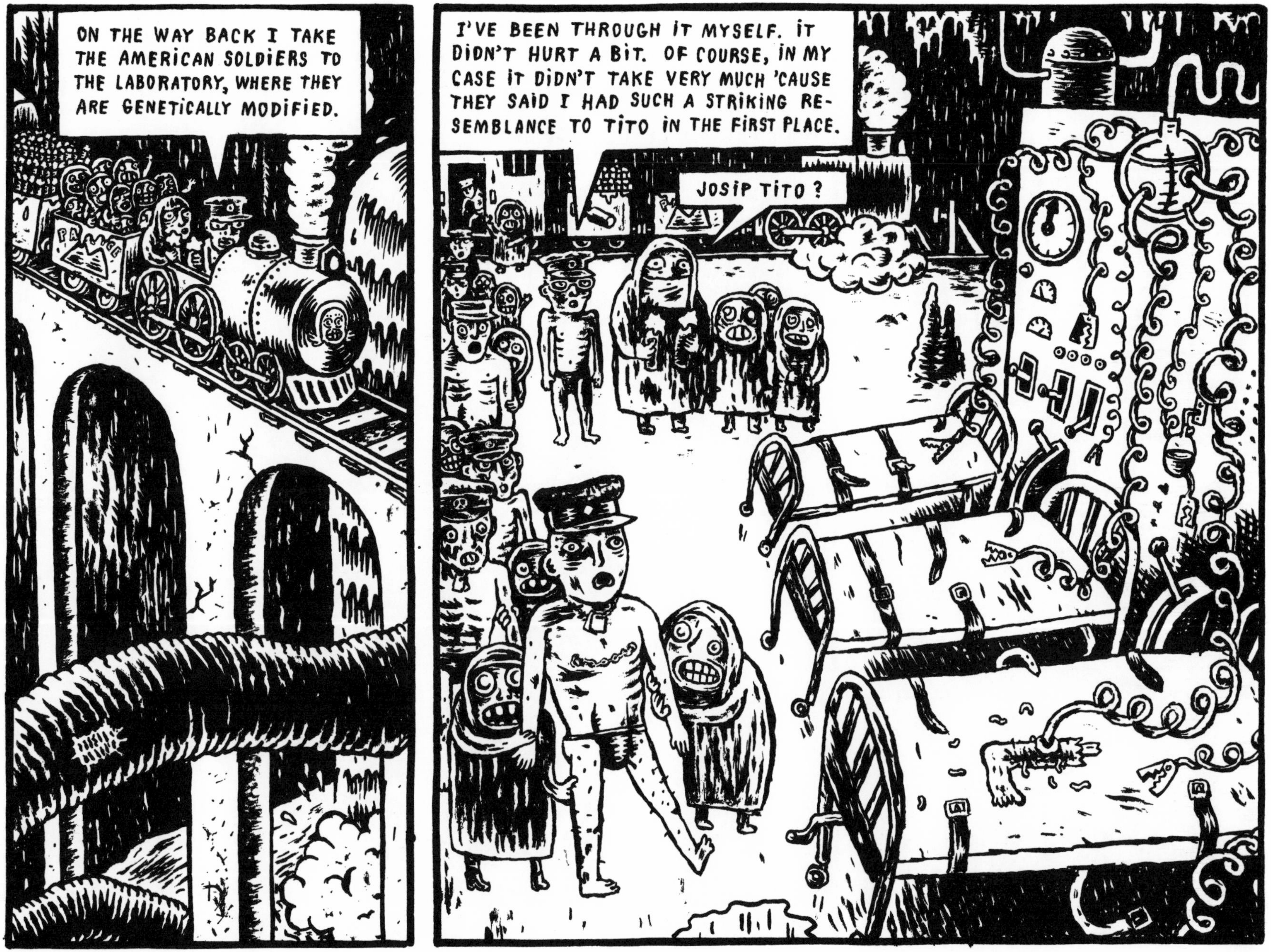
ON THE WAY BACK I TAKE THE AMERICAN SOLDIERS TO THE LABORATORY, WHERE THEY ARE GENETICALLY MODIFIED.
I'VE BEEN THROUGH IT MYSELF. IT DIDN'T HURT A BIT. OF COURSE, IN MY CASE IT DIDN'T TAKE VERY MUCH 'CAUSE THEY SAID I HAD SUCH A STRIKING RESEMBLANCE TO TITO IN THE FIRST PLACE.
JOSIP TITO?

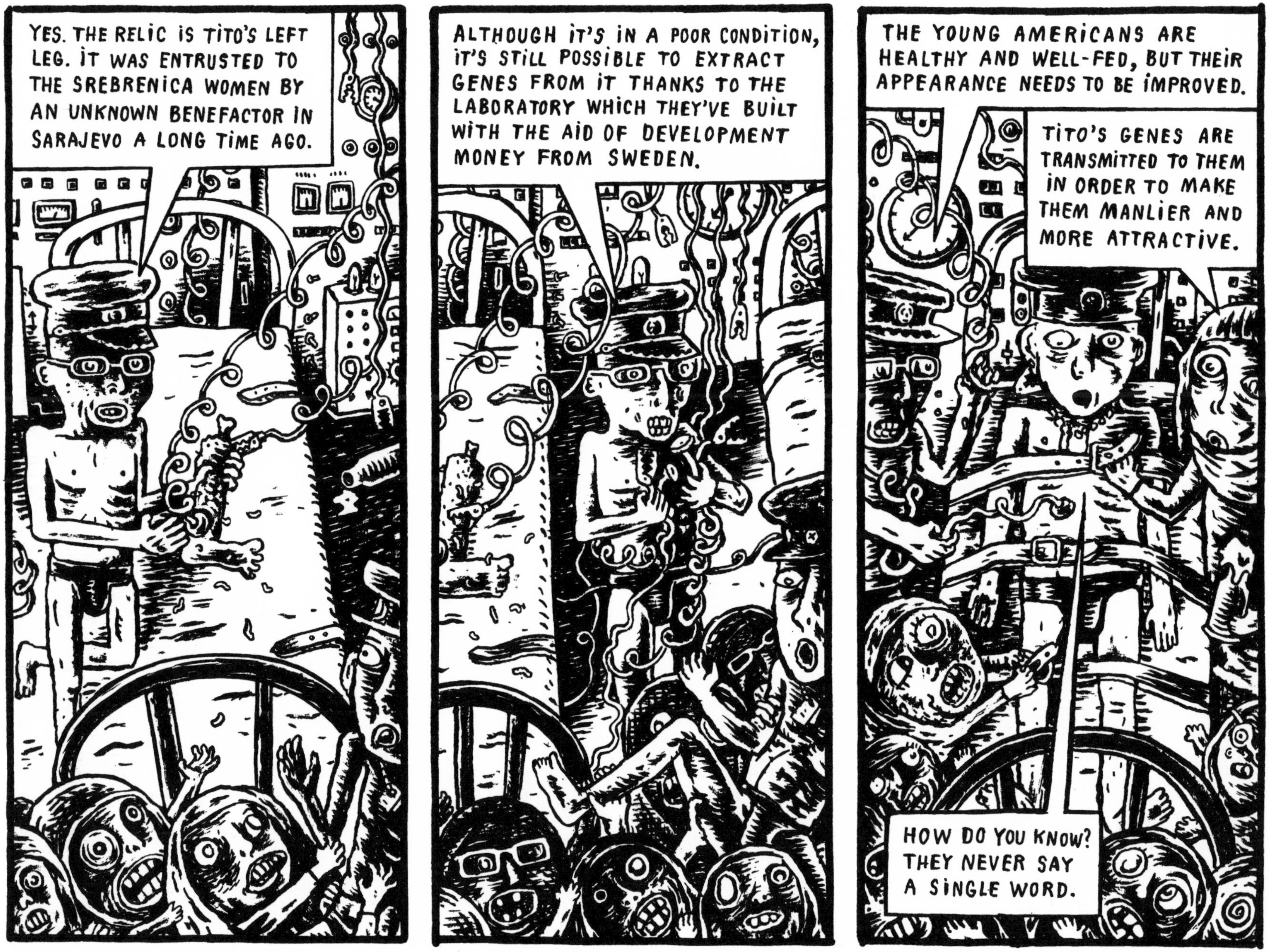
YES. THE RELIC IS TITO'S LEFT LEG. IT WAS ENTRUSTED TO THE SREBRENICA WOMEN BY AN UNKNOWN BENEFACTOR IN SARAJEVO A LONG TIME AGO.
ALTHOUGH IT'S IN A POOR CONDITION, IT'S STILL POSSIBLE TO EXTRACT GENES FROM IT THANKS TO THE LABORATORY WHICH THEY'VE BUILT WITH THE AID OF DEVELOPMENT MONEY FROM SWEDEN.
THE YOUNG AMERICANS ARE HEALTHY AND WELL-FED, BUT THEIR APPEARANCE NEEDS TO BE IMPROVED.
TITO'S GENES ARE TRANSMITTED TO THEM IN ORDER TO MAKE THEM MANLIER AND MORE ATTRACTIVE.
HOW DO YOU KNOW? THEY NEVER SAY A SINGLE WORD.

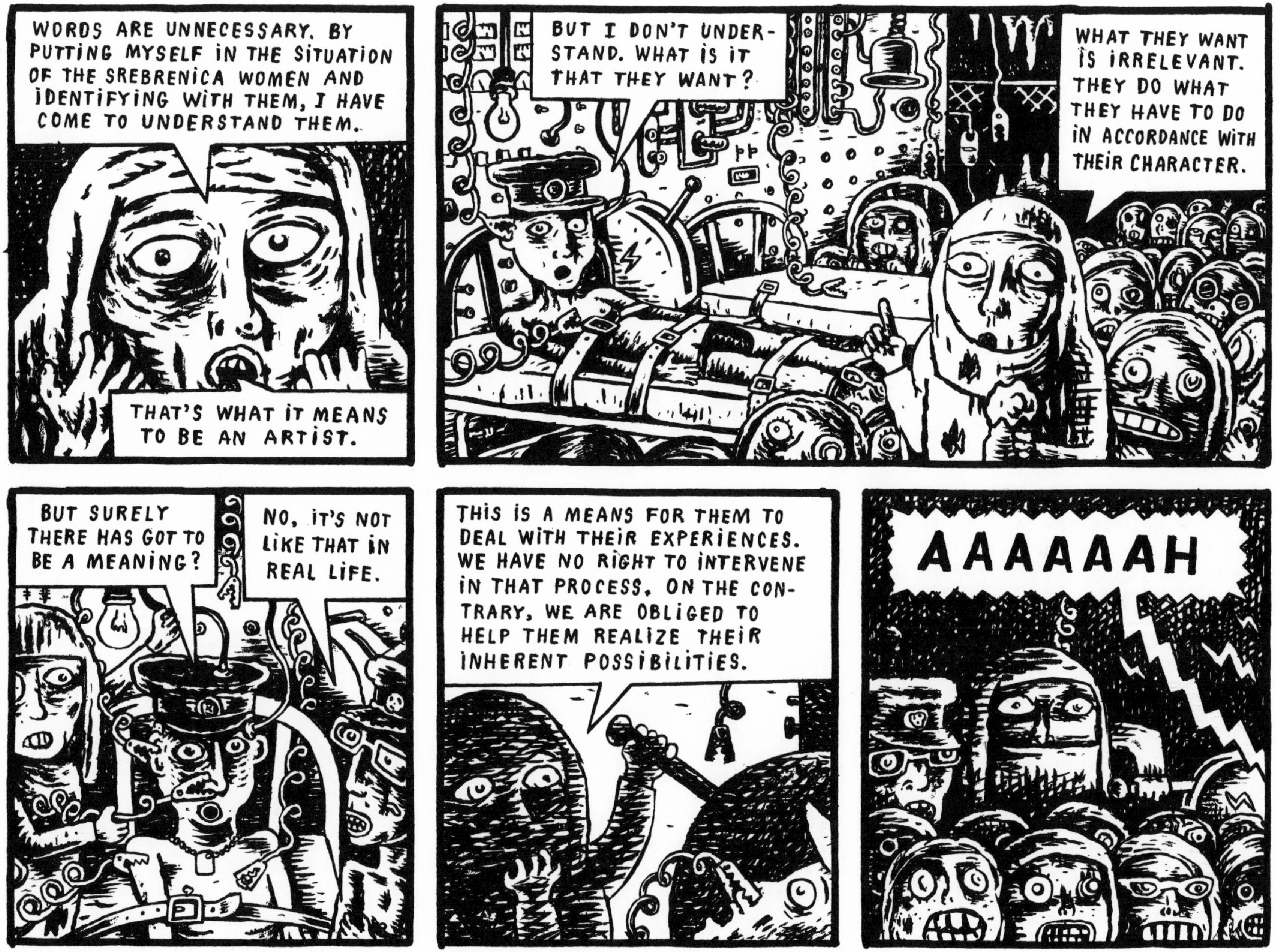
WORDS ARE UNNECESSARY. BY PUTTING MYSELF IN THE SITUATION OF THE SREBRENICA WOMEN AND IDENTIFYING WITH THEM, I HAVE COME TO UNDERSTAND THEM.
THAT'S WHAT IT MEANS TO BE AN ARTIST.
BUT I DON'T UNDER-STAND. WHAT IS IT THAT THEY WANT?
WHAT THEY WANT IS IRRELEVANT. THEY DO WHAT THEY HAVE TO DO IN ACCORDANCE WITH THEIR CHARACTER.
BUT SURELY THERE HAS GOT TO BE A MEANING?
NO, IT'S NOT LIKE THAT IN REAL LIFE.
THIS IS A MEANS FOR THEM TO DEAL WITH THEIR EXPERIENCES. WE HAVE NO RIGHT TO INTERVENE IN THAT PROCESS. ON THE CON-TRARY, WE ARE OBLIGED TO HELP THEM REALIZE THEIR INHERENT POSSIBILITIES.
AAAAAAH

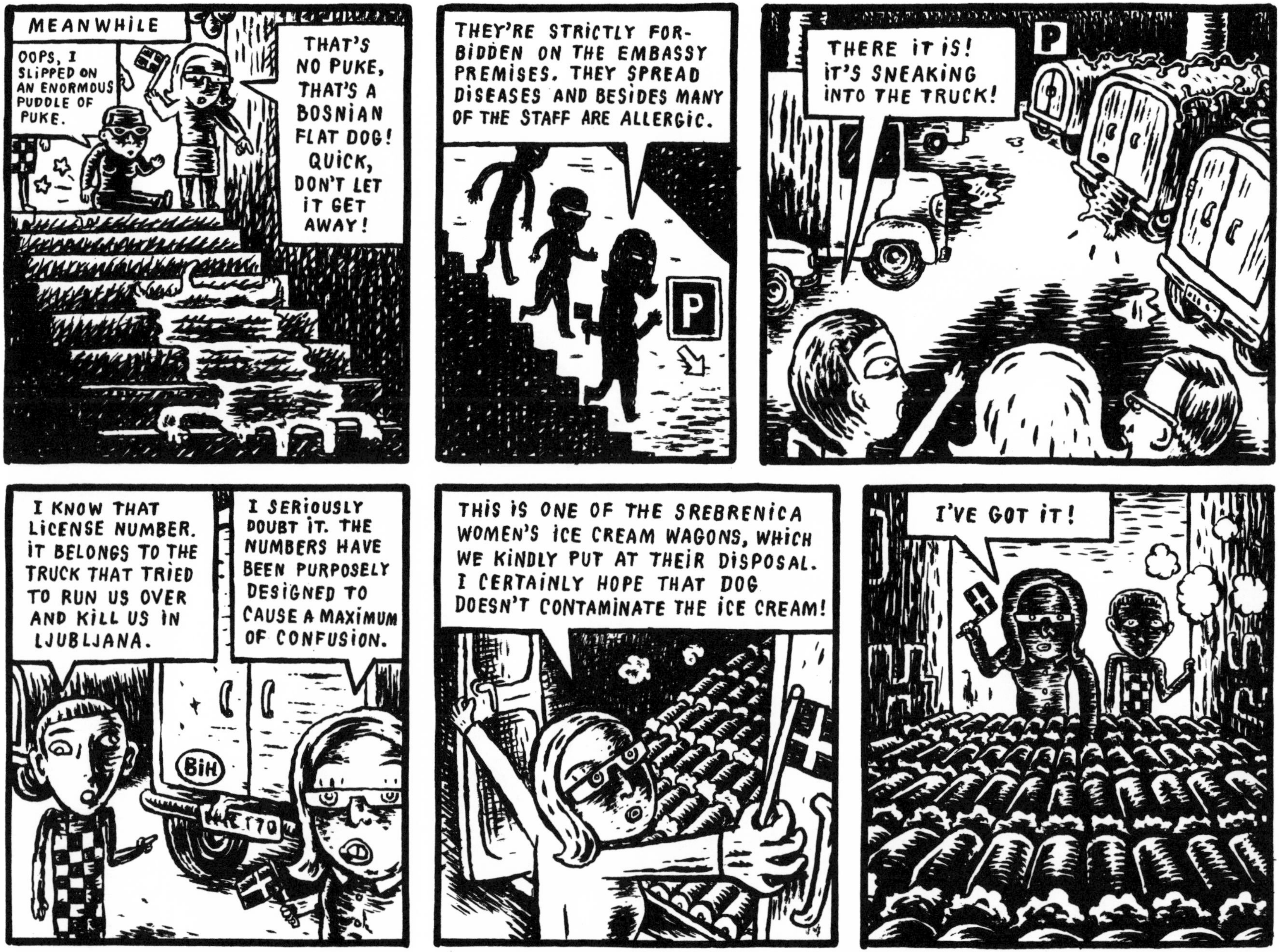
MEANWHILE
OOPS, I SLIPPED ON AN ENORMOUS PUDDLE OF PUKE.
THAT'S NO PUKE, THAT'S A BOSNIAN FLAT DOG! QUICK, DON'T LET IT GET AWAY!
THEY'RE STRICTLY FORBIDDEN ON THE EMBASSY PREMISES. THEY SPREAD DISEASES AND BESIDES MANY OF THE STAFF ARE ALLERGIC.
P
THERE IT IS! IT'S SNEAKING INTO THE TRUCK!
P
I KNOW THAT LICENSE NUMBER. IT BELONGS TO THE TRUCK THAT TRIED TO RUN US OVER AND KILL US IN LJUBLJANA.
I SERIOUSLY DOUBT IT. THE NUMBERS HAVE BEEN PURPOSELY DESIGNED TO CAUSE A MAXIMUM OF CONFUSION.
BiH
THIS IS ONE OF THE SREBRENICA WOMEN'S ICE CREAM WAGONS, WHICH WE KINDLY PUT AT THEIR DISPOSAL. I CERTAINLY HOPE THAT DOG DOESN'T CONTAMINATE THE ICE CREAM!
I'VE GOT IT!

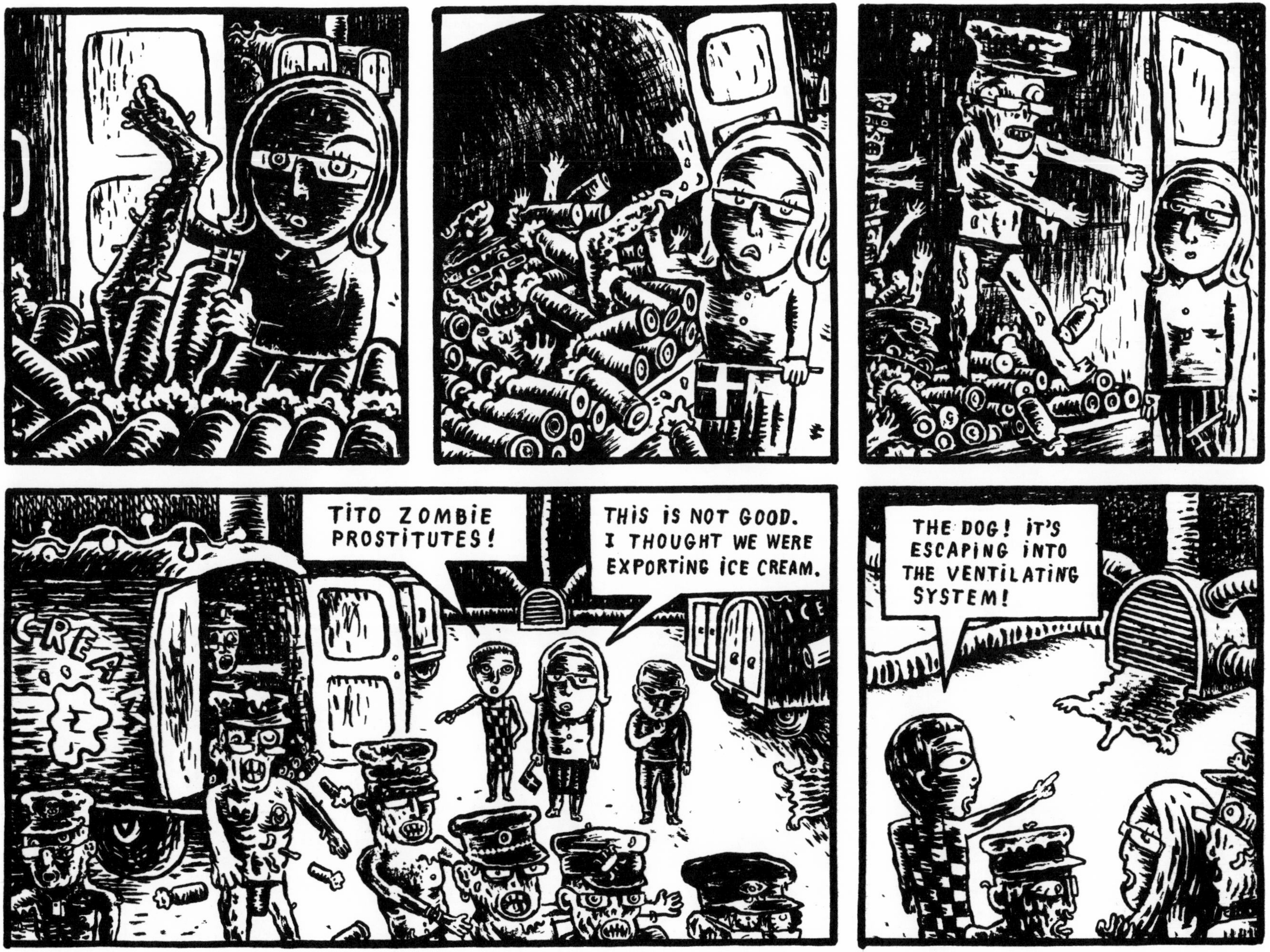
TITO ZOMBIE PROSTITUTES!
THIS IS NOT GOOD. I THOUGHT WE WERE EXPORTING ICE CREAM.
CREAK
ICE
THE DOG! IT'S ESCAPING INTO THE VENTILATING SYSTEM!

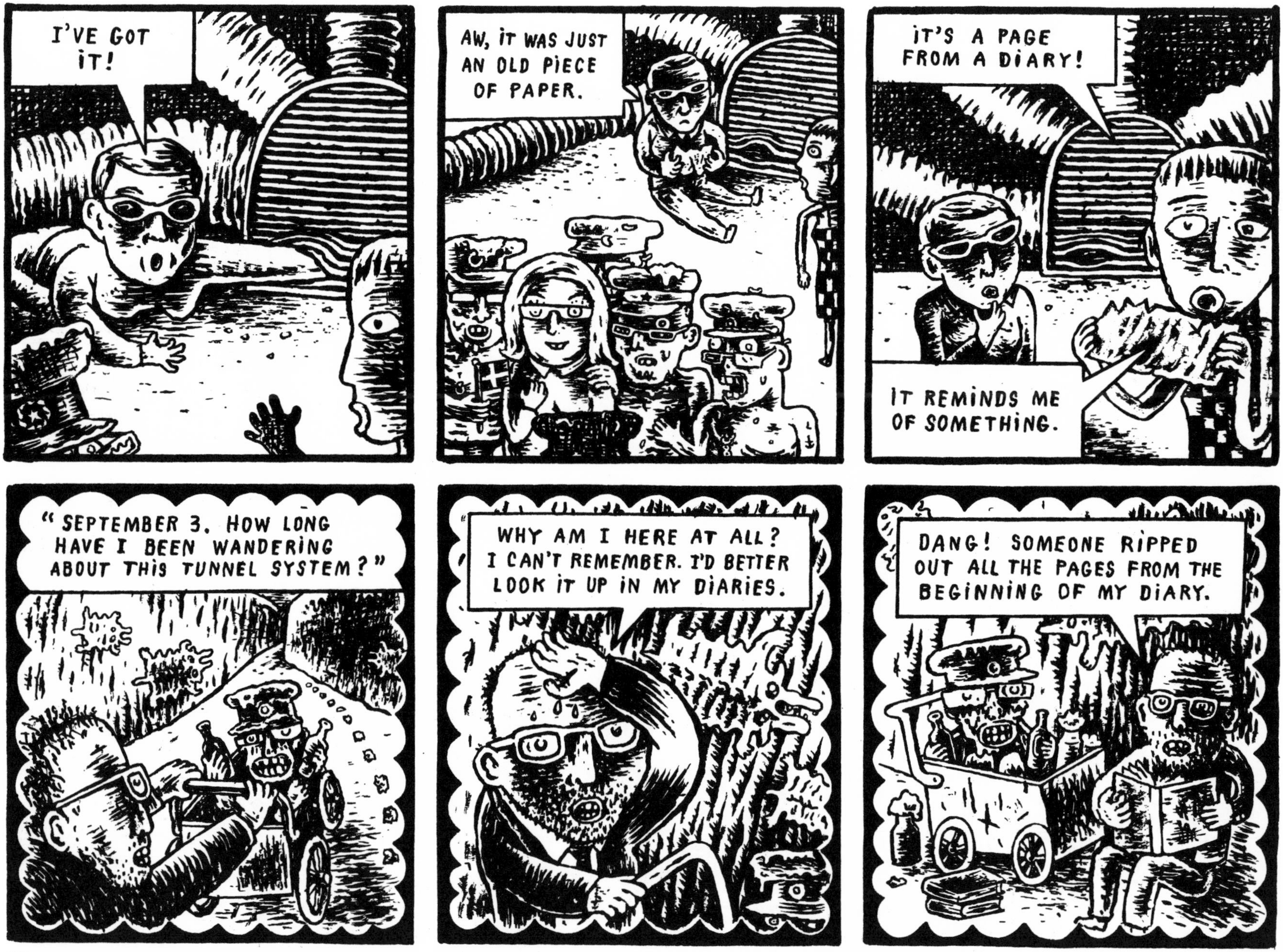
I'VE GOT IT!
AW, IT WAS JUST AN OLD PIECE OF PAPER.
IT'S A PAGE FROM A DIARY!
IT REMINDS ME OF SOMETHING.
"SEPTEMBER 3. HOW LONG HAVE I BEEN WANDERING ABOUT THIS TUNNEL SYSTEM?"
WHY AM I HERE AT ALL? I CAN'T REMEMBER. I'D BETTER LOOK IT UP IN MY DIARIES.
DANG! SOMEONE RIPPED OUT ALL THE PAGES FROM THE BEGINNING OF MY DIARY.

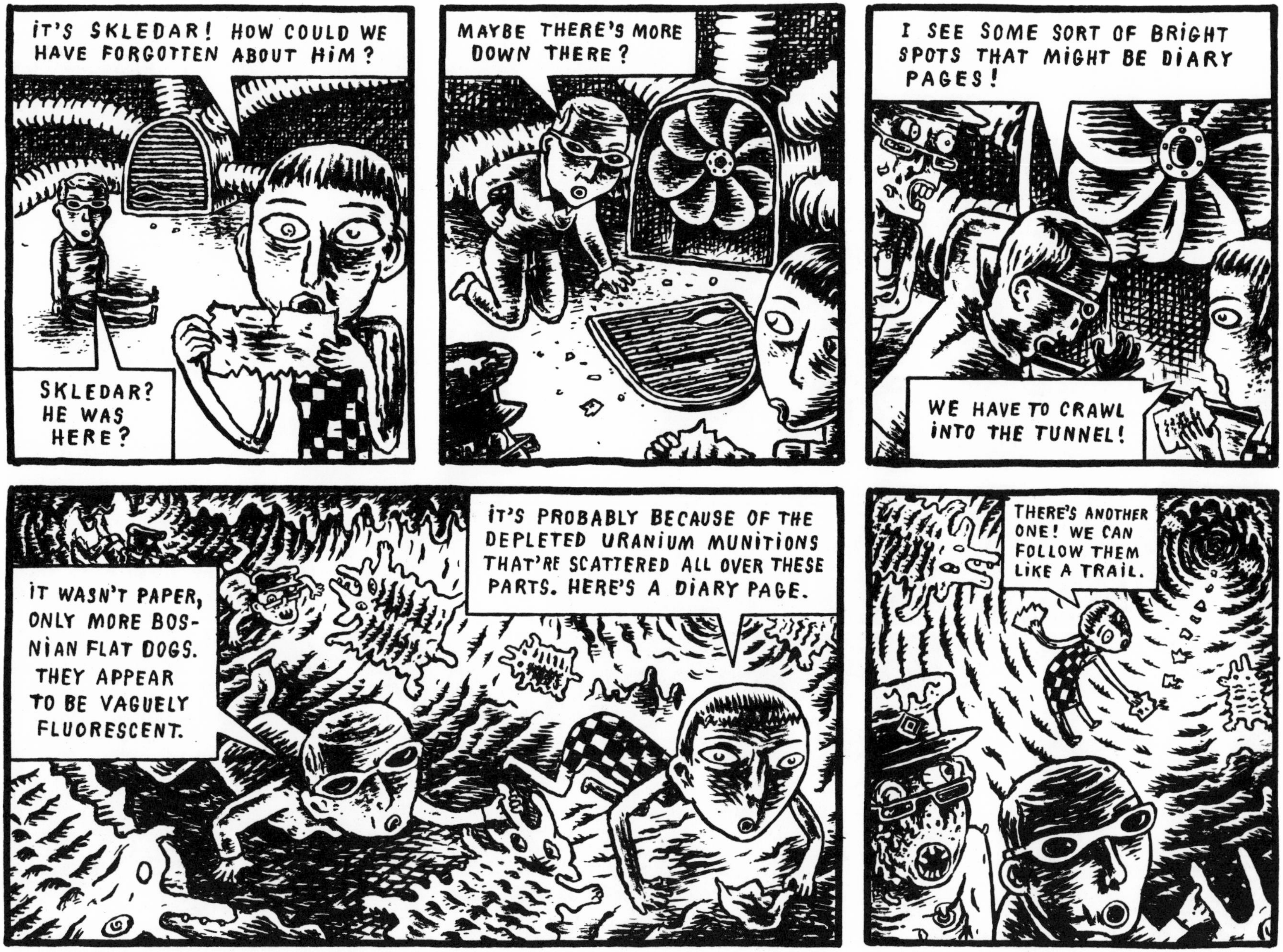
IT'S SKLEDAR! HOW COULD WE HAVE FORGOTTEN ABOUT HIM?
SKLEDAR? HE WAS HERE?
MAYBE THERE'S MORE DOWN THERE?
I SEE SOME SORT OF BRIGHT SPOTS THAT MIGHT BE DIARY PAGES!
WE HAVE TO CRAWL INTO THE TUNNEL!
IT WASN'T PAPER, ONLY MORE BOS-NIAN FLAT DOGS. THEY APPEAR TO BE VAGUELY FLUORESCENT.
IT'S PROBABLY BECAUSE OF THE DEPLETED URANIUM MUNITIONS THAT'RE SCATTERED ALL OVER THESE PARTS. HERE'S A DIARY PAGE.
THERE'S ANOTHER ONE! WE CAN FOLLOW THEM LIKE A TRAIL.

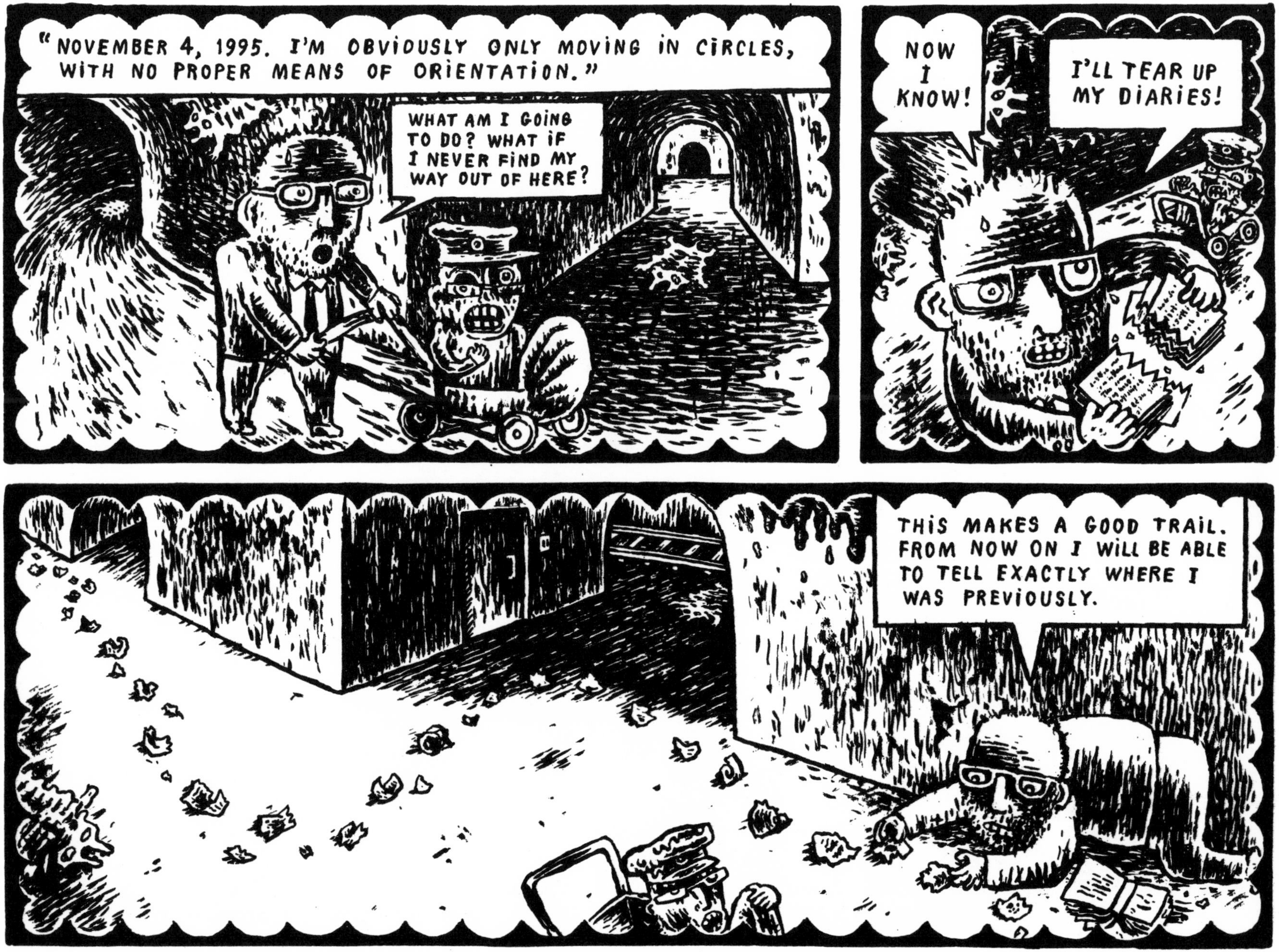
"NOVEMBER 4, 1995. I'M OBVIOUSLY ONLY MOVING IN CIRCLES, WITH NO PROPER MEANS OF ORIENTATION."
WHAT AM I GOING TO DO? WHAT IF I NEVER FIND MY WAY OUT OF HERE?
NOW I KNOW!
I'LL TEAR UP MY DIARIES!
THIS MAKES A GOOD TRAIL. FROM NOW ON I WILL BE ABLE TO TELL EXACTLY WHERE I WAS PREVIOUSLY.

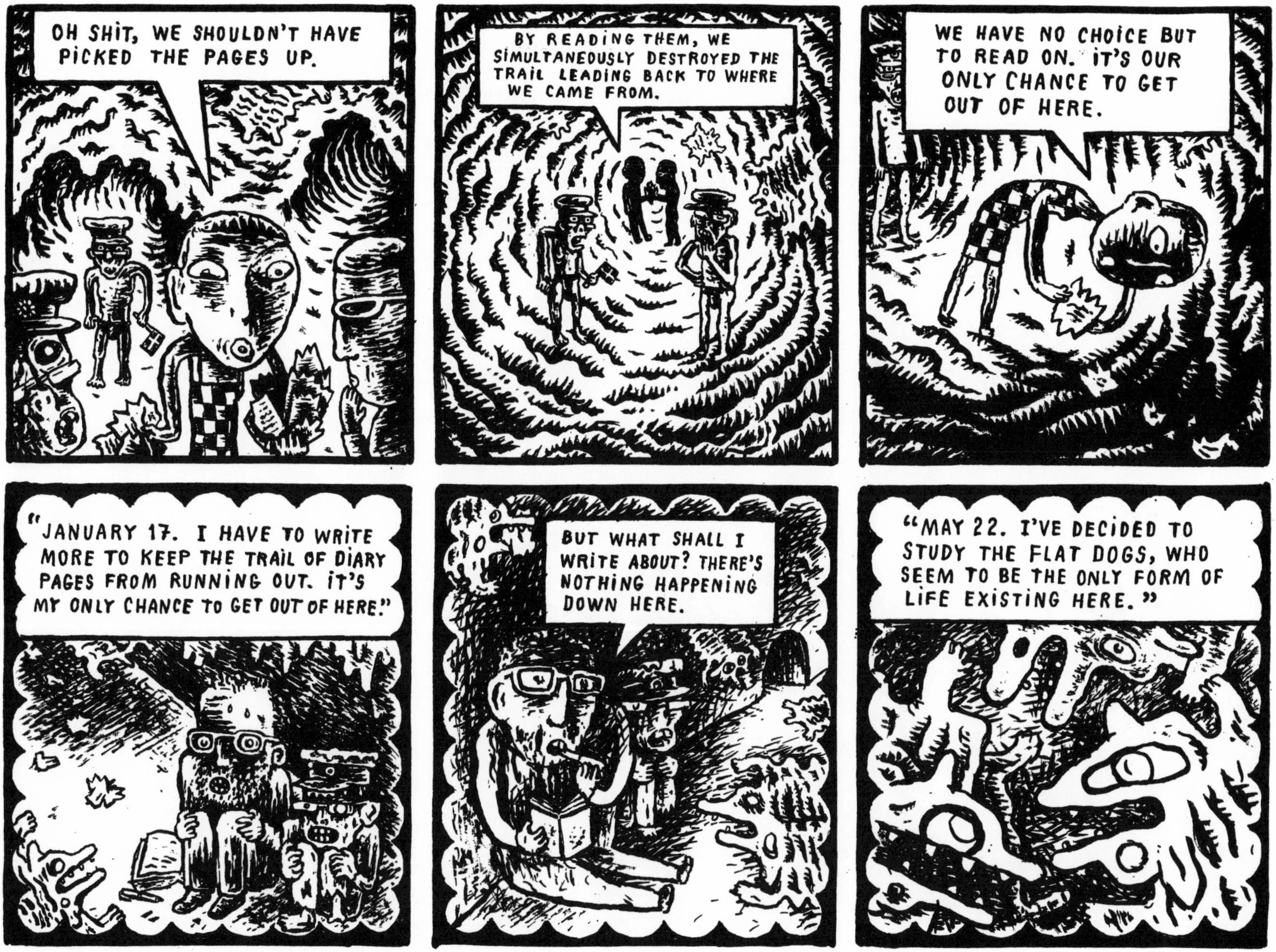
OH SHIT, WE SHOULDN'T HAVE PICKED THE PAGES UP.
BY READING THEM, WE SIMULTANEOUSLY DESTROYED THE TRAIL LEADING BACK TO WHERE WE CAME FROM.
WE HAVE NO CHOICE BUT TO READ ON. IT'S OUR ONLY CHANCE TO GET OUT OF HERE.
"JANUARY 17. I HAVE TO WRITE MORE TO KEEP THE TRAIL OF DIARY PAGES FROM RUNNING OUT. IT'S MY ONLY CHANCE TO GET OUT OF HERE."
BUT WHAT SHALL I WRITE ABOUT? THERE'S NOTHING HAPPENING DOWN HERE.
"MAY 22. I'VE DECIDED TO STUDY THE FLAT DOGS, WHO SEEM TO BE THE ONLY FORM OF LIFE EXISTING HERE."

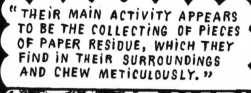

"AUGUST 11. THE DOGS LEAD A RELATIVELY SECLUDED AND MONOTONOUS LIFE."

"THEIR MAIN ACTIVITY APPEARS TO BE THE COLLECTING OF PIECES OF PAPER RESIDUE, WHICH THEY FIND IN THEIR SURROUNDINGS AND CHEW METICULOUSLY."

"THE RESULTING SUBSTANCE IS SPEWED UP AND SUBSEQUENTLY USED AS A BUILDING MATERIAL FOR EXPANDING THEIR NESTS."

THAT'S THE END OF THE TRAIL OF NOTES. WE'RE NOT GETTING ANY FURTHER.

NO, WAIT!

I CAN SEE REMAINS OF DIARY PAGES EMBEDDED IN THE WALLS.

THEY HAVE BEEN CHEWED AND MIXED WITH SALIVA UNTIL THEY'VE REACHED A CEMENT-LIKE CONSISTENCY, BUT CERTAIN FRAGMENTS ARE STILL RECOGNIZABLE.

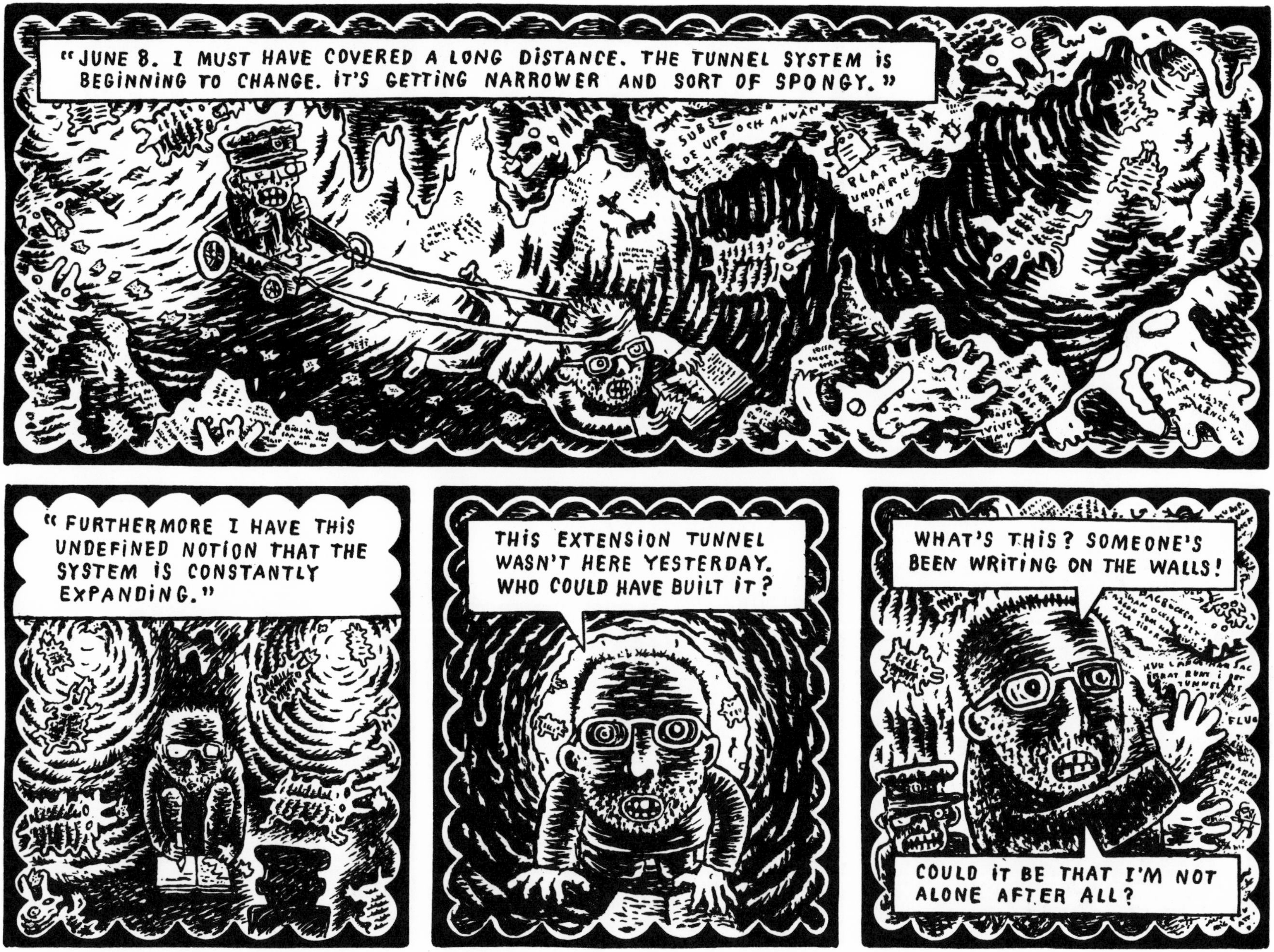
"JUNE 8. I MUST HAVE COVERED A LONG DISTANCE. THE TUNNEL SYSTEM IS BEGINNING TO CHANGE. IT'S GETTING NARROWER AND SORT OF SPONGY."
"FURTHERMORE I HAVE THIS UNDEFINED NOTION THAT THE SYSTEM IS CONSTANTLY EXPANDING."
THIS EXTENSION TUNNEL WASN'T HERE YESTERDAY. WHO COULD HAVE BUILT IT?
WHAT'S THIS? SOMEONE'S BEEN WRITING ON THE WALLS!
COULD IT BE THAT I'M NOT ALONE AFTER ALL?

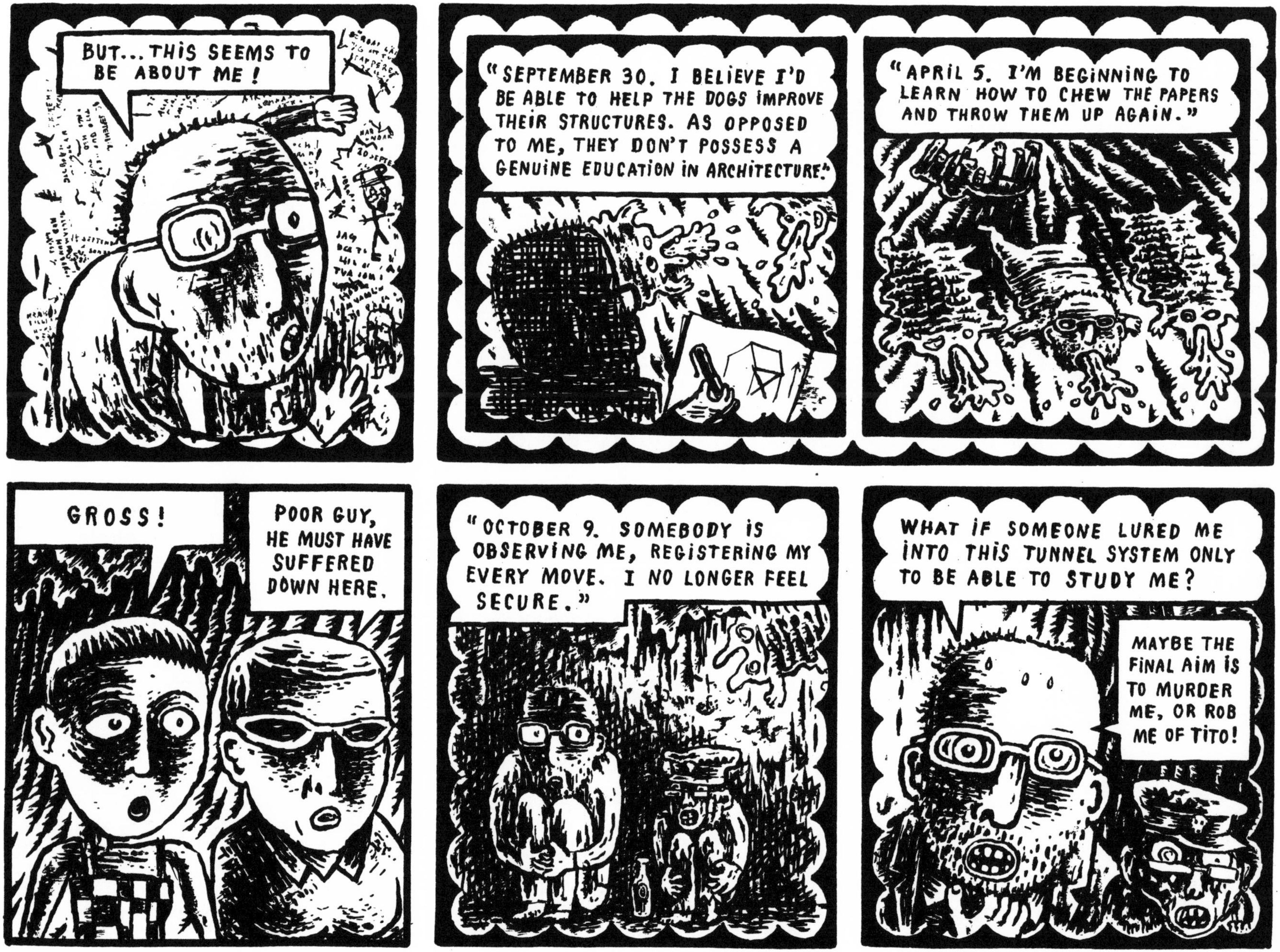

BUT... THIS SEEMS TO BE ABOUT ME!
"SEPTEMBER 30. I BELIEVE I'D BE ABLE TO HELP THE DOGS IMPROVE THEIR STRUCTURES. AS OPPOSED TO ME, THEY DON'T POSSESS A GENUINE EDUCATION IN ARCHITECTURE."
"APRIL 5. I'M BEGINNING TO LEARN HOW TO CHEW THE PAPERS AND THROW THEM UP AGAIN."
GROSS!
POOR GUY, HE MUST HAVE SUFFERED DOWN HERE.
"OCTOBER 9. SOMEBODY IS OBSERVING ME, REGISTERING MY EVERY MOVE. I NO LONGER FEEL SECURE."
WHAT IF SOMEONE LURED ME INTO THIS TUNNEL SYSTEM ONLY TO BE ABLE TO STUDY ME?
MAYBE THE FINAL AIM IS TO MURDER ME, OR ROB ME OF TITO!

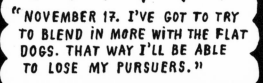

"NOVEMBER 17. I'VE GOT TO TRY TO BLEND IN MORE WITH THE FLAT DOGS. THAT WAY I'LL BE ABLE TO LOSE MY PURSUERS."

THE FRAGMENTS ARE GETTING SMALLER AND SMALLER!

WE'VE GOT TO TRY TO MAKE THEM OUT, OR WE'RE FINISHED!

"JULY 29. THE DOGS HAVE ACCEPTED ME AND TITO AS MEMBERS OF THE PACK. TOGETHER WE MOVE TOWARDS WHAT APPEARS TO BE A COMMON GOAL."

"SEPTEMBER 13. I SEEM TO DETECT A DARK SPOT AT THE FAR END OF OUR DIRECTION. COULD IT BE..."

... THE END OF THE TUNNEL!

THE LAST LEGIBLE DIARY ENTRY!

TELL ME! WHAT DOES IT SAY?

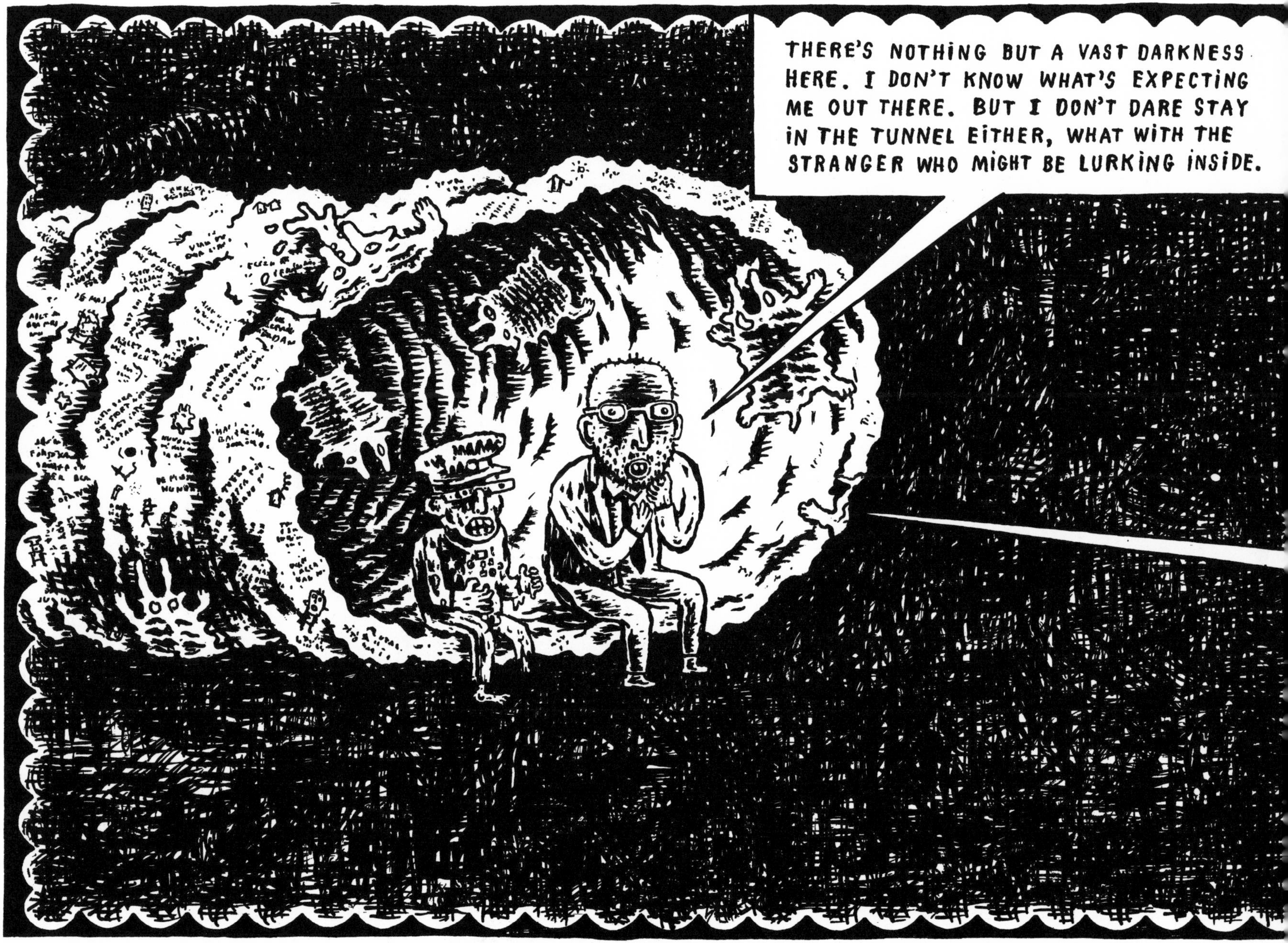
THERE'S NOTHING BUT A VAST DARKNESS HERE. I DON'T KNOW WHAT'S EXPECTING ME OUT THERE. BUT I DON'T DARE STAY IN THE TUNNEL EITHER, WHAT WITH THE STRANGER WHO MIGHT BE LURKING INSIDE.

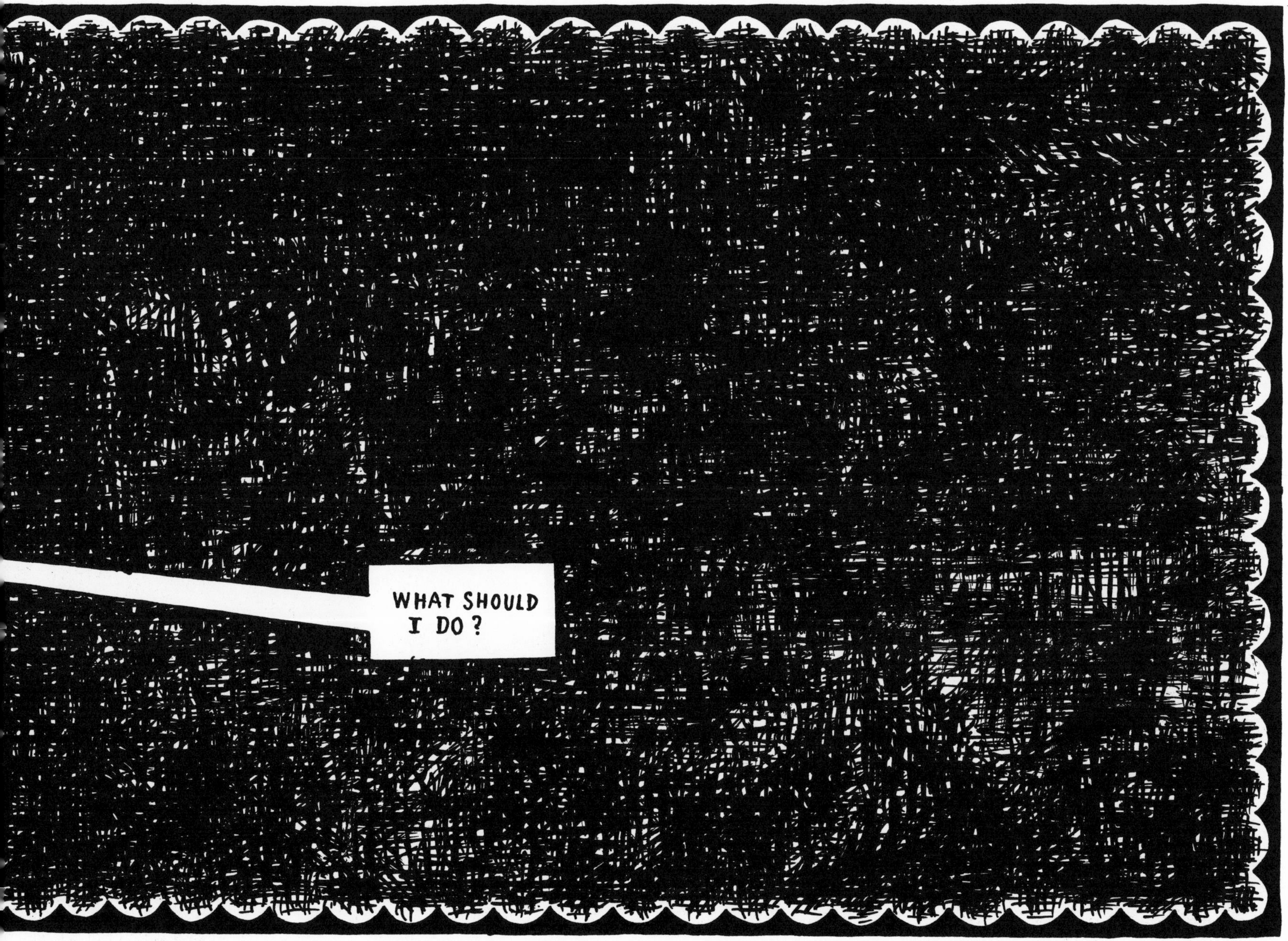
WHAT SHOULD I DO?

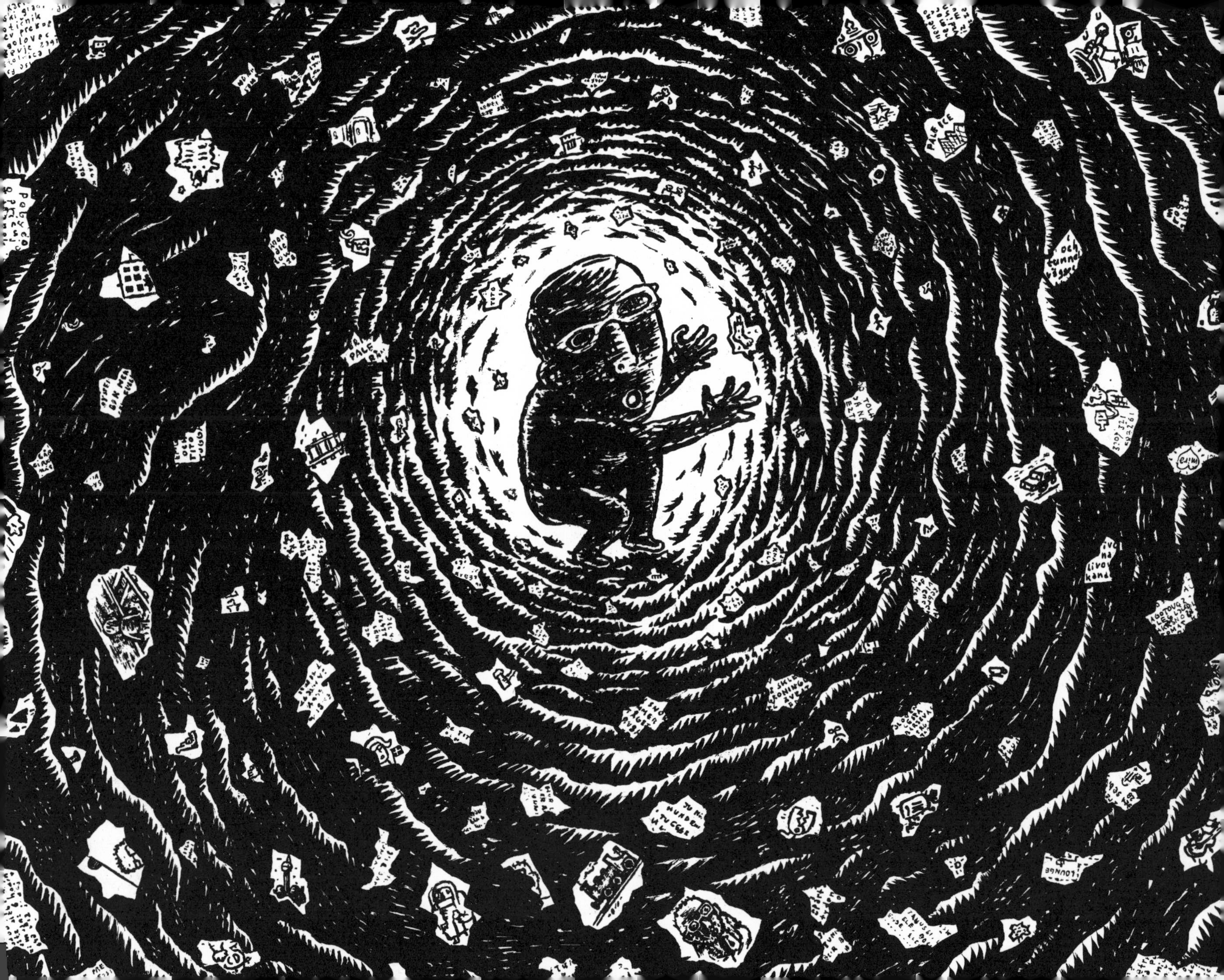

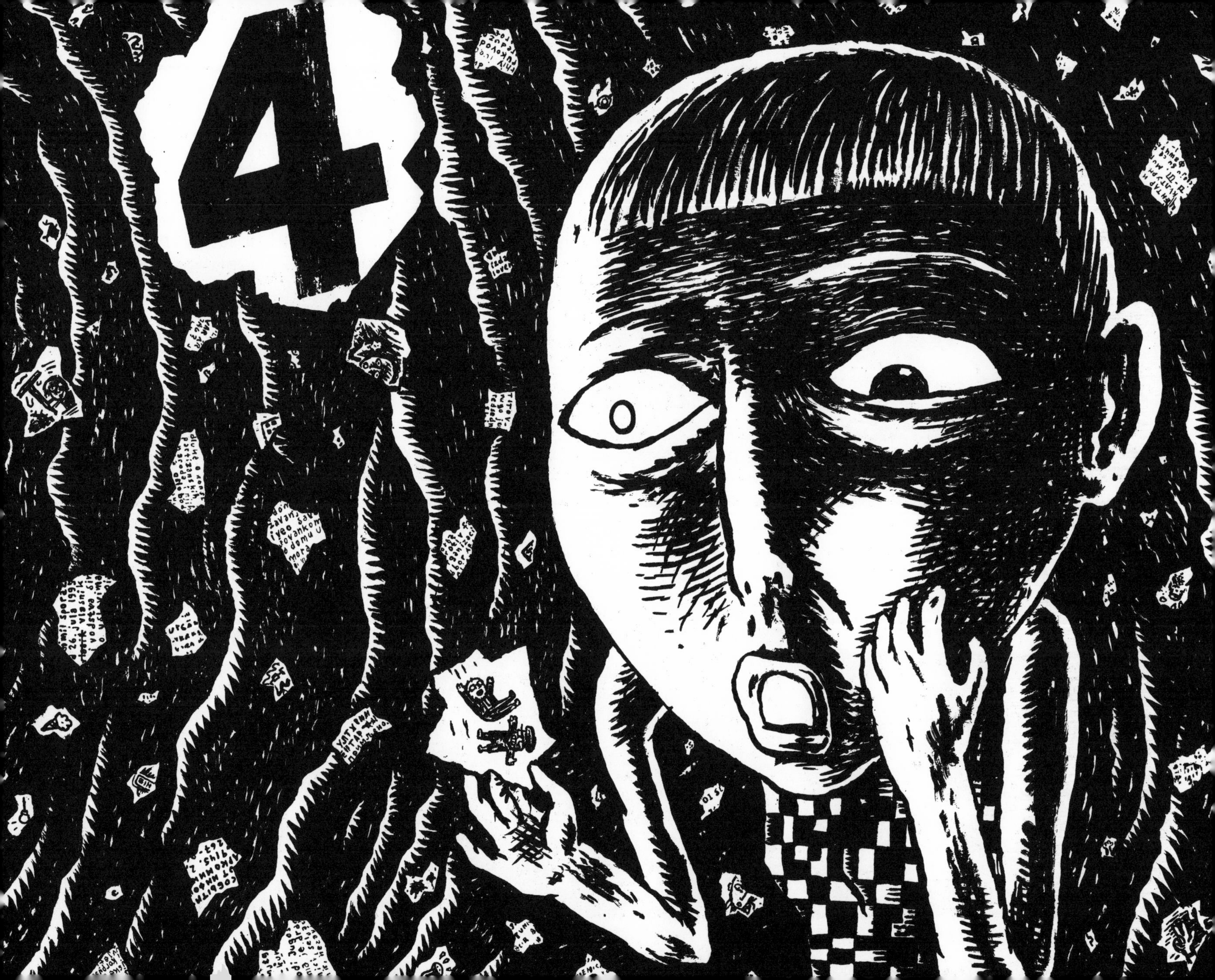
4

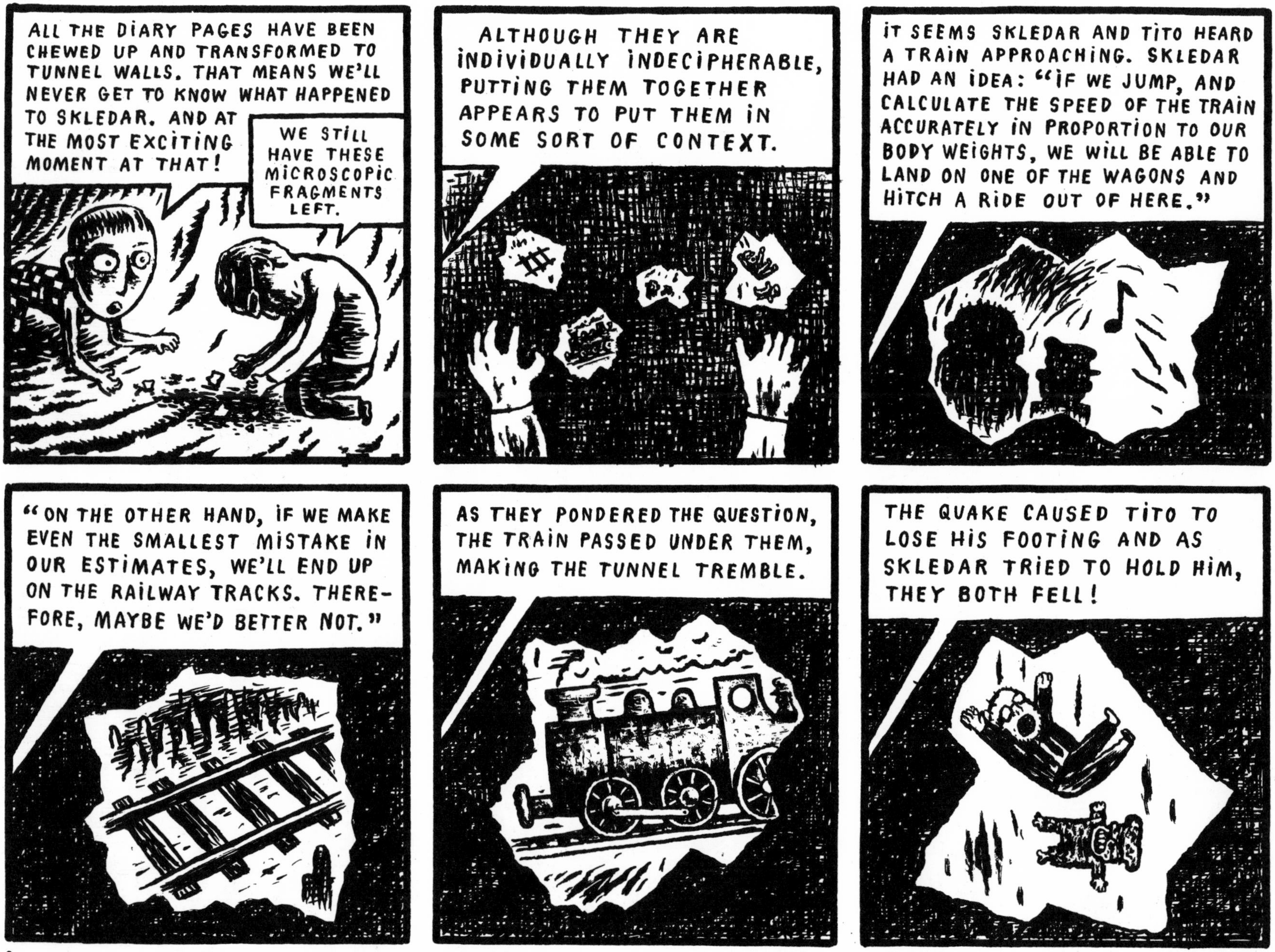
ALL THE DIARY PAGES HAVE BEEN CHEWED UP AND TRANSFORMED TO TUNNEL WALLS. THAT MEANS WE'LL NEVER GET TO KNOW WHAT HAPPENED TO SKLEDAR. AND AT THE MOST EXCITING MOMENT AT THAT!
WE STILL HAVE THESE MICROSCOPIC FRAGMENTS LEFT.
ALTHOUGH THEY ARE INDIVIDUALLY INDECIPHERABLE, PUTTING THEM TOGETHER APPEARS TO PUT THEM IN SOME SORT OF CONTEXT.
IT SEEMS SKLEDAR AND TITO HEARD A TRAIN APPROACHING. SKLEDAR HAD AN IDEA: "IF WE JUMP, AND CALCULATE THE SPEED OF THE TRAIN ACCURATELY IN PROPORTION TO OUR BODY WEIGHTS, WE WILL BE ABLE TO LAND ON ONE OF THE WAGONS AND HITCH A RIDE OUT OF HERE."
"ON THE OTHER HAND, IF WE MAKE EVEN THE SMALLEST MISTAKE IN OUR ESTIMATES, WE'LL END UP ON THE RAILWAY TRACKS. THEREFORE, MAYBE WE'D BETTER NOT."
AS THEY PONDERED THE QUESTION, THE TRAIN PASSED UNDER THEM, MAKING THE TUNNEL TREMBLE.
THE QUAKE CAUSED TITO TO LOSE HIS FOOTING AND AS SKLEDAR TRIED TO HOLD HIM, THEY BOTH FELL!

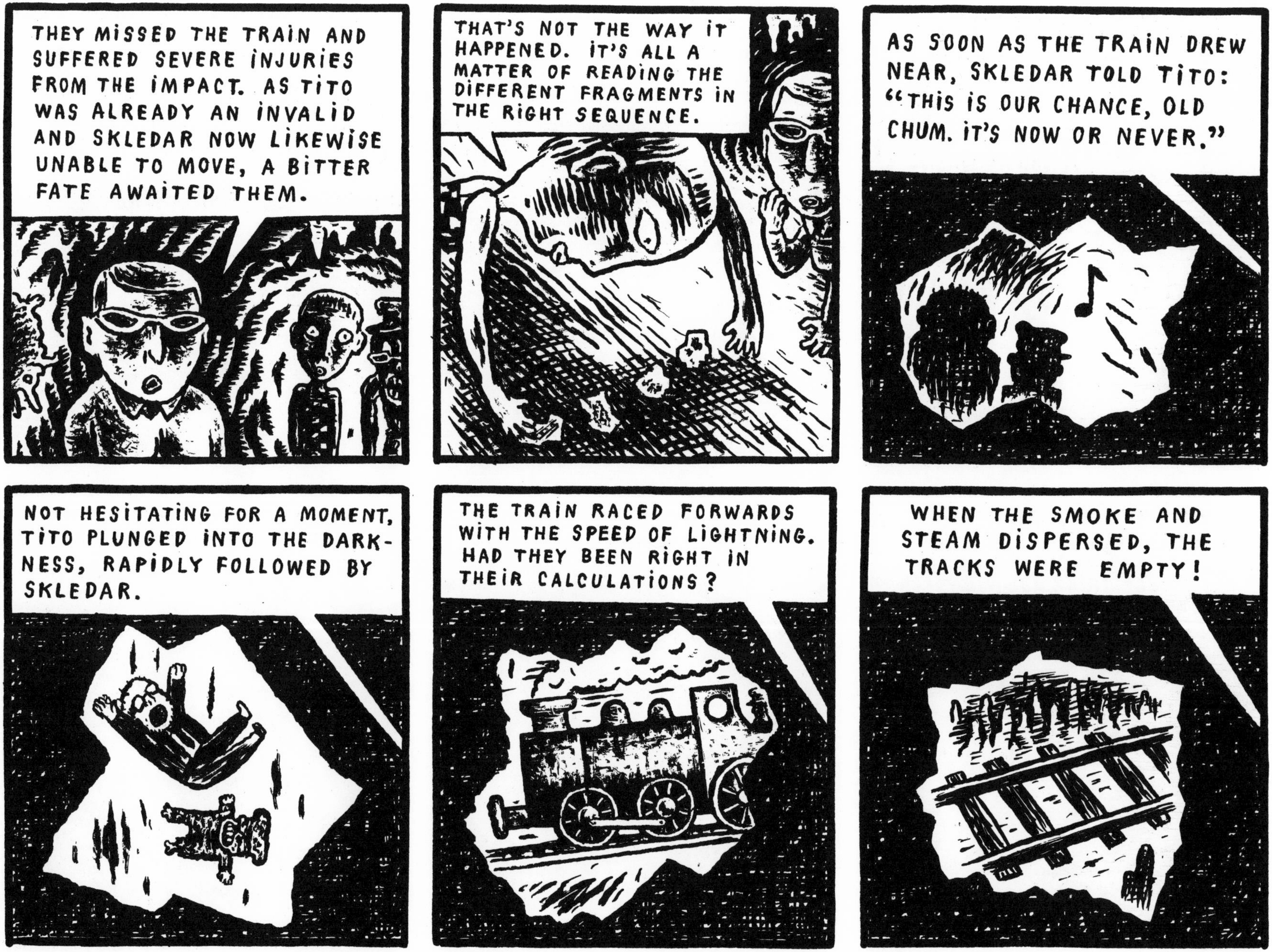
THEY MISSED THE TRAIN AND SUFFERED SEVERE INJURIES FROM THE IMPACT. AS TITO WAS ALREADY AN INVALID AND SKLEDAR NOW LIKEWISE UNABLE TO MOVE, A BITTER FATE AWAITED THEM.
THAT'S NOT THE WAY IT HAPPENED. IT'S ALL A MATTER OF READING THE DIFFERENT FRAGMENTS IN THE RIGHT SEQUENCE.
AS SOON AS THE TRAIN DREW NEAR, SKLEDAR TOLD TITO: "THIS IS OUR CHANCE, OLD CHUM. IT'S NOW OR NEVER."
NOT HESITATING FOR A MOMENT, TITO PLUNGED INTO THE DARKNESS, RAPIDLY FOLLOWED BY SKLEDAR.
THE TRAIN RACED FORWARDS WITH THE SPEED OF LIGHTNING. HAD THEY BEEN RIGHT IN THEIR CALCULATIONS?
WHEN THE SMOKE AND STEAM DISPERSED, THE TRACKS WERE EMPTY!

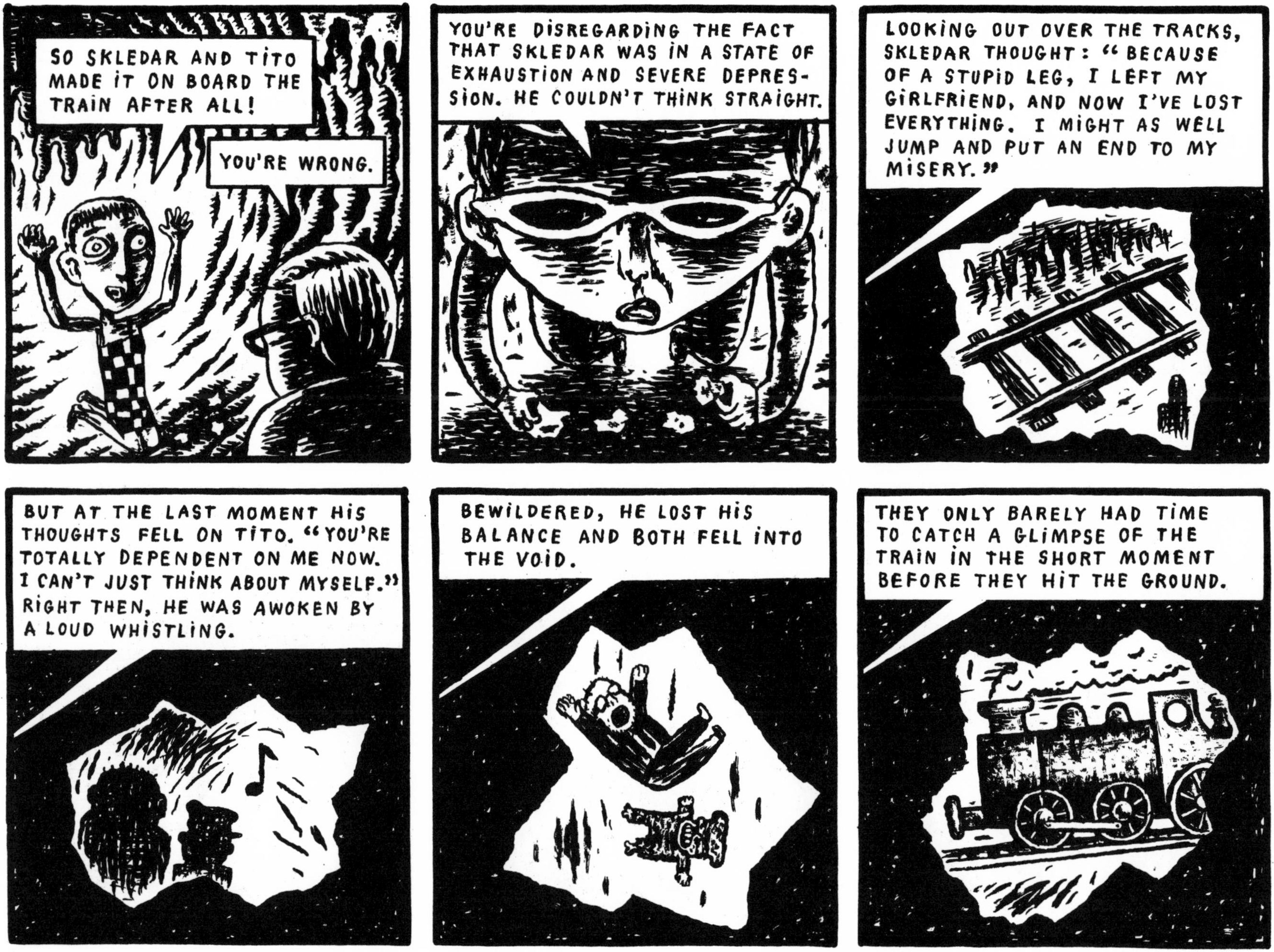
SO SKLEDAR AND TITO MADE IT ON BOARD THE TRAIN AFTER ALL!
YOU'RE WRONG.
YOU'RE DISREGARDING THE FACT THAT SKLEDAR WAS IN A STATE OF EXHAUSTION AND SEVERE DEPRESSION. HE COULDN'T THINK STRAIGHT.
LOOKING OUT OVER THE TRACKS, SKLEDAR THOUGHT: "BECAUSE OF A STUPID LEG, I LEFT MY GIRLFRIEND, AND NOW I'VE LOST EVERYTHING. I MIGHT AS WELL JUMP AND PUT AN END TO MY MISERY."
BUT AT THE LAST MOMENT HIS THOUGHTS FELL ON TITO. "YOU'RE TOTALLY DEPENDENT ON ME NOW. I CAN'T JUST THINK ABOUT MYSELF." RIGHT THEN, HE WAS AWOKEN BY A LOUD WHISTLING.
BEWILDERED, HE LOST HIS BALANCE AND BOTH FELL INTO THE VOID.
THEY ONLY BARELY HAD TIME TO CATCH A GLIMPSE OF THE TRAIN IN THE SHORT MOMENT BEFORE THEY HIT THE GROUND.

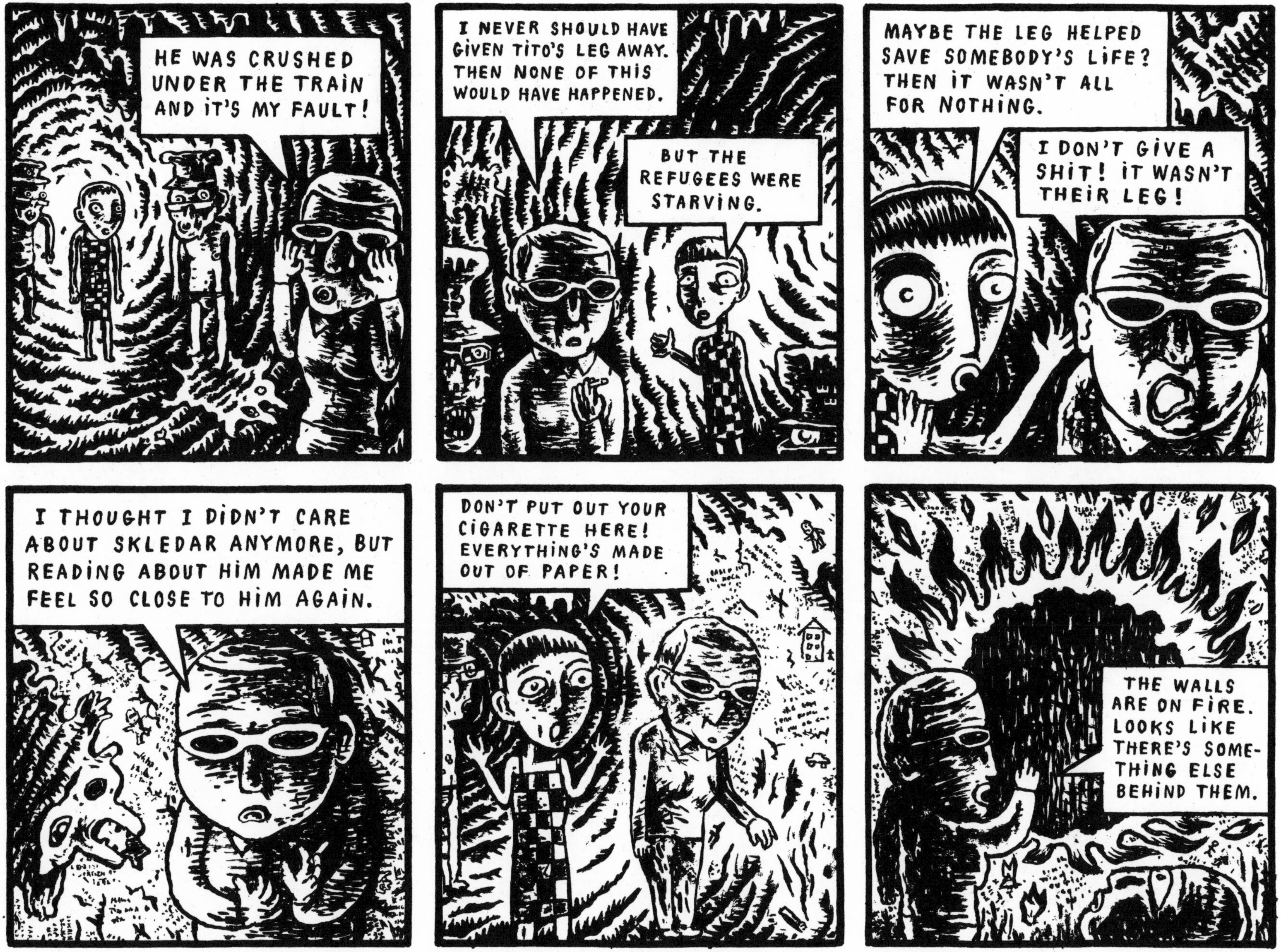

HE WAS CRUSHED UNDER THE TRAIN AND IT'S MY FAULT!
I NEVER SHOULD HAVE GIVEN TITO'S LEG AWAY. THEN NONE OF THIS WOULD HAVE HAPPENED.
BUT THE REFUGEES WERE STARVING.
MAYBE THE LEG HELPED SAVE SOMEBODY'S LIFE? THEN IT WASN'T ALL FOR NOTHING.
I DON'T GIVE A SHIT! IT WASN'T THEIR LEG!
I THOUGHT I DIDN'T CARE ABOUT SKLEDAR ANYMORE, BUT READING ABOUT HIM MADE ME FEEL SO CLOSE TO HIM AGAIN.
DON'T PUT OUT YOUR CIGARETTE HERE! EVERYTHING'S MADE OUT OF PAPER!
THE WALLS ARE ON FIRE. LOOKS LIKE THERE'S SOMETHING ELSE BEHIND THEM.

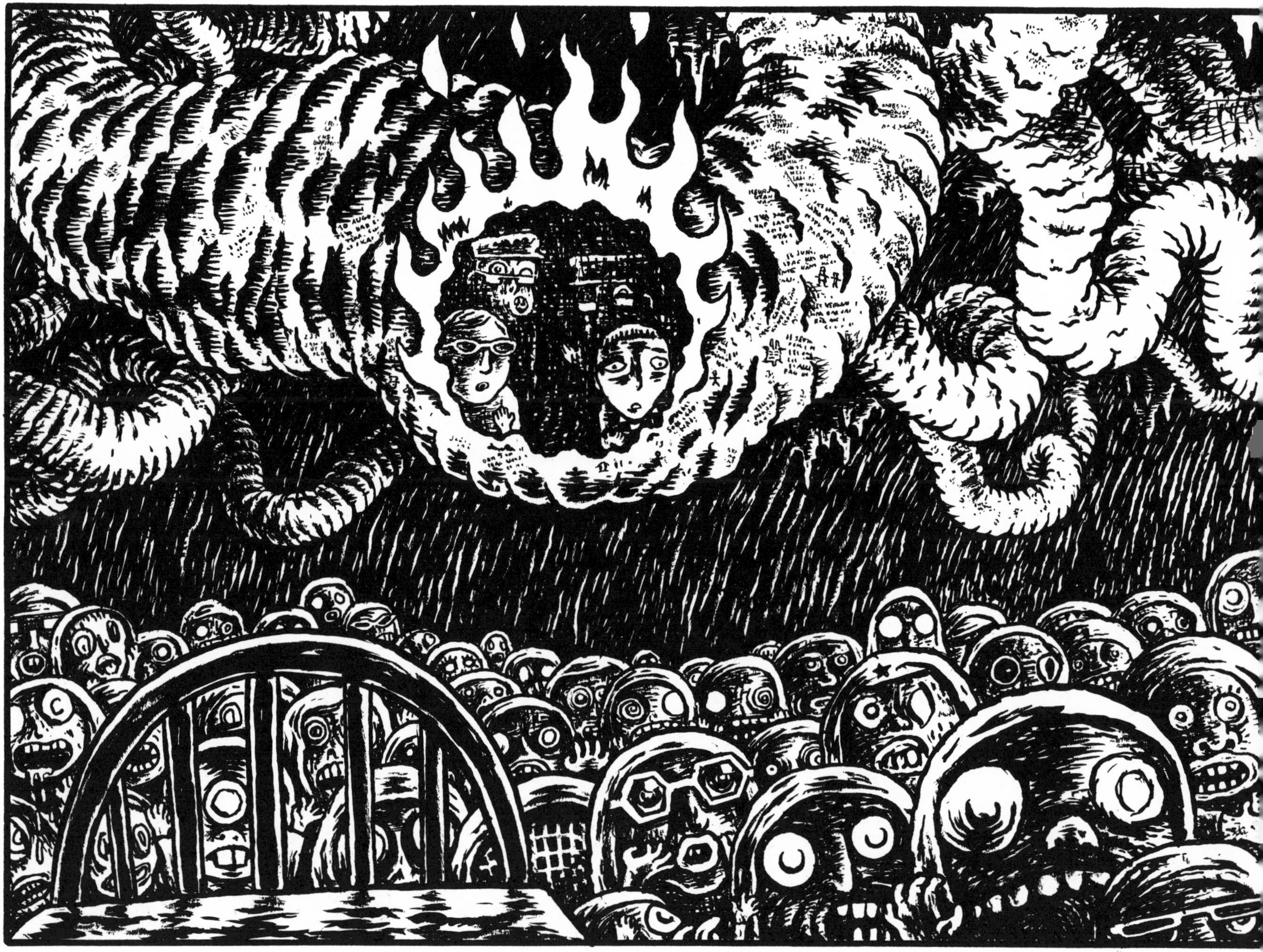

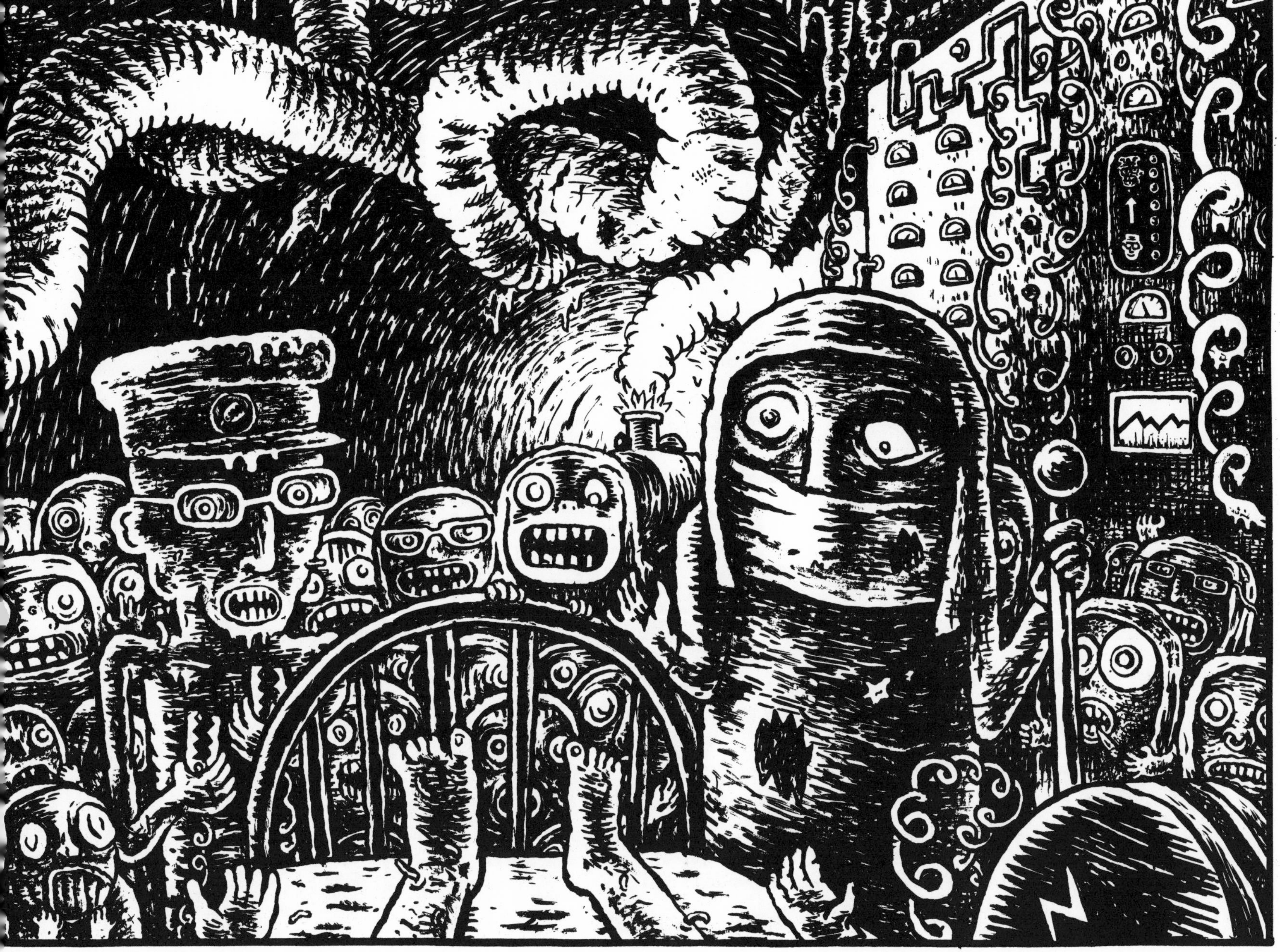

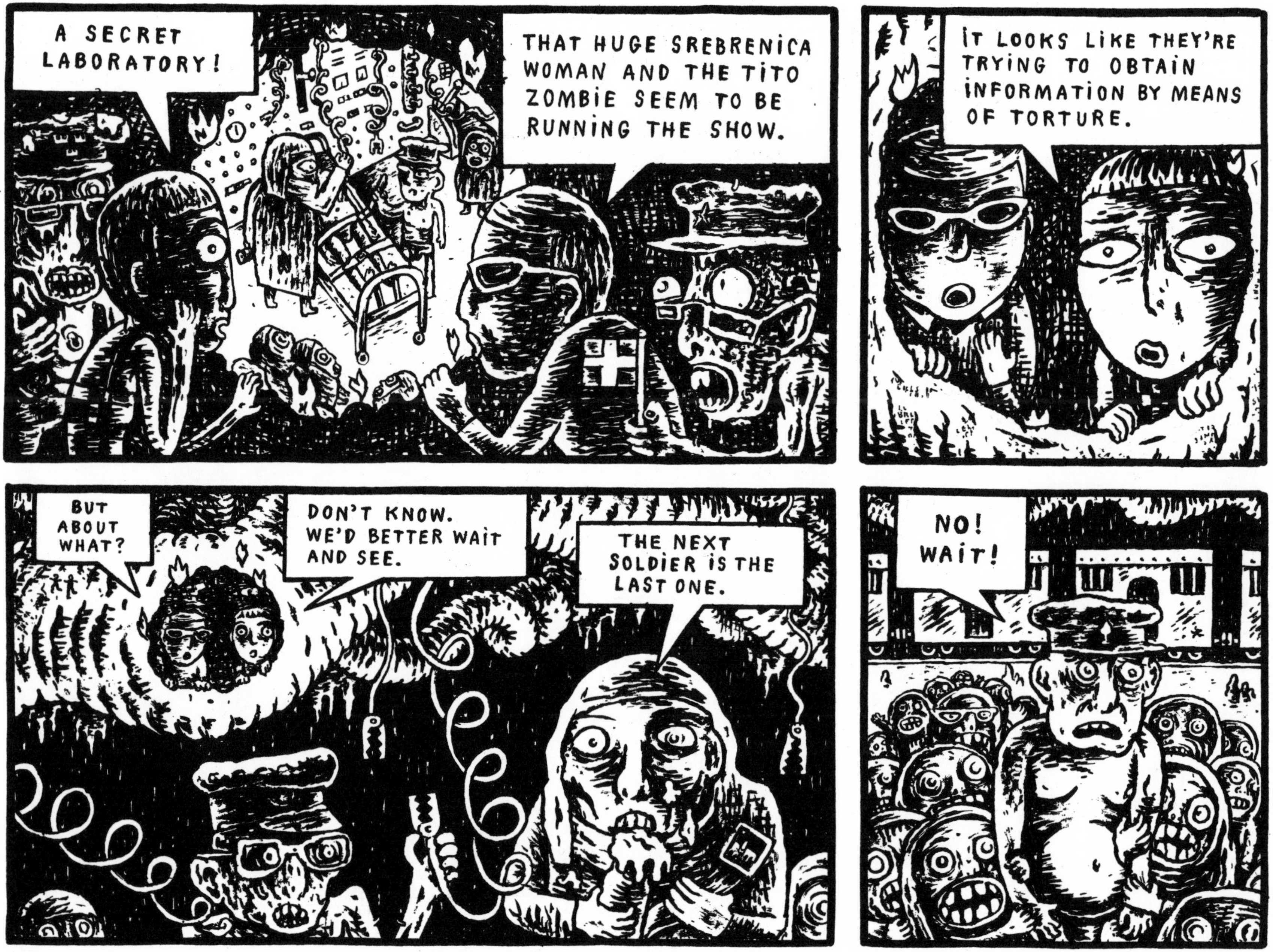
A SECRET LABORATORY!
THAT HUGE SREBRENICA WOMAN AND THE TITO ZOMBIE SEEM TO BE RUNNING THE SHOW.
IT LOOKS LIKE THEY'RE TRYING TO OBTAIN INFORMATION BY MEANS OF TORTURE.
BUT ABOUT WHAT?
DON'T KNOW. WE'D BETTER WAIT AND SEE.
THE NEXT SOLDIER IS THE LAST ONE.
NO! WAIT!

I'M NOT A GENUINE SFOR SOLDIER. I'M A FACTORY OWNER. I JUST DISGUISED MYSELF SO AS NOT TO BE EXPOSED.

THAT'S WHAT THEY ALL SAY.

BUT IT'S TRUE! I'M JUST AN ORDINARY BUSINESSMAN FROM PALE. I HAD AN ICE CREAM FACTORY!

AN ICE CREAM FACTORY?

YES. IT WAS THE BEST AND THE BIGGEST IN ALL OF BOSNIA. IT WAS AN UNDERGROUND FACTORY. IT WAS LOCATED IN PALE, WHICH IS A WINTER SPORTS RESORT RIGHT OUTSIDE SARAJEVO.

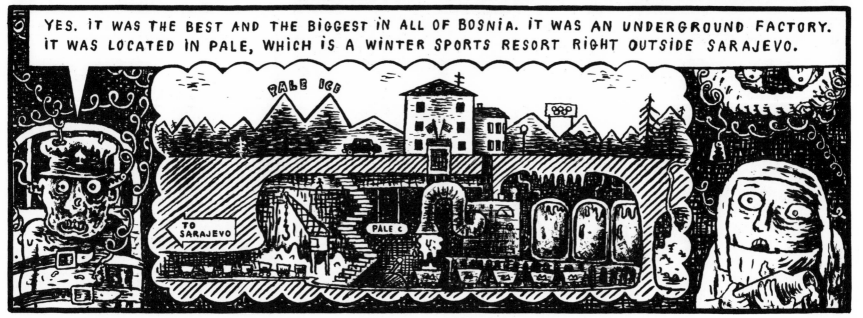

PALE ICE

TO SARAJEVO

PALE C

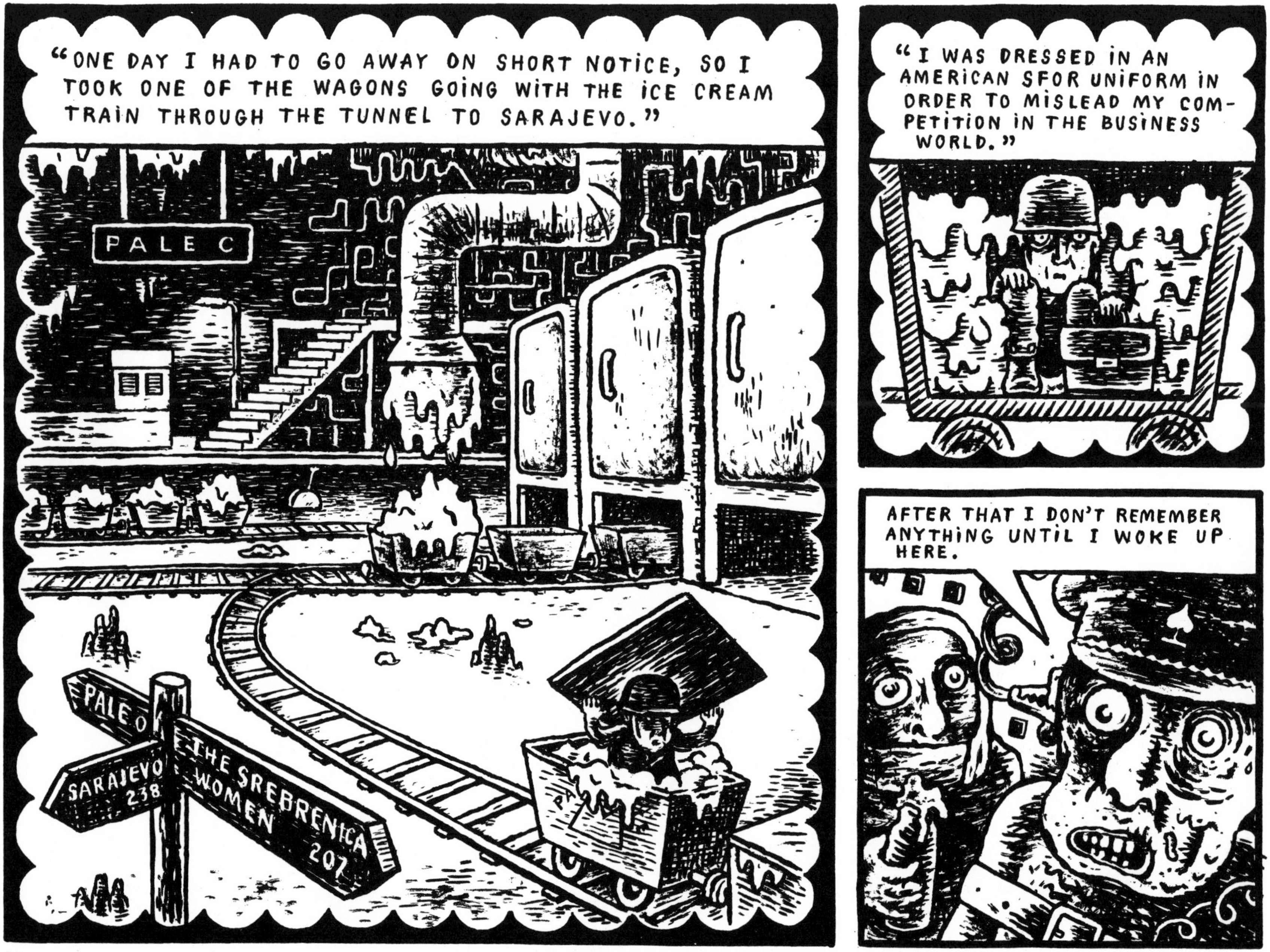
"ONE DAY I HAD TO GO AWAY ON SHORT NOTICE, SO I TOOK ONE OF THE WAGONS GOING WITH THE ICE CREAM TRAIN THROUGH THE TUNNEL TO SARAJEVO."
PALE C
PALE
SARAJEVO 238
THE SREBRENICA WOMEN 207
"I WAS DRESSED IN AN AMERICAN SFOR UNIFORM IN ORDER TO MISLEAD MY COMPETITION IN THE BUSINESS WORLD."
AFTER THAT I DON'T REMEMBER ANYTHING UNTIL I WOKE UP HERE.

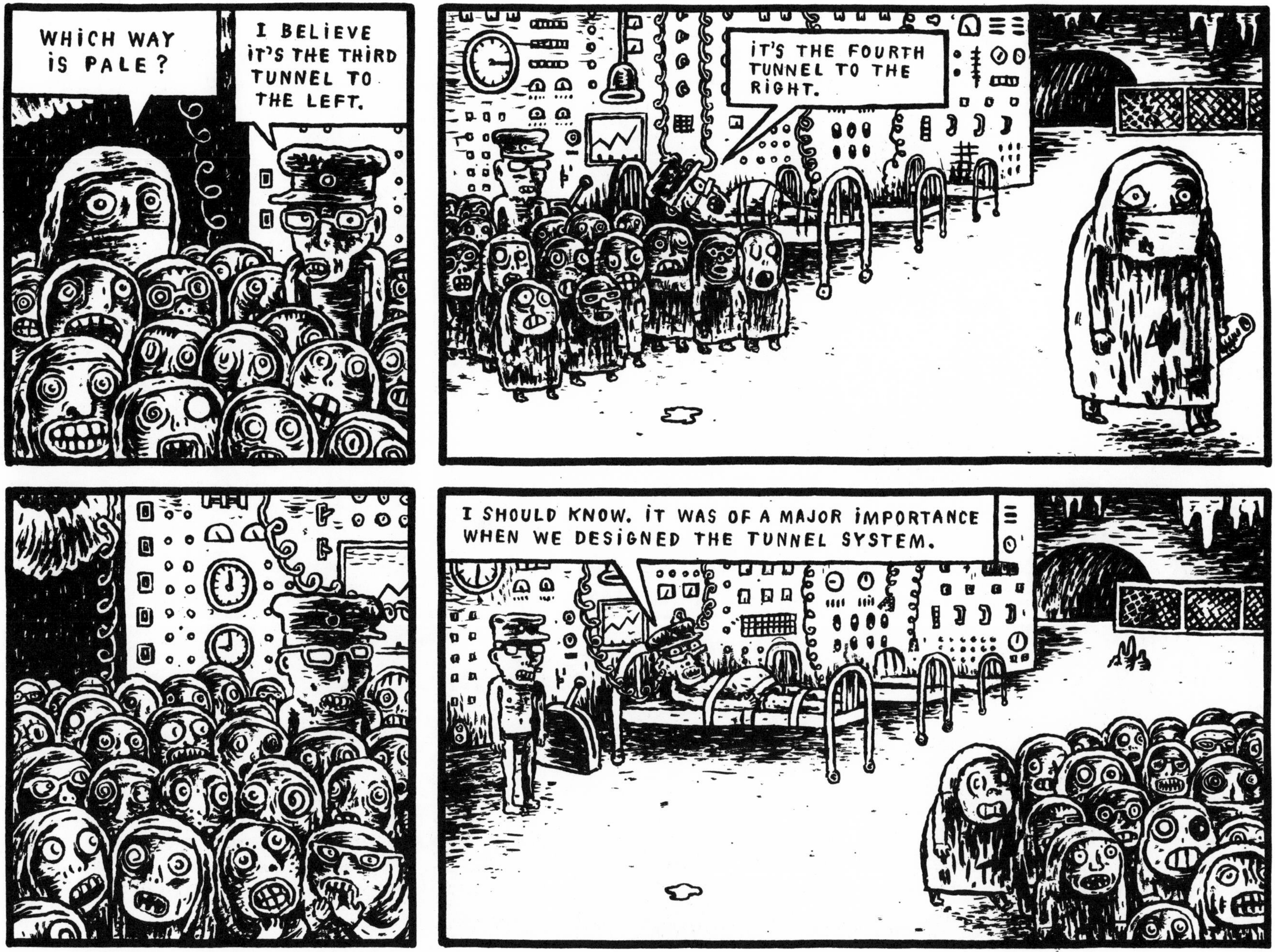
WHICH WAY IS PALE?
I BELIEVE IT'S THE THIRD TUNNEL TO THE LEFT.
IT'S THE FOURTH TUNNEL TO THE RIGHT.
I SHOULD KNOW. IT WAS OF A MAJOR IMPORTANCE WHEN WE DESIGNED THE TUNNEL SYSTEM.

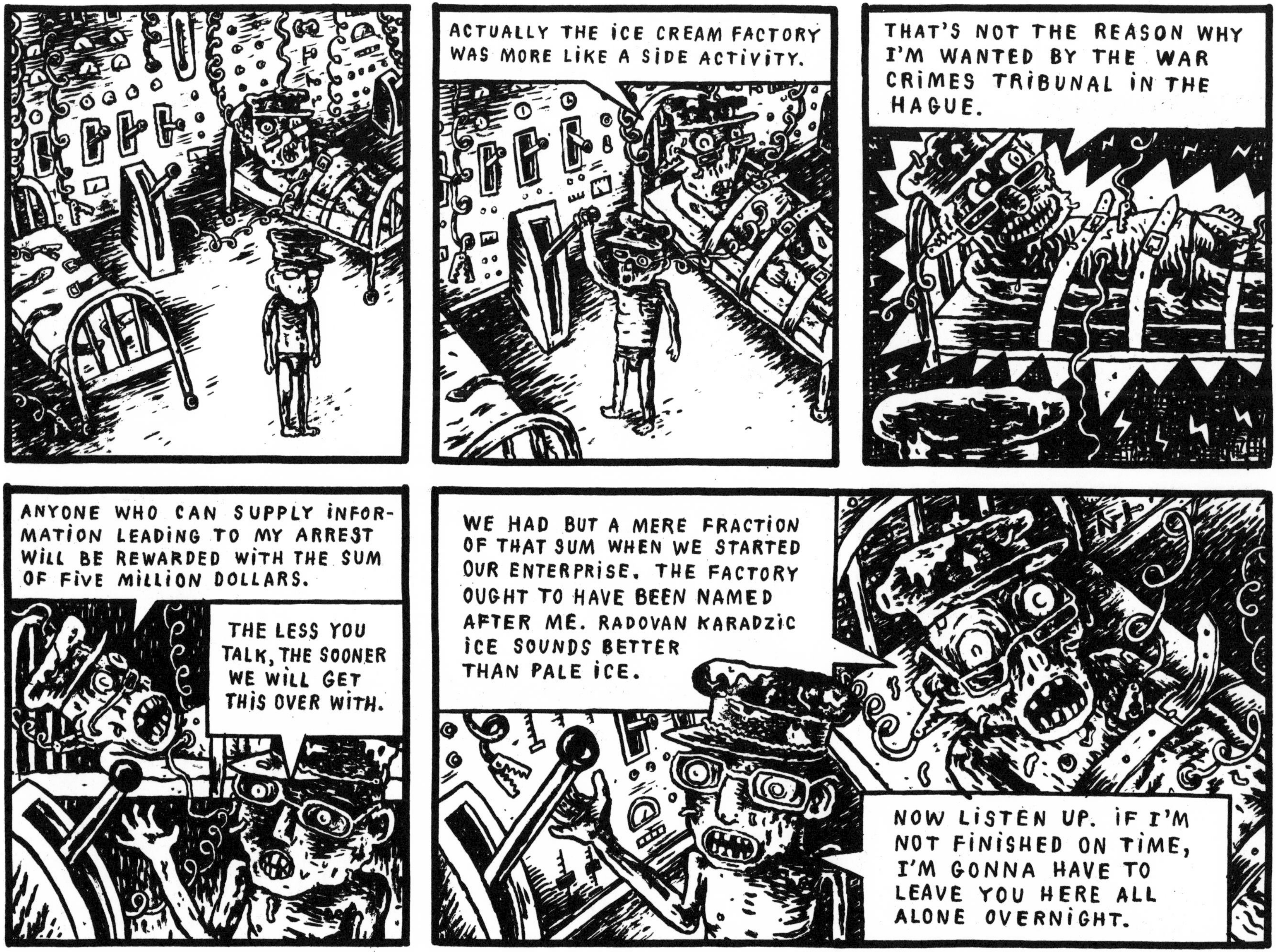
ACTUALLY THE ICE CREAM FACTORY WAS MORE LIKE A SIDE ACTIVITY.
THAT'S NOT THE REASON WHY I'M WANTED BY THE WAR CRIMES TRIBUNAL IN THE HAGUE.
ANYONE WHO CAN SUPPLY INFORMATION LEADING TO MY ARREST WILL BE REWARDED WITH THE SUM OF FIVE MILLION DOLLARS.
THE LESS YOU TALK, THE SOONER WE WILL GET THIS OVER WITH.
WE HAD BUT A MERE FRACTION OF THAT SUM WHEN WE STARTED OUR ENTERPRISE. THE FACTORY OUGHT TO HAVE BEEN NAMED AFTER ME. RADOVAN KARADZIC ICE SOUNDS BETTER THAN PALE ICE.
NOW LISTEN UP. IF I'M NOT FINISHED ON TIME, I'M GONNA HAVE TO LEAVE YOU HERE ALL ALONE OVERNIGHT.

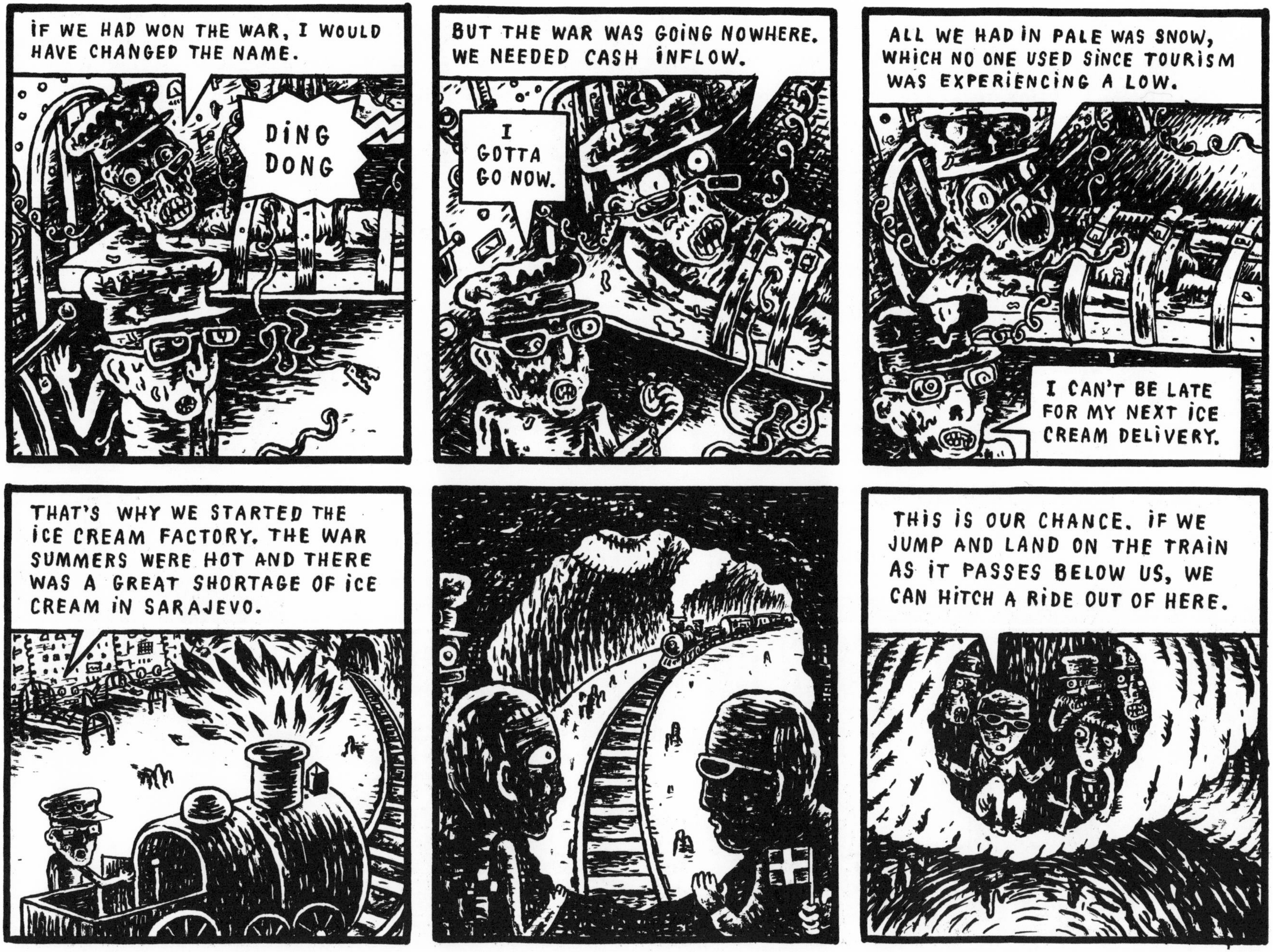
IF WE HAD WON THE WAR, I WOULD HAVE CHANGED THE NAME.
DING DONG
BUT THE WAR WAS GOING NOWHERE. WE NEEDED CASH INFLOW.
I GOTTA GO NOW.
ALL WE HAD IN PALE WAS SNOW, WHICH NO ONE USED SINCE TOURISM WAS EXPERIENCING A LOW.
I CAN'T BE LATE FOR MY NEXT ICE CREAM DELIVERY.
THAT'S WHY WE STARTED THE ICE CREAM FACTORY. THE WAR SUMMERS WERE HOT AND THERE WAS A GREAT SHORTAGE OF ICE CREAM IN SARAJEVO.
THIS IS OUR CHANCE. IF WE JUMP AND LAND ON THE TRAIN AS IT PASSES BELOW US, WE CAN HITCH A RIDE OUT OF HERE.

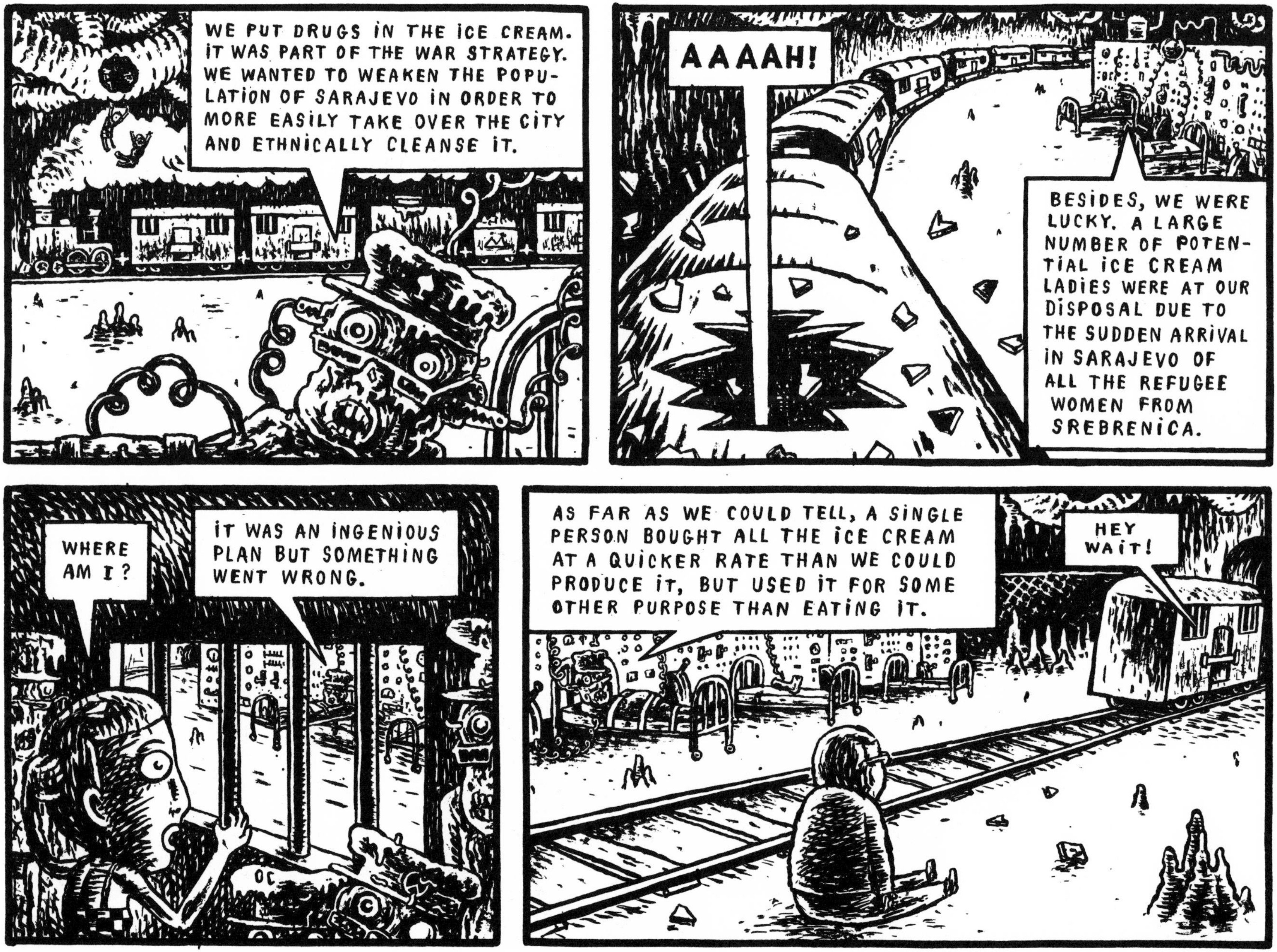
WE PUT DRUGS IN THE ICE CREAM. IT WAS PART OF THE WAR STRATEGY. WE WANTED TO WEAKEN THE POPULATION OF SARAJEVO IN ORDER TO MORE EASILY TAKE OVER THE CITY AND ETHNICALLY CLEANSE IT.
AAAAH!
BESIDES, WE WERE LUCKY. A LARGE NUMBER OF POTENTIAL ICE CREAM LADIES WERE AT OUR DISPOSAL DUE TO THE SUDDEN ARRIVAL IN SARAJEVO OF ALL THE REFUGEE WOMEN FROM SREBRENICA.
WHERE AM I?
IT WAS AN INGENIOUS PLAN BUT SOMETHING WENT WRONG.
AS FAR AS WE COULD TELL, A SINGLE PERSON BOUGHT ALL THE ICE CREAM AT A QUICKER RATE THAN WE COULD PRODUCE IT, BUT USED IT FOR SOME OTHER PURPOSE THAN EATING IT.
HEY WAIT!

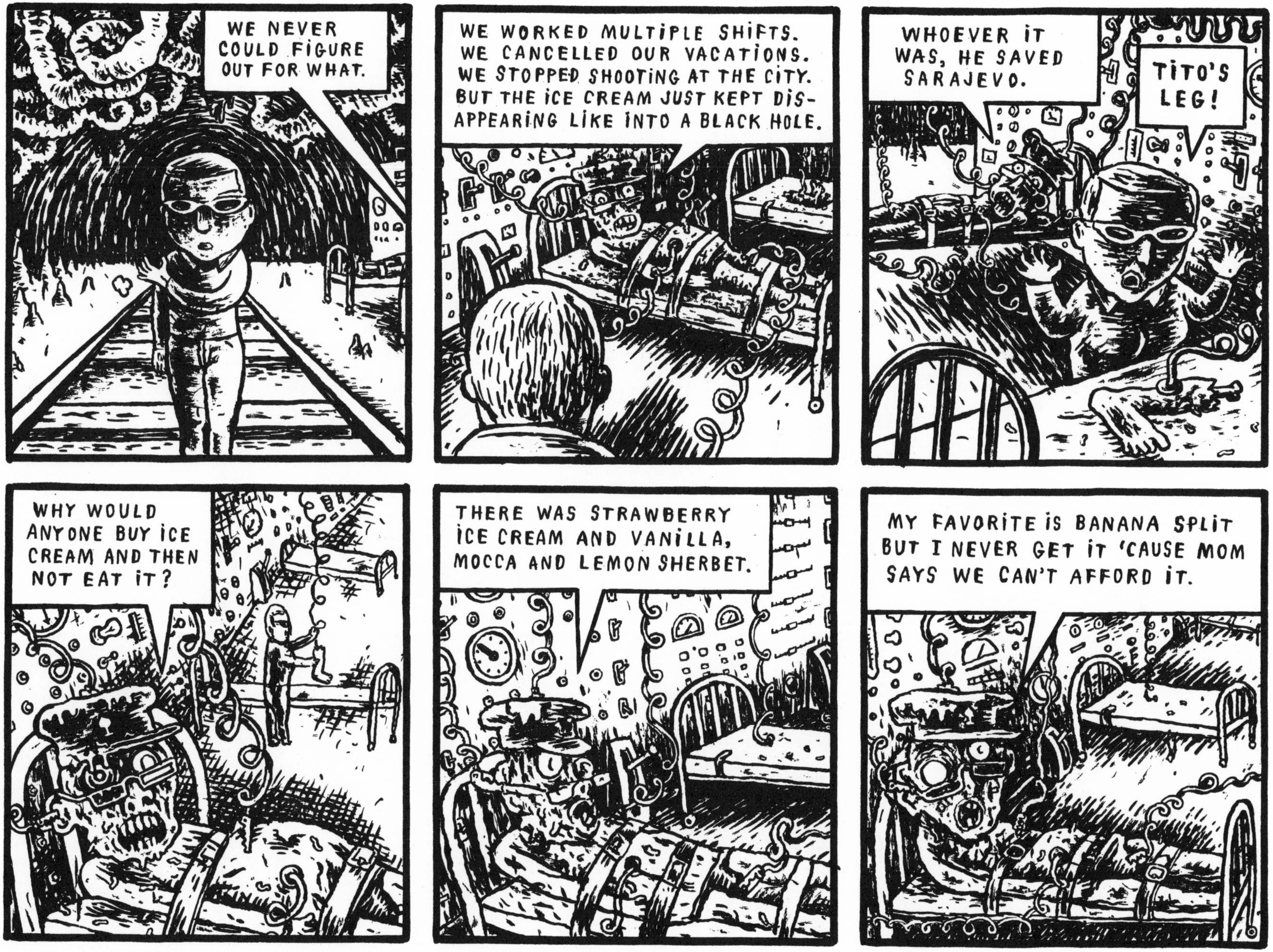
WE NEVER COULD FIGURE OUT FOR WHAT.
WE WORKED MULTIPLE SHIFTS. WE CANCELLED OUR VACATIONS. WE STOPPED SHOOTING AT THE CITY. BUT THE ICE CREAM JUST KEPT DIS-APPEARING LIKE INTO A BLACK HOLE.
WHOEVER IT WAS, HE SAVED SARAJEVO.
TITO'S LEG!
WHY WOULD ANYONE BUY ICE CREAM AND THEN NOT EAT IT?
THERE WAS STRAWBERRY ICE CREAM AND VANILLA, MOCCA AND LEMON SHERBET.
MY FAVORITE IS BANANA SPLIT BUT I NEVER GET IT 'CAUSE MOM SAYS WE CAN'T AFFORD IT.

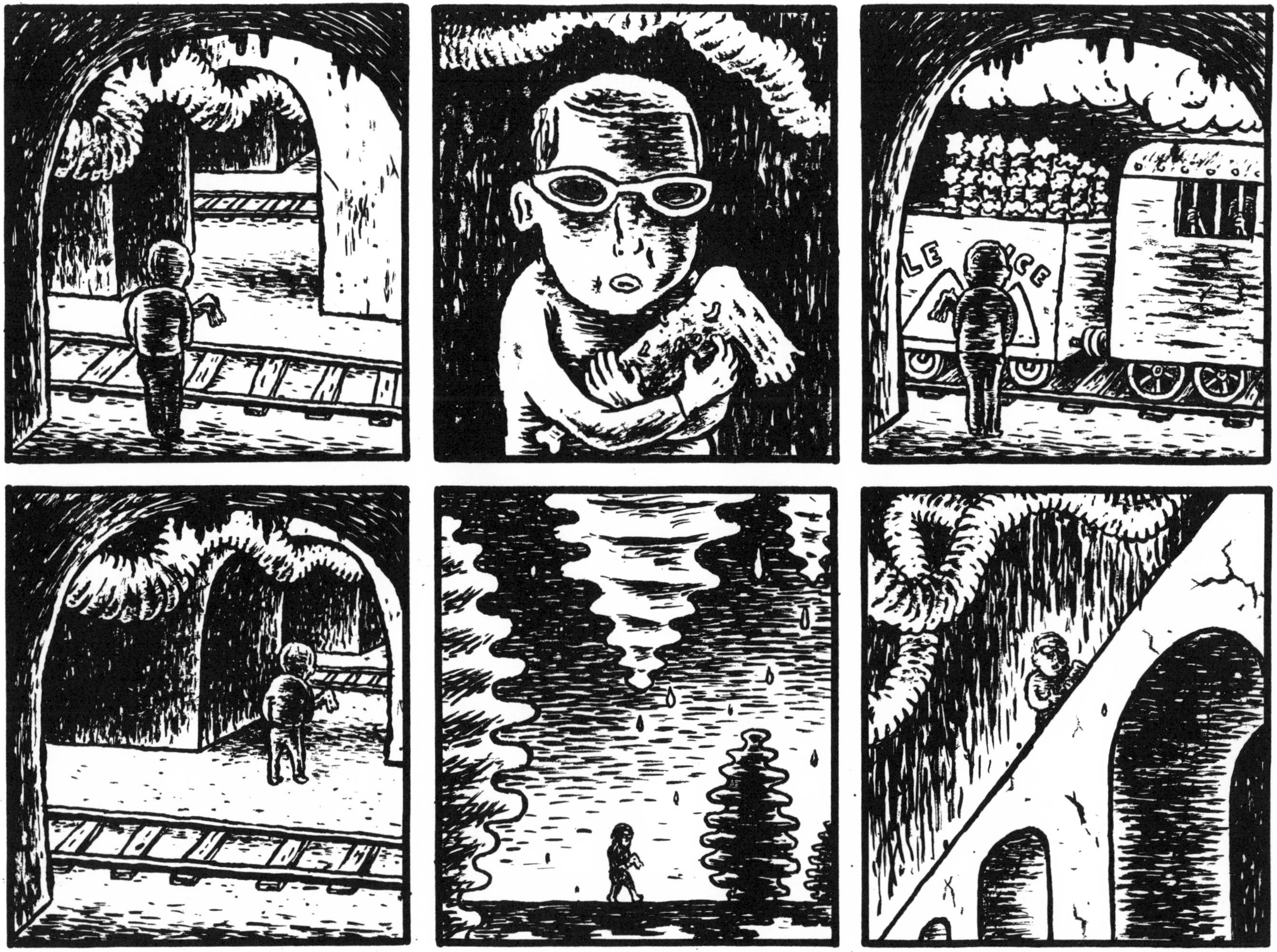
LE ICE

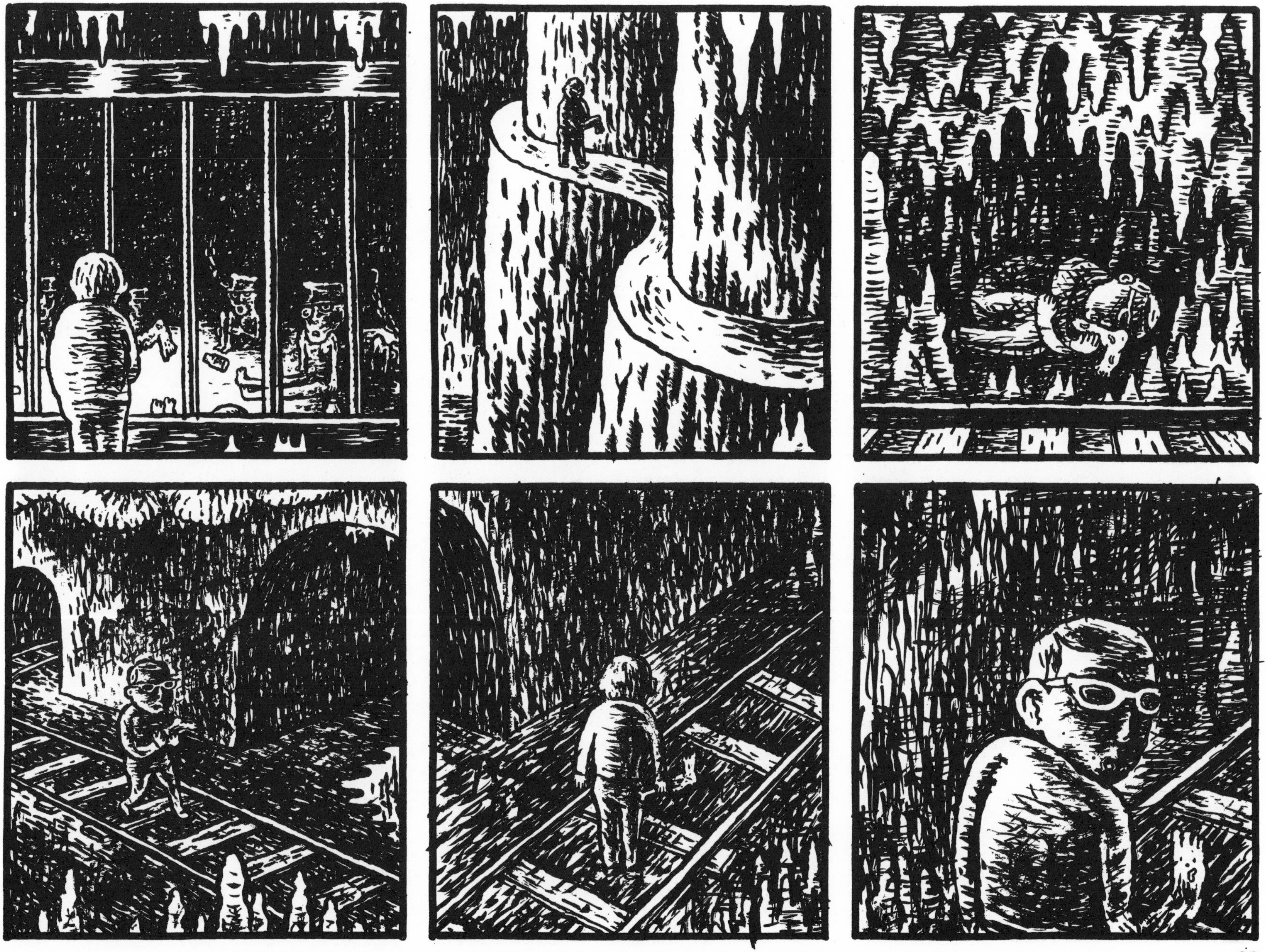

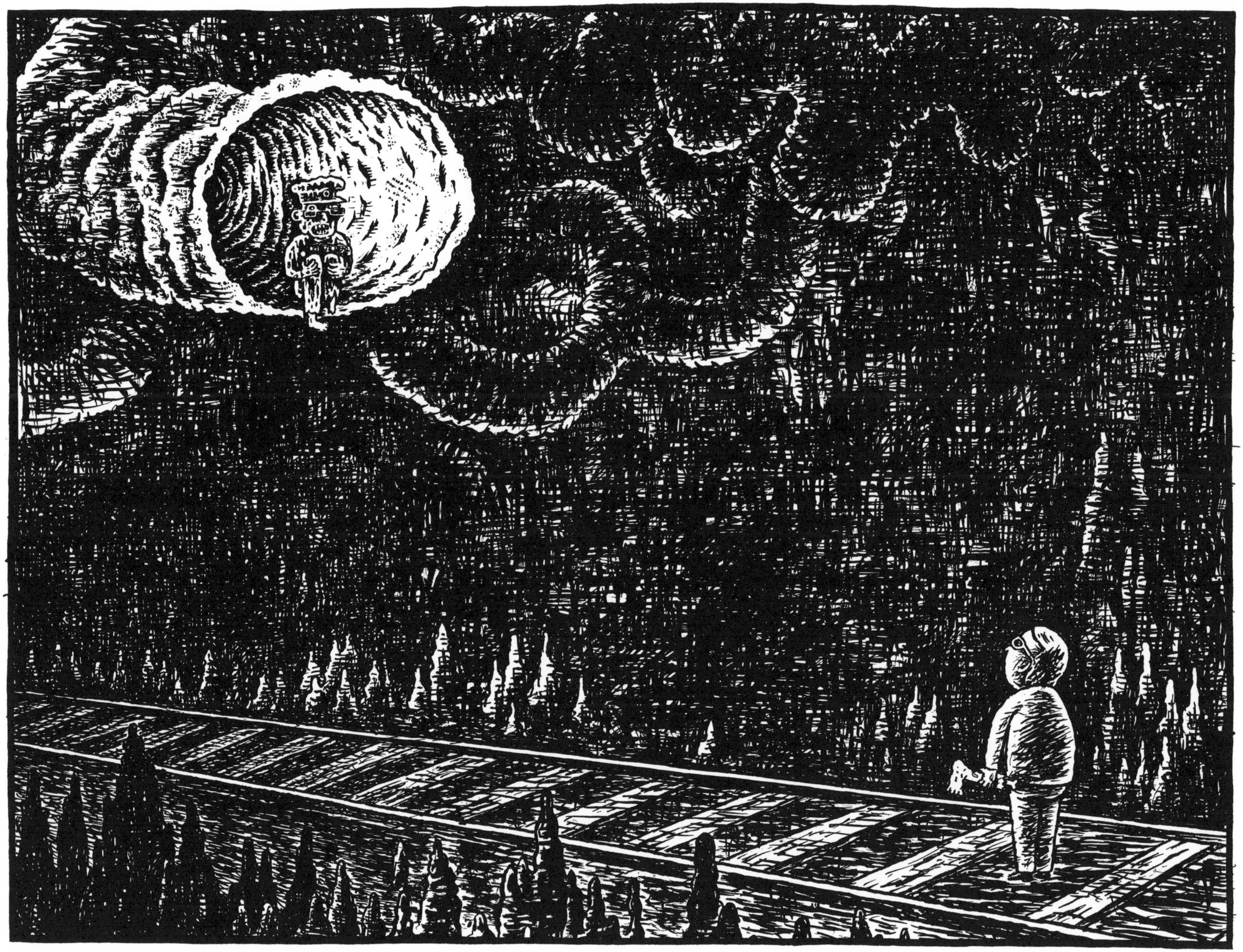

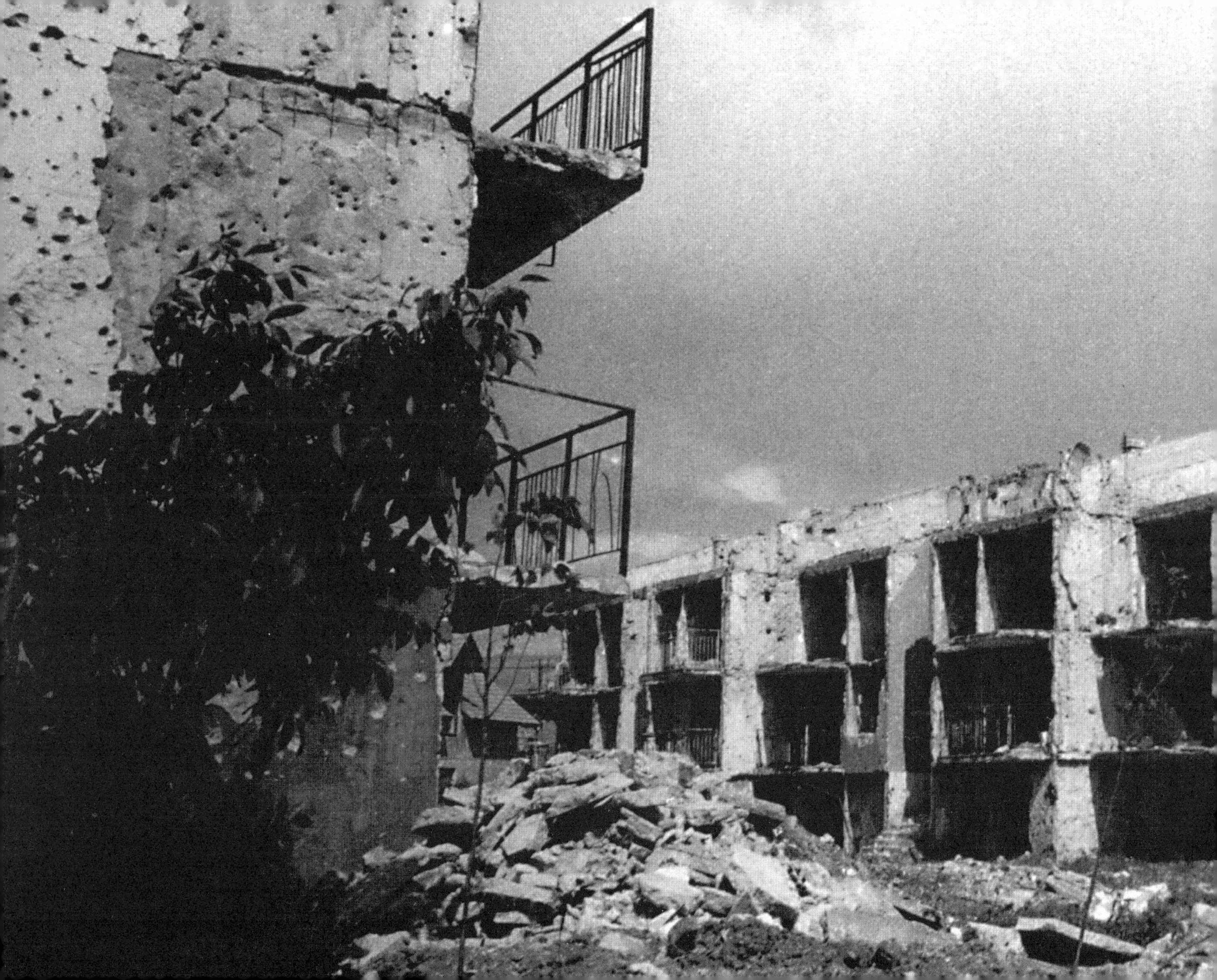

GLOSSARY

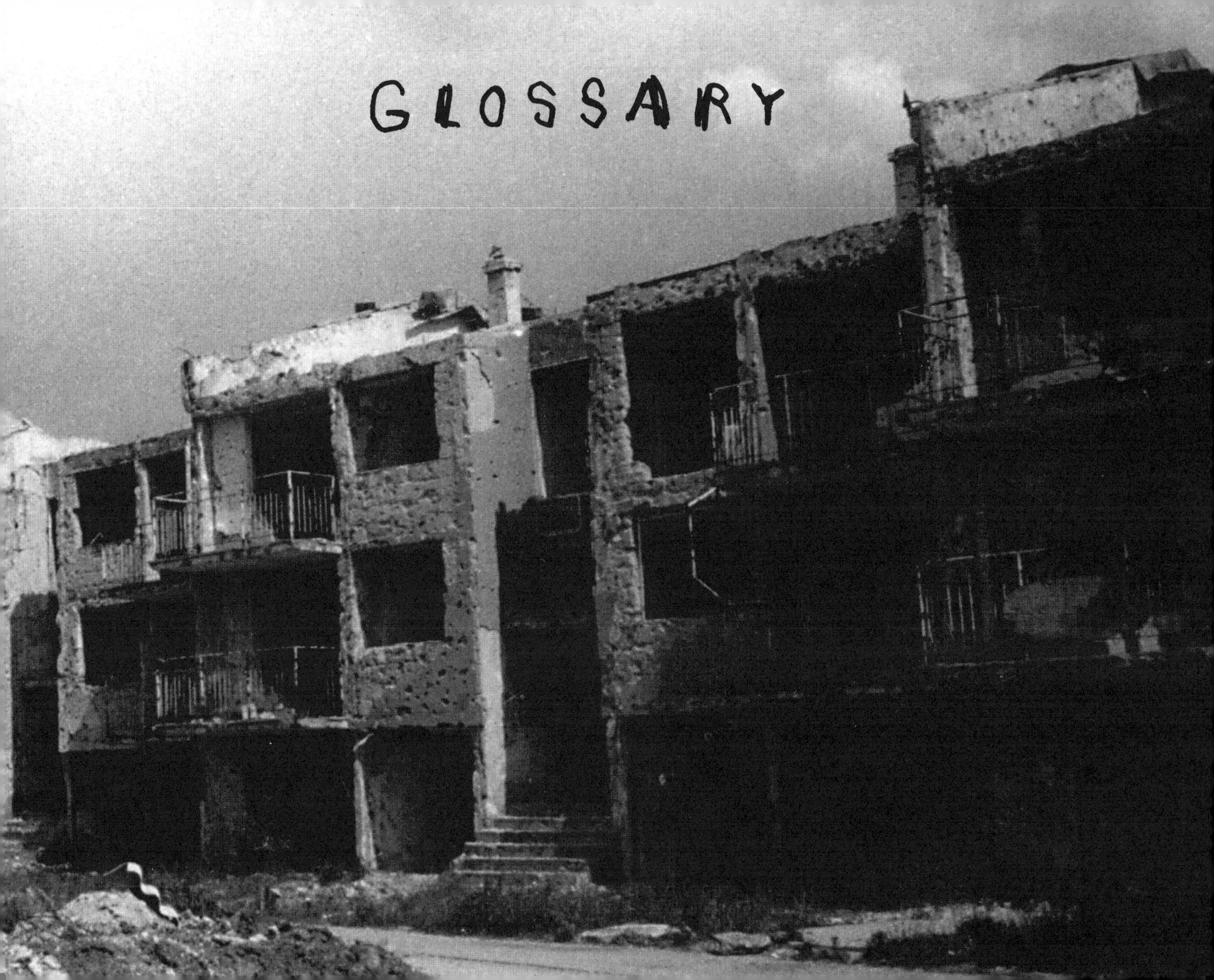

Alternative position of explosives

Alternative position of explosives

Fig. 6:20. Placing of explosives on different types of helicopter

APACHE HELICOPTER

Heavily armed American so-called attack helicopter, particularly effective when used against "soft" targets in open terrain. Named after an indigenous ethnic group now found in special reservations (see ethnic cleansing).

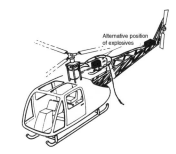

ARIZONA ROAD

Unofficial free trade zone and settlement in Bosnia, situated at a road crossing where three ethnic entities and a U.S. air force base meet. Used to be called something else that was more difficult to pronounce.
Renamed by the U.S. army after an area in the USA where an indigenous ethnic group is now found in special camps (see apache helicopter).

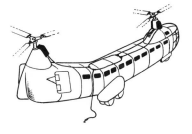

BALKANS, the

strategically located yet inaccessible region in southeastern Europe. Has lately come to refer to what was formerly known as Yugoslavia, a federation comprised of a number of republics and two autonomous regions, also a psychological condition – "balkanization" – the feeling of having vanished into different directions.
War breaks out in 1991, as B. in part declares its independence from itself. The Yugoslav army attacks and ex-Yugoslavia is born. (see Dayton, The peace talks in).

CD Shop
TEL/FAX: 076/861-034
LONČARI
ORAŠJE
BRČKO
500m
CD
TUZLA
BANJA LUKA

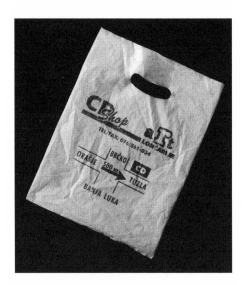

BILDT, CARL

Swedish former prime minister, who made a political career in Bosnia after the peace agreement of 1995.
(see Dayton, The peace talks in)

BAŠČARŠIJA The oldest, Ottoman part of Sarajevo. Centre for the ancient Bosnian tradition of engraving used ammunition with ornamental designs and picturesque views.

BOSNIA

Former Yugoslav republic. Home of the excellent beer "Sarajevsko Pivo".

CROATIA

Former Yugoslav republic. ~~Home of the~~ the most popular beer brand, Ožjusko, is not so good.

DAYTON, THE PEACE TALKS IN

A meeting that took place in 1995 at a U.S. air force base within the U.S., where the decision was made to cancel the war in Bosnia. Also made permanent the division of the country into three ethnic entities which had been a creation of the war. The products "IFOR" and "High Representative" were launched internationally (see SFOR and High representative).

ETHNIC CLEANSING The removal of an undesired ethnic group or groups from a geographic territory. Should the ethnic group not consent to the removal, various forms of violence, or threats of violence, are applied. The earliest known description, or manual, is to be found in the Old Testament.

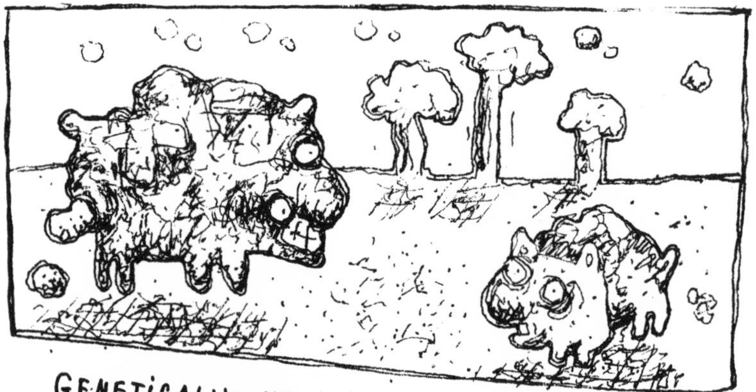

EUROVISION SONG CONTEST
A televised event that has managed to bring all the different nations and ~~nationalities~~, plus Israel, together for an evening of friendly competition and good clean family entertainment for well over 4 decades.

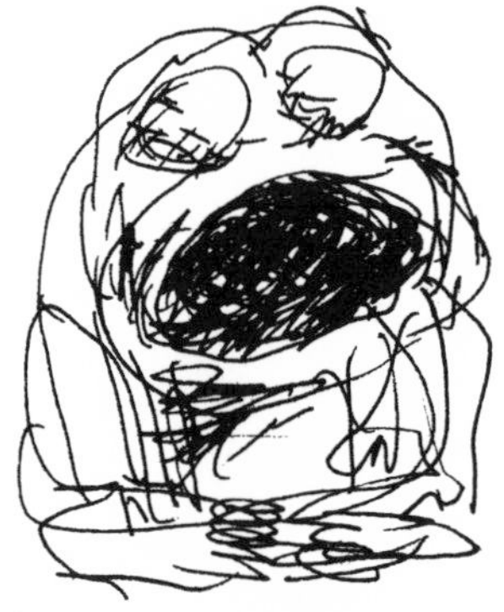

GENETICALLY MODIFIED ORGANISMS
(Genetic cleansing) The removal of undesired DNA from an organic territory. In its place, new genes are inserted which should increase the ability of the territory to assert itself in terms of competition.

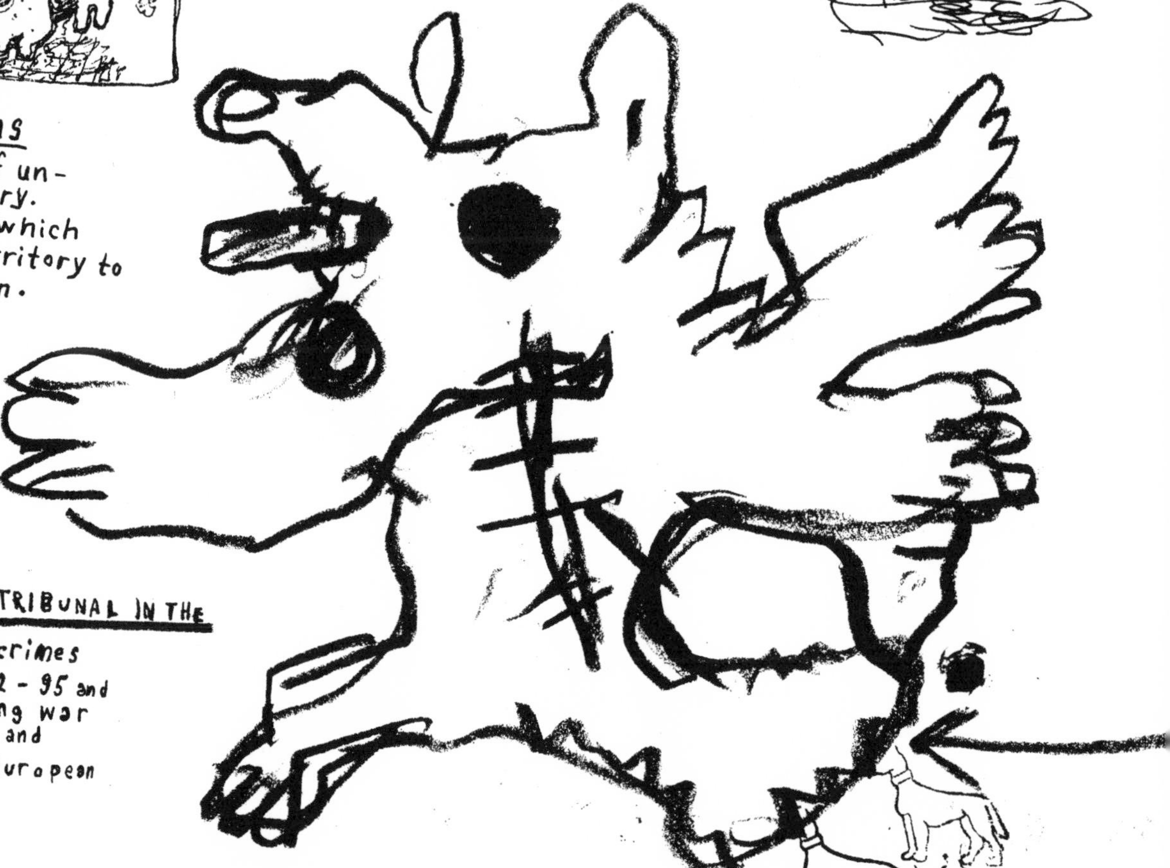

HAMAS, the Former resistance group which made a political career within an ethnic group now found in Special reservations (see **ethnic cleansing**).

HAGUE, THE INTERNATIONAL WAR CRIMES TRIBUNAL IN THE
Court established to investigate war crimes committed in Croatia and Bosnia from 1992 - 95 and in ~~1999~~ Kosovo in 1999. All participating war parties can be subject to prosecution and sentencing, with the exception of West European or U.S. American forces.

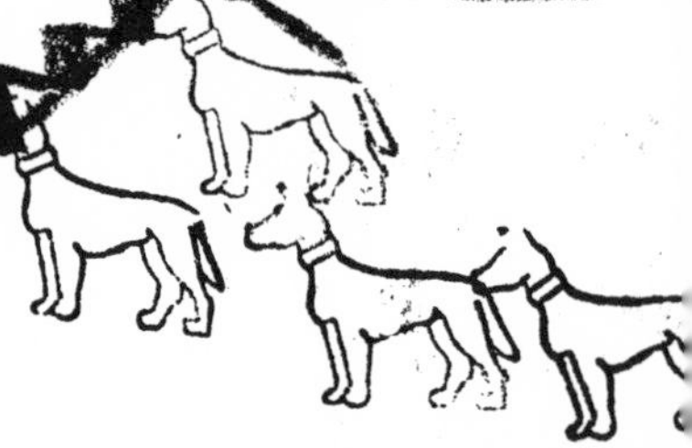

HIGH REPRESENTATIVE
New supranational authority with more or less unlimited powers in present-day Bosnia. May remove democratically elected representatives from office and enact laws of its own.

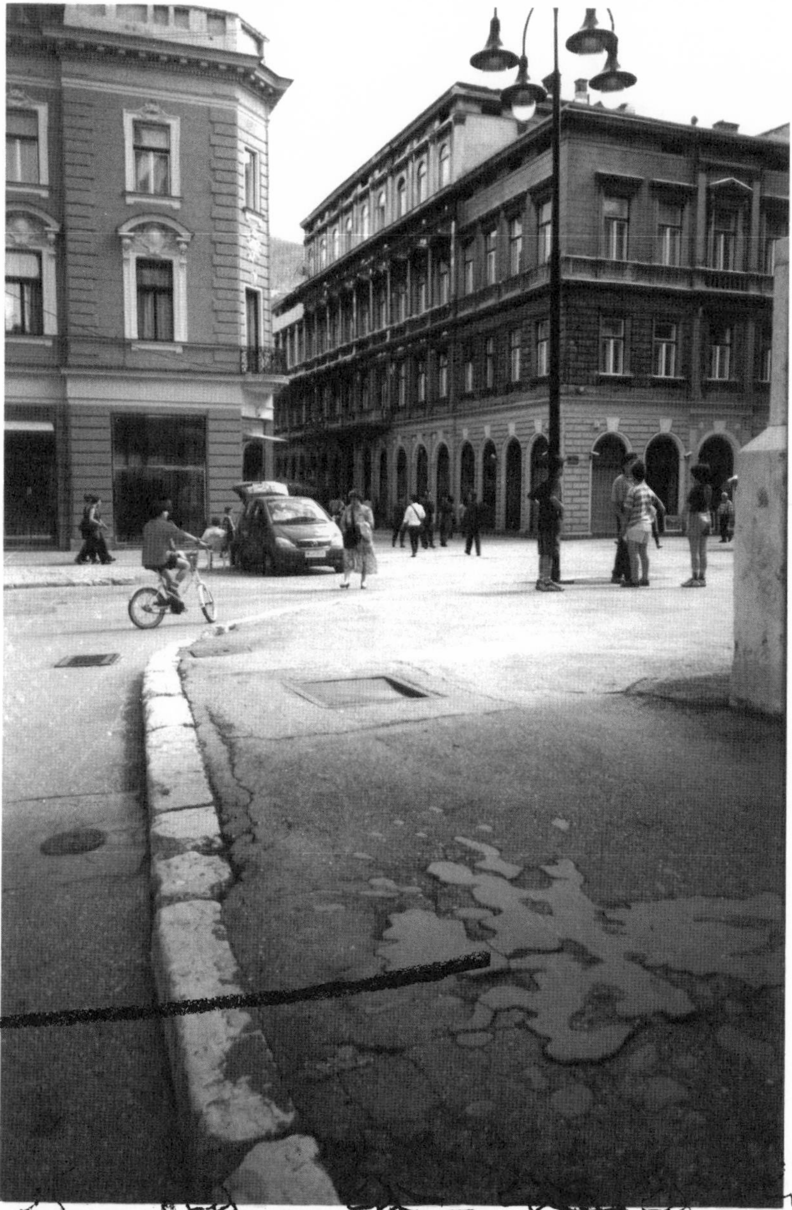

KALASHNIKOV Popular Russian automatic weapon. On account of its comparatively low price and reliable, robust mechanism it is particularly favored by privately funded armed organizations.

KARADZIĆ, RADOVAN, DR.

Bosnian Serb poet and psychiatrist, who made a ~~poli~~- political career in Republika Srpska until the peace agreement of 1995 (see Dayton)

KRAJINA

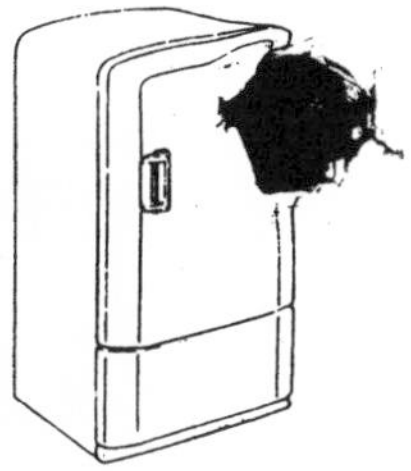

Mountainous region in southwestern Croatia, with a population mainly of Serb heritage. In 1995, supported by the USA and other parties, the Croat army carried out the Blitzkrieg-like "Operation Storm" resulting in the vanishing of the Serb population (see ethnic cleansing).

KOSOVO

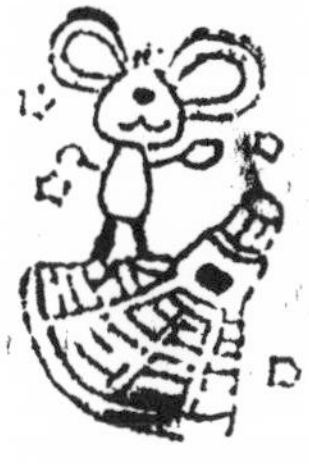

Former autonomous region within Yugoslavia. In 1999 it was discovered to contain parts of the Serb population that had been balkanized from Croatia (see Krajina). After NATO had completed its bombing campaign, said parts vanished again. Currently a U.S. air force base.

LEOPARD

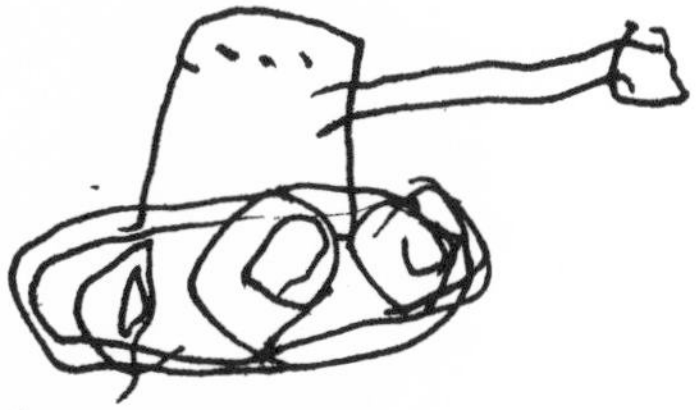

Originally an African feline, currently a Bavarian tank. The animal, which is threatened by extinction, has over time proved to be significantly inferior to the tank, which is one of the world's most popular (see Genetically modified organisms)

LJUBLJANA capital of Slovenia.

MIG-21 popular Soviet jet fighter from the 1960's.

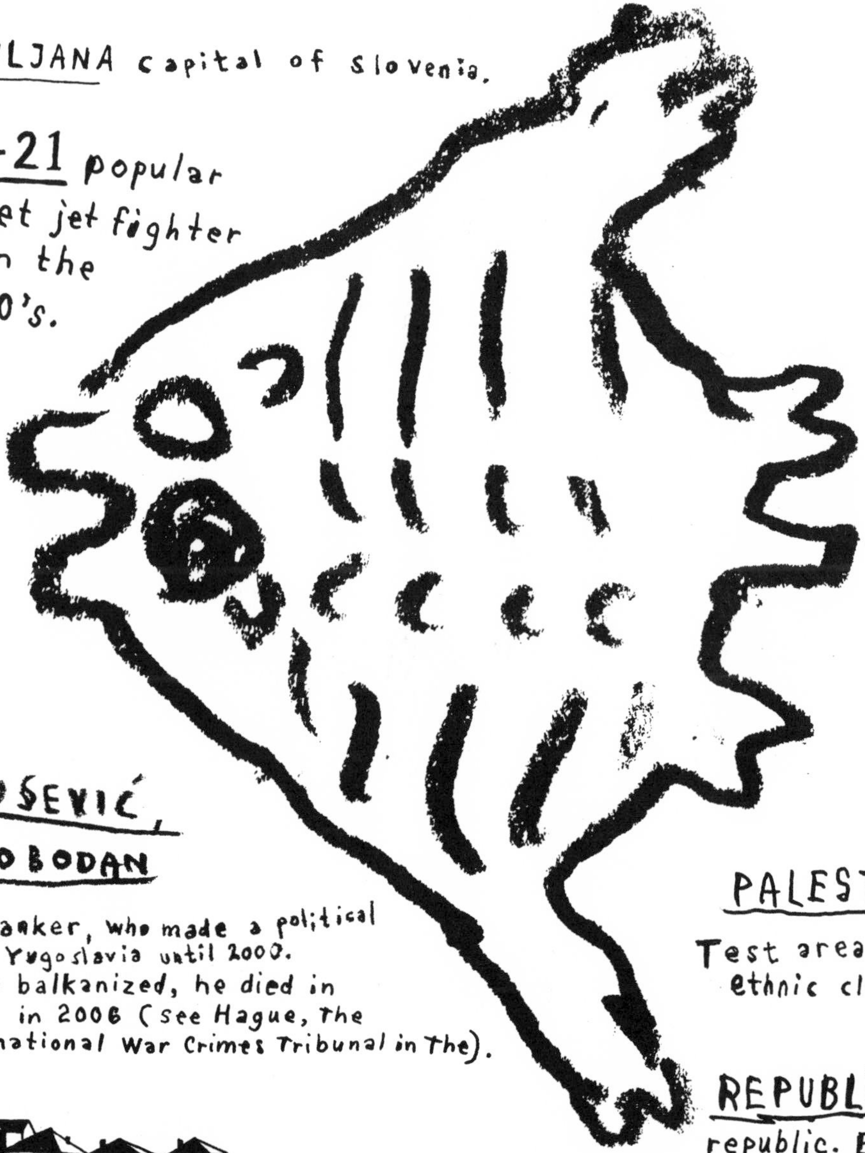

NATO

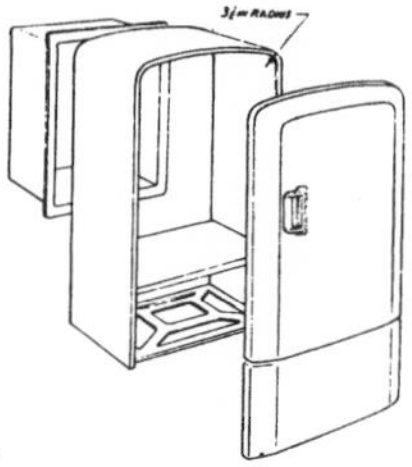

Defense pact founded during the Cold War with the Warsaw pact as its counterpart. Went through an identity crisis following the disintegration of the Soviet Union. Attacked Serbia in 1999.

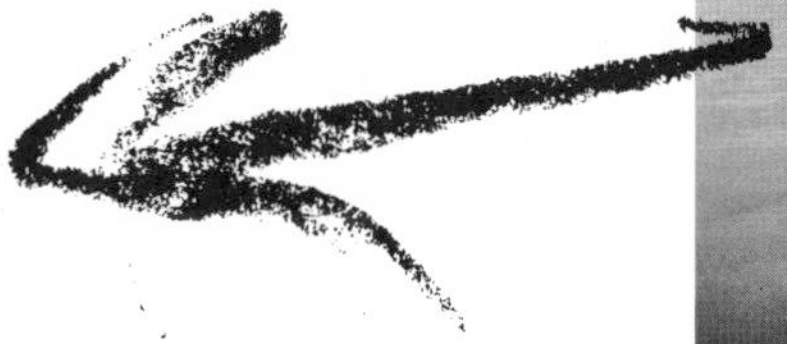

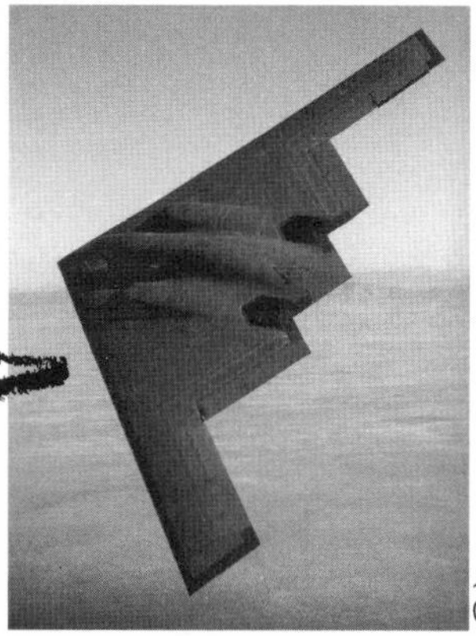

©X

MILOŠEVIĆ, SLOBODAN

Serb banker, who made a political career in Yugoslavia until 2000. Severely balkanized, he died in Holland in 2006 (see Hague, The International War Crimes Tribunal in The).

PALESTINE

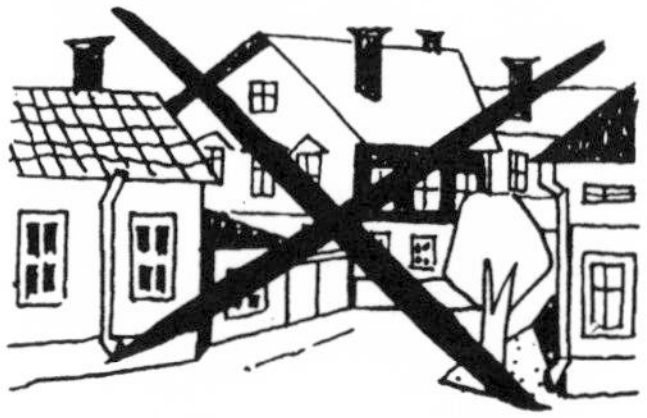

Test area for balkanization and ethnic cleansing.

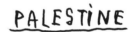

REPUBLIKA SRPSKA Bosnian Serb separatist republic. Established its first seat of government and military central command in the former tourist lodgings of the Hotel Panorama in the – since the Winter Olympics of 1984 – largely forgotten ski resort of Pale. The siege of the Bosnian capital was directed from here (see Sarajevo).

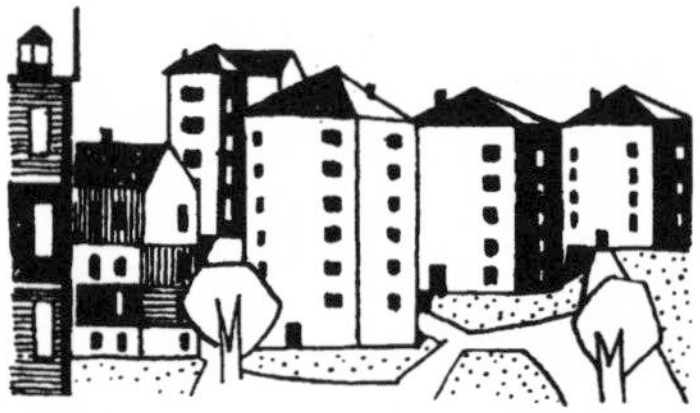

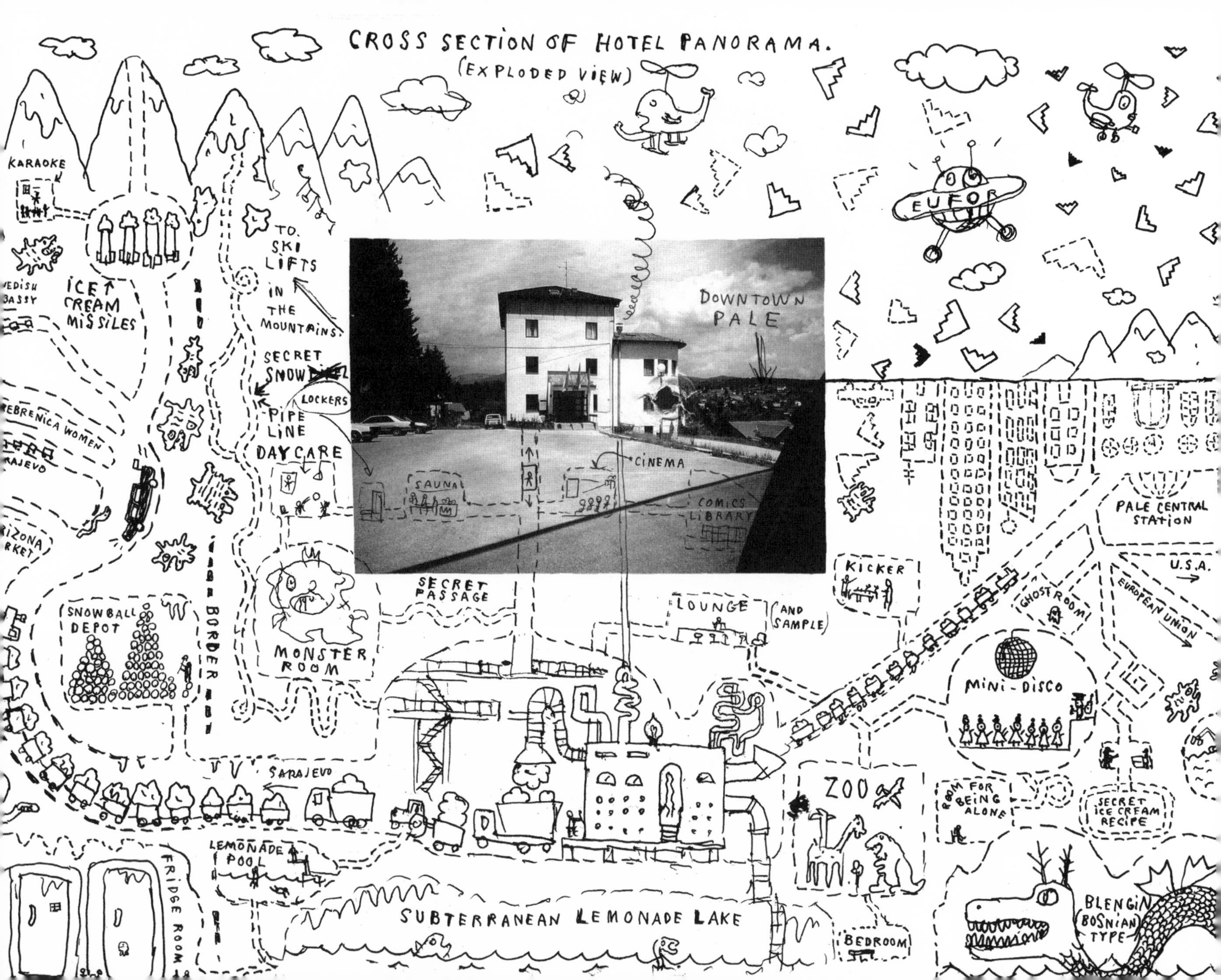

CROSS SECTION OF HOTEL PANORAMA.
(EXPLODED VIEW)

EUFOR

DOWNTOWN PALE

KARAOKE

SWEDISH EMBASSY

ICE CREAM MISSILES

TO SKI LIFTS IN THE MOUNTAINS.

SECRET SNOW PIXEL

LOCKERS

PIPE LINE

DAY CARE

SREBRENICA WOMEN

SARAJEVO

ARIZONA MARKET

BORDER

SNOWBALL DEPOT

MONSTER ROOM

SAUNA

CINEMA

COMICS LIBRARY

SECRET PASSAGE

LOUNGE (AND SAMPLE)

KICKER

PALE CENTRAL STATION

U.S.A.

EUROPEAN UNION

GHOST ROOM

MINI-DISCO

ROOM FOR BEING ALONE

SECRET ICE CREAM RECIPE

ZOO

SARAJEVO

LEMONADE POOL

FRIDGE ROOM

SUBTERRANEAN LEMONADE LAKE

BEDROOM

BLENGIN BOSNIAN TYPE

SARAJEVO Capital of Bosnia with a majority population of Muslims. Besieged by constant artillery fire by Bosnian serb forces 1992-1995.

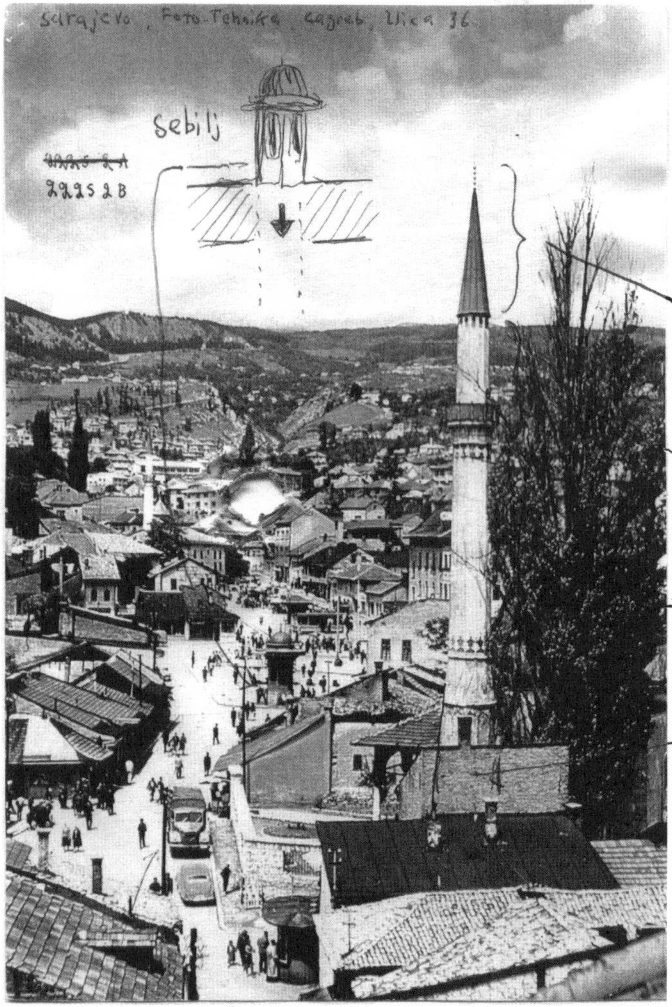
Sebilj

SCUD

German rocket from World War II. Modified in the Soviet Union in the 1960's.

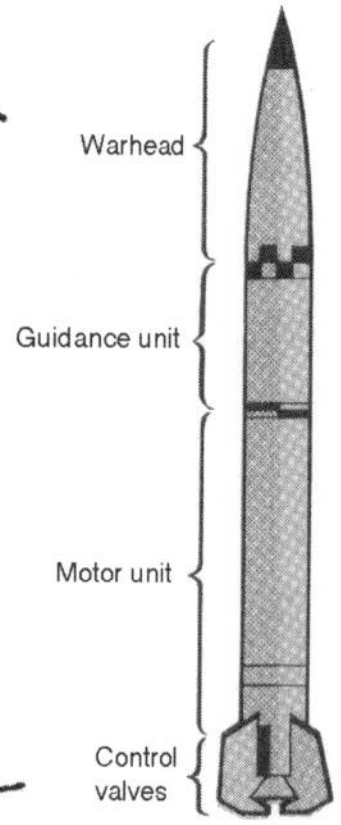
Warhead
Guidance unit
Motor unit
Control valves

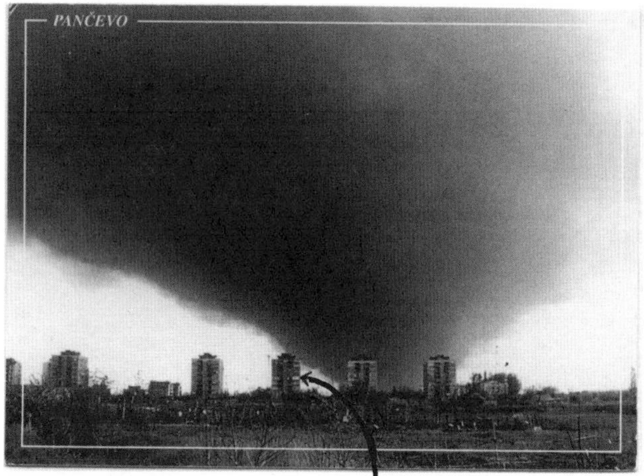
PANČEVO

SAŠA'S APARTMENT

SERBIA Former Yugoslavia

SFOR New brand name launched by NATO for the Bosnian market whereby the "S" stands for stability. Replaced the previous model IFOR in 1996. Currently being sold in Kosovo under the name KFOR. Later changed to the more positive-sounding EUFOR.

SLIVOVICA Traditional liquid intoxicant made from plums. Strong balkanizing effect.

SLOVENIA Former Yugoslav republic. Home of the pop group Laibach and the excellent beer Laško.

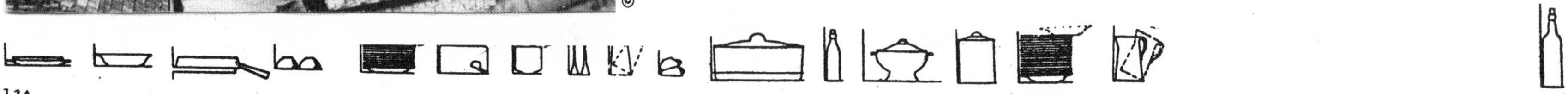

SREBRENICA Bosnian community within the area occupied by Bosnian Serb forces, but with a mainly Muslim population. Proclaimed a "safe area" by the UN. In July 1995 the Serbs entered the city, whereupon the male population was separated from the women and children and executed in what became the largest example of mass murder in Europe since World War II.

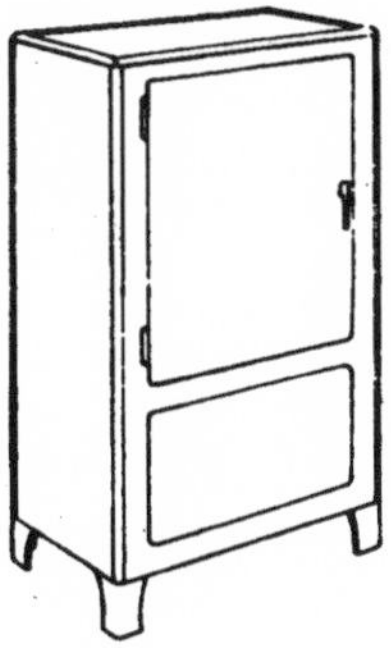

TITO, JOSIP BROZ

Yugoslav head of state from 1945 until his death in 1980.

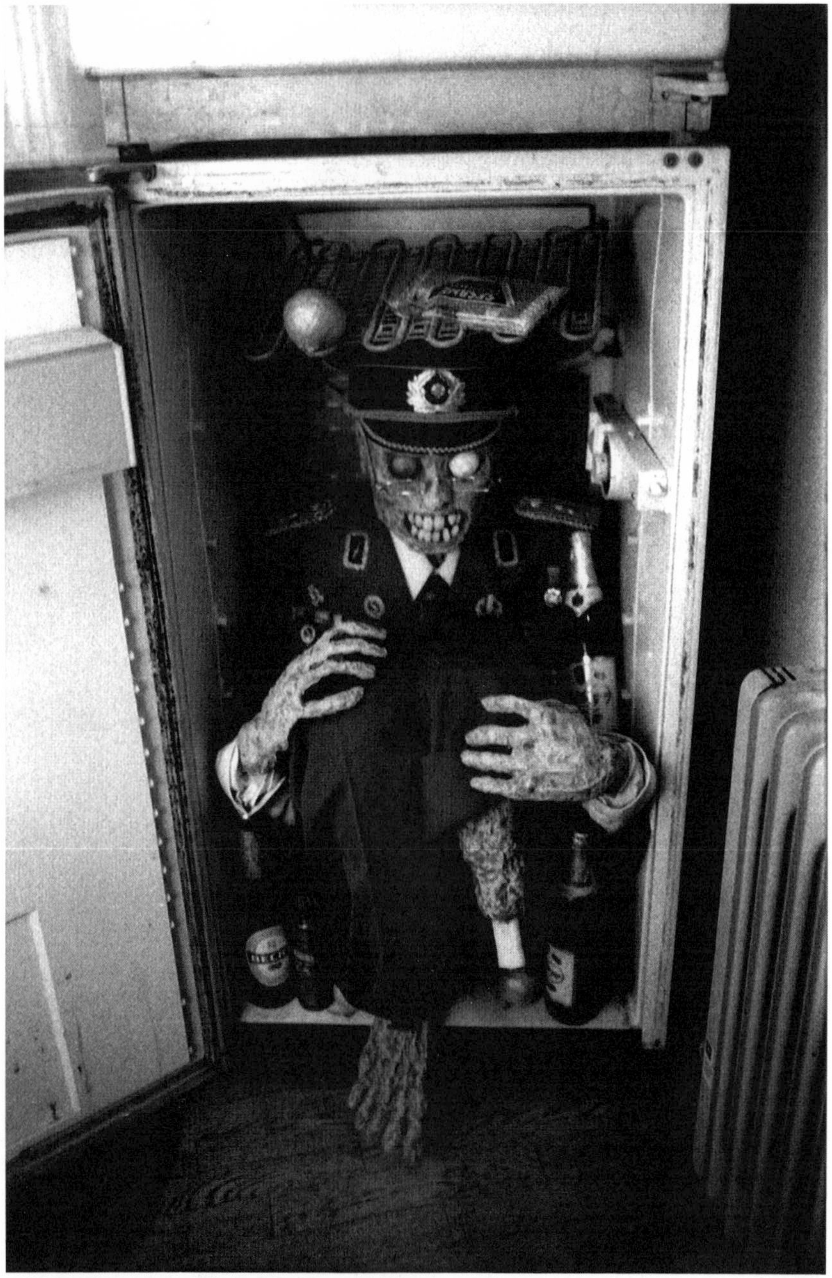

URANIUM MUNITION Projectiles containing depleted uranium, a cheap, poisonous and strongly radioactive waste product of the nuclear power industry. Used in large ~~quant.~~ quantities by NATO forces as armor-piercing ammunition in Bosnia, Serbia and Kosovo.

UZI Popular, pocket-size Israeli automatic weapon.

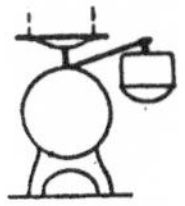
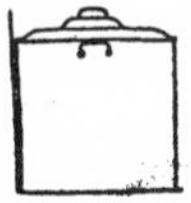
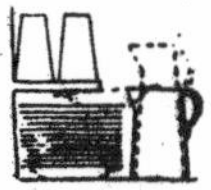
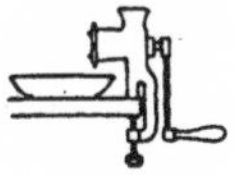

Special thanks to:

Helena Ahonen, Maria Tengroth, Štefan Skledar, Igor Prassel, Katerina Mirović,
Ivan Mitrevski, Alexandra Stratimirović, Ivana Armanini, Igor Hofbauer, Ljudmila Stratimirović,
Dejan Ubović, Saša Rakezić, Vladimir Nedeljković, Nedim Cišic, Igor Banjac, Elettra Stamboulis,
Gianluca Costantini, Jelena Radosavljević, Sven Cvek, Marko Brečelj, Rolf Classon, Daniel Munoz,
Matthias Schneider, Johan Melbi, Jens Ågren, Thomas Olsson, Aleksandar Perović.
Strip Core (Ljubljana), Club Močvara (Zagreb), refract (Belgrad), Centar za kulturu Pančevo,
Alternativni Institut (Mostar), Club Access (Sarajevo), Mirada (Ravenna),
Lichtblick Kino (Berlin), IASPIS.